Horst Siebert

Economics of the Environment

Theory and Policy

Second, Revised and Enlarged Edition

Springer-Verlag
Berlin Heidelberg New York
London Paris Tokyo

Prof. Dr. Horst Siebert
Universität Konstanz
Lehrstuhl für internationale Wirtschaftsbeziehungen
Universitätsstraße 10
7750 Konstanz 1, Federal Republic of Germany

The first edition was published in 1981 by Lexington Books,
D.C. Heath and Company, Lexington.

ISBN 3-540-17283-1 Springer-Verlag Berlin Heidelberg New York
ISBN 0-387-17283-1 Springer-Verlag New York Berlin Heidelberg

Library of Congress Cataloging-in-Publication Data. Siebert, Horst, 1938-. Economics
of the environment. Bibliography: p. Includes index. 1. Environmental policy–Economic aspects. I. Title. HC79.E5S437   1987   363.7   87-4703
ISBN 0-387-17283-1 (U.S.)

Printing: Druckhaus Beltz, Hemsbach;
Bookbinding: J. Schäffer GmbH & Co. KG, Grünstadt
2142/3140-543210

Contents

List of Figures
and Tables

Figures

Tables

Preface

"The labor of nature is paid, not because she does little. In proportion as she becomes niggardly in her gifts, she exacts a greater price for her work. Where she is munificently beneficient, she always works gratis."   David Ricardo*

This book interprets nature and the environment as a scarce resource. Whereas in the past people lived in a paradise of environmental superabundance, at present environmental goods and services are no longer in ample supply. The environment fulfills many functions for the economy: it serves as a public-consumption good, as a provider of natural resources, and as receptacle of wastes. These different functions compete with each other. Releasing more pollutants into the environment reduces environmental quality, and a better environmental quality implies that the environment's use as a receptacle of wastes has to be restrained. Consequently, environmental disruption and environmental use are by nature allocation problems. This is the basic message of this book.

If a resources is scarce and if a zero price is charged for its use, then misallocation will result. The environment as a receptacle of wastes is heavily overused, and consequently environmental quality declines. Scarcity requires a price. This book analyzes how this price should be set, whether a correct price can be established through the market mechanism, and what role the government should play. The book offers a theoretical study of the allocation problem and describes different policy approaches to the environmental problem. The entire spectrum of the allocation issue is studied: the use of the environment in a static context, international and trade aspects of environmental allocation, regional dimensions, environmental use over time and under uncertainty. The book incorporates a variety of economic approaches, including neoclassical analysis, the public-goods approach, benefit-cost analysis, property-rights ideas, economic policy and public-finance reasoning, international trade theory, regional science, optimization theory, and risk analysis.

This book grew out of may research at the Universities of Konstanz and Mannheim, Germany, and visiting positions at the University of Aberdeen, Scotland, the Australian National University in Canberra, the Energy Laboratory of the Massachusetts Institute of Technology as well as the Sloan School of Management, the University of California at Riverside, the University of New Mexico at Albuquerque, New York University, and Resources for the Future. I would like to thank Ralph d'Arge, Ron Cummings, Allen V. Kneese, John V. Krutilla, Ngo Van Long, Toby Page, David Pearce, Cliff Russell, Walter Spofford, and Ingo Walter for stimulating discussions. I am also grateful to Rüdiger Pethig (University of Oldenburg) and to Hans Werner Sinn (University of Munich), to Ferdi Dudenhöfer, Helga Gebauer, Ralf Gronych, Helmut Meder, Sabine Toussaint and Wolfgang Vogt (all Mannheim) and Ernst Mohr (Konstanz) with whom I worked on the environmental issue and on intertemporal allocation. Further, I appreciatively acknowledge financial support by the Deutsche Forschungsgemeinschaft.

This book only considers environmental issues and does not discuss natural resource scarcity for nonrenewable and renewable resources such as oil and fish. Of course, there are interrelations between the environmental and resource scarcity problem, for instance the common property rights issue and the intertemporal aspect of environmental use and resource allocation. I have studied the intertemporal allocation problem of natural resource scarcity in my German Book "Ökonomische Theorie natürlicher Ressorucen" (J. C. B. Mohr, Tübingen, 1983). With the environmental problem having already a sufficiently broad spectrum of facets, it is a topic in its own right. Both of my books, however, should be viewed as an ensemble attempting an answer as to how to incorporate the environment and natural resource scarcity into the doctrine of economics.

This book was originally published by D. C. Heath in 1981. In this thoroughly and extendedly revised edition, chapter 9 on the political economy of environmental scarcity as well as chapter 14 on environmental risks and their impact on allocation have been added whereas chapter 12 on depletable resources of the first edition has been omitted. Besides these major changes, the whole text has been completely revised. The regulatory approach to environmental policy, the bubble concept, and some practical aspects of regional environmental policy have been added or extended. The role of transaction costs in the Coase theorem and the distinction between public goods and common properties has been clarified. New data have been introduced, the bibliography has been updated and extended and the new literature has been incorporated into the text. Moreover, teaching a text over several years brings to light some shortcomings. Ernst Mohr scrutinized the complete manuscript for improvements, and he has pointed out quite a few. Finally, Gudrun Kugler has typed the bulk of the revisions.

It should be mentioned that some parts of the book were originally published in German under the title "Ökonomische Theorie der Umwelt" in 1978. However, chapters 4, 6, 7, 8, 9, 14 and parts of 5 as well as 11 were not included in the original publication. Of course, the profession does not read, and simplifications are called for. But it is not justified to classify this book as an English version of the original German Text.

I hope that the analysis presented in this book contributes some insights to the emotional debate on environmental disruption, and I wish that it incorporates nature and the environment as a scarce good into the body of economic thought and that it provides an answer of economics as a discipline to a problem of great importance to our societies.   H. S.

Note

* D. Ricardo, *Principles of Political Economy and Taxation,* 1817, quoted accordingly to Everyman's Library, London 1911, Dent, p. 39.

**Part I
Introduction**

The Problem

Air and water have long been prototypes of free goods, available in unlimited quantities with no price attached to their use. The Rhine River, with its fairy tales and romantic songs, is an example. It has been used as a common-property resource in a manner similar to the ozone layer and the oceans. Natural resources have been employed in economic activities without consideration of the long-run effects on the life-supporting systems of the planet or the potential losses to future generations. The joint outputs of consumption and production activities have not been factored into the calculation of the economic system. In short, the environment, as the set of natural conditions defining the human living space, has not been taken into consideration by economic theory.

Since the late 1960s and the early 1970s, we have become increasingly aware of environmental disruption. The environment has fallen from the paradise of free goods to the realm of scarcity:

> The Los Angeles *Times* publishes a daily smog report in which is noted the local level of pollution concentrations, such as carbon monoxide and nitrogen oxide. The Los Angeles resident is very happy when the report states, "No eye irritation today."

> There was no oxygen in the atmosphere when the earth came into existence; rather, it took 3 billion years for oxygen to appear through the photosynthesis of slowly evolving plants. Today, the photosynthesis of phytoplankton in the oceans supplies about 70 percent of the oxygen demand of the earth. The biologist Wuster states that already a concentration of 0.1 parts per million (ppm) of DDT in the oceans will reduce the photosynthesis of phytoplankton.[1]

> Numerous statistical studies seem to suggest that there is a relationship between air and water pollution and a variety of illnesses.[2]

From the economist's point of view, the environment has become a scarce commodity. Scarcity means that competing uses exist for a given good and that not all demands for its use can be satisfied. The environment is used as a public-consumption good, as a provider of natural resources, and as a receptacle of wastes. Since the demand for different uses is greater than the supply, some of the competing uses have to be reduced or eliminated. The challenge is to determine which potential uses deserve priority.

Environmental use poses an allocation problem. That is the message of this book. In chapter 2 we study the basic structure of this allocation problem. In the past, the environment was used as a common-property resource at a zero price. This was especially true of its role as a receptacle of wastes. This institutional setting of a zero price implies an overuse of the environment and a decline in environmental quality. It also causes private and social costs of production and consumption to diverge. Commodity prices do not indicate the true opportunity costs of economic activities, and so pollution-intensive activities become too large relative to an allocation optimum. Sector structure is distorted in favor of the pollution-intensive sector, and too many resources of production are attracted to the pollution-intensive sector. The solution to the environmental problem lies in reducing the divergence of private and social costs and introducing an institutional framework for market economies such that all costs of economic activities are attributed to the individual unit.

After introducing the economic dimension of the environmental problem in part I, we analyze its static allocation aspect in part II. Policy implementation is discussed in part III. The spatial aspect of the environmental problem is examined in part IV. Finally, in part V we consider the intertemporal allocation problems including uncertainty.

Throughout the book, the same basic model is used. The underlying assumptions with respect to the production side are presented in chapter 3. Emissions are interpreted as joint products of output. Also it is assumed that factors of production are used for abatement. For simplicity, a two-sector model of the economy is considered. The transformation space, that is, the production possibilities with respect to private goods and the public-good environmental quality, is analyzed. It is shown that there is a tradeoff between the production of private goods and environmental quality. A higher environmental quality results in fewer private goods, and concomitantly, more private goods can be obtained only at the cost of a lower environmental quality.

In chapter 4 optimal environmental allocation is defined so that a frame of reference for environmental policy is established. The implications of the optimum are studied. We can indicate how the price mechanism has to be corrected in order to take into account environmental quality. We can specify how a shadow price for pollutants, that is, an emission tax, has to be set. Also we can show that if a correct emission tax is chosen, the optimum can be reached with a competitive equilibrium.

Chapter 5 focuses on the public-goods approach to the environmental problem. If environmental quality is a public good, property rights cannot be defined and government intervention becomes necessary. The problem arises as to how the government determines environmental quality. The social-welfare function, benefit/cost analysis, and the aggregation of individual preferences are studied as alternative approaches. According to the Lindahl solution, a Pareto-optimal allocation of the environment requires individualized prices of environmental quality to be differentiated according to the individual's willingness to pay. The individual, however, can take the position of the free rider and not reveal his or her true preference. Therefore we have to investigate institutional arrangements which will reveal and aggregate individual preferences.

The property-rights approach described in chapter 6 represents the counterpoint to the public-goods discussion. If property rights can be adequately defined, optimal allocation will be attained through private decisions, and government intervention will be necessary only in order to define and secure property rights. In fact, it is conceivable that property rights could even be established through private bargaining without any government intervention. The Coase (1960) theorem shows that under specific conditions the allocation result is independent of the attribution of property rights. The salient point is that property rights must be assigned. It may not be feasible to make the freerider problem disappear by defining property rights, but in any case new property rights have to be set up for the use of the environment as a receptacle of wastes.

In part II, the static allocation aspect is discussed from a theoretical point of view. In part III, policy aspects are studied. From a pragmatic standpoint, we may start from the assumption that environmental policy has set an environmental-quality target. The problem, then, is to determine how this target can be transformed to the emission behavior of the polluters. In chapter 7 we use the theoretical framework of our model to consider how producers react to an emission tax. First, we use partial equilibrium analysis for a given commodity price and for perfect competition. We also look into the question of whether a monopolist can shift the emission tax. Finally, we use a general equilibrium framework in which the emission tax also affects relative price and in which the demand side of the economy is taken into consideration. In chapter 8, we contrast regulation through permits, emission taxes, pollution licenses, the bubble concept and cost sharing as mechanisms for translating quality targets into individual behavior. The advantages and the disadvantages of the four policy instruments are reviewed. In chapter 9, we study some issues of the political economy of environmental scarcity. The basic principles of a rational environmental policy are developed such as recognizing the opportunity costs, attributing them to the decentralized units, having a long-run orientation in preventing future damages, securing continuity in the policy approach and not neglecting the interdepence among pollutants and among environmental media. We then discuss why these rational principles are not adhered to in environmental policy in the real world.

In part III, we introduce the spatial dimension of the environmental system to our analysis. In reality, environmental systems are defined over space. We may distinguish among global systems, such as the ozone layer; international environmental goods, such as the quality of the Mediterranean Sea; transfrontier pollution systems, such as the international diffusion of acid rains; national environmental media and regional assets as subsystems of nations, such as the air region of a metropolitan area. In chapter 10, the international aspects of environmental pollution are highlighted. We look into the problem of how environmental abundance or scarcity affects comparative advantage, the terms of trade, and trade flows. Since environmental policy must be embedded in an international context, the trade repercussions of environmental policy are of utmost importance. In chapter 11, regional environmental allocation is analyzed. Should all areas of a country strive for an identical environmental quality, or should the quality targets be differentiated among regions? Should policy instruments be uniform for a nation, or should they be different for different areas? What are the implications of an environmental policy that is established by autonomous regional authorities compared to a nationally formulated environmental policy?

In part V, the time and risk dimension of environmental allocation is examined. The environment will be used not only by the present generation but also by future generations. Pollutants such as DDT may accumulate over time so that future generations will inherit our stock of pollutants. Or, on the positive side, succeeding generations will enjoy the benefits of abatement capital and abatement technology which we have invented. In chapter 12 we determine the optimal intertemporal allocation of environmental use and its implications. The problem is to decide which stock of pollutants can be safely passed on to future generations if we take their well-being into consideration. In this context, the optimal time path of an emission tax is studied. In chapter 13, we deal with the problem of economic growth; here we are interested in the extent to which environmental quality targets may represent a brake on economic growth. Also the interrelationship between growth and natural resources is investigated. Finally, in chapter 14, we study the use of the environment in its different functions when damages in the future are uncertain. The implications of such a risk on the optimal environmental quality to be reached and on the policy instruments are discussed. Moreover, other problems relating to risk management such as irreversibilities and approaches to allocate the costs of risk reduction to the decentralized units of an economy are described.

Notes

1. Ch. Wuster, "DDT Reduces Photosynthesis by Marine Phytoplankton," *Science* 159 (1968).

2. Examples of environmental problems are given in H. Siebert and A. Berthorn Antal, *The Political Economy of Environmental Protection* (Greenwich, Conn.: JAI Press, Inc., 1979).

2

Using the Environment—
An Allocation Problem

Externalities

Technological externalities are nonmarket interdependencies among economic activities. Consider, for example, two production activities i and j. An externality exists if the output Q_i in activity i depends on the output Q_j or on the inputs R_j of the other activity. Thus

$$Q_i = F_i(R_i; Q_j, R_j) \qquad (2.1)$$

where
$$\frac{\partial Q_i}{\partial Q_j} \neq 0 \quad \text{or} \quad \frac{\partial Q_i}{\partial R_j} \neq 0$$

If the output of good i increases while the output of good j is rising, then positive externalities exist. If the output of good i decreases while the output of good j is rising, then negative externalities will prevail (for example, open-pit mining may reduce the water-table level and consequently affect the productivity of surrounding agricultural fields). In addition to interdependencies among production activities, there are technological interactions among consumption activities (the thesis of "conspicuous consumption" by Veblen[1]) and between production and consumption activities (cement plant and housing areas, for example).

In the past, economists have taken an interest in externalities (for example, Pigou 1920) because externalities violate a condition for the optimality of a market equilibrium. In this case, the question arises as to whether the set of autonomous decisions by individual units constitutes an optimal allocation. While analyzing externalities, however, the economists have not taken into account the "technological" systems by which the economic activities are linked to one another (for example, the groundwater system in the open-pit mining example). One such system linking economic activities is the environment. The examination of these intervening systems permits new insights into the problem of externalities.

Relationship between the Environment and the Economic System

The environment may be understood to be the set of natural conditions that defines the human living space. It has become customary to distinguish among different environmental systems such as air, water, and land. Within these categories, one may consider such subdivisions as the meteorological region of a metropolitan area, atmospheric conditions in a region of the world such as the Northern Hemisphere, or global systems such as the earth's atmosphere or the ozone layer. In the following analysis, the term *environment* may be understood to be a specific environmental system.

In an economic interpretation, the environment has four functions. Figure 2-1 illustrates these functions.

Consumption Good

The environment provides public goods for consumption such as air to breathe, the amenity of the landscape, and the recreational function of nature (arrow 5 in Figure 2-1). A public good is characterized by two features: First, a public good, contrary to a private good, can be used by several individuals at the same time without the users competing with one another. There is no rivalry in use. This possibility of collective use or non-rivalry is not a sufficient characteristic of a public good because collective consumption also exists for many private goods (for example, a bullfight). Second, a public good does not permit the exclusion of competing users. An outstanding example is the lighthouse which can be used as a checkpoint at sea by every fisherman regardless of whether he wishes to share the costs. In addition to this technical impossibility of exclusion, there are several goods for which an exclusion technically could be possible (television cable or fees at a university), however, one dispenses with the exclusion of potential users owing to normative considerations. Therefore, we have to define a *public good* as a commodity from whose use no one can or should be excluded. The *or should* is decisive. The nonexclusive character of the public good can be very often traced to a value judgment (compare chapter 5).

Environmental quality as a consumption good is such a public good. A technical exclusion, as far as it is possible, is not desirable, and the good can be used by all individuals. The environment as a public good for consumption can be used in two ways: First, the environment provides consumption goods that are measurable in physical units, such as oxygen in pounds inhaled per minute. Second, the environment provides consumption inputs which are only qualitatively valued (say, the amenity of the landscape). While in the first case mass flows from the environment to consumption, this does not necessarily apply in the second case.

In order to simplify the following analysis, we consider environmental quality to be a public good without delineating different kinds of consumptive inputs.[4] A more detailed analysis of the public-good "environment" should—beginning with the consumption theory by Lancaster[2]—define acts of consumption such as swimming, breathing, and so on. Then one would view these acts as

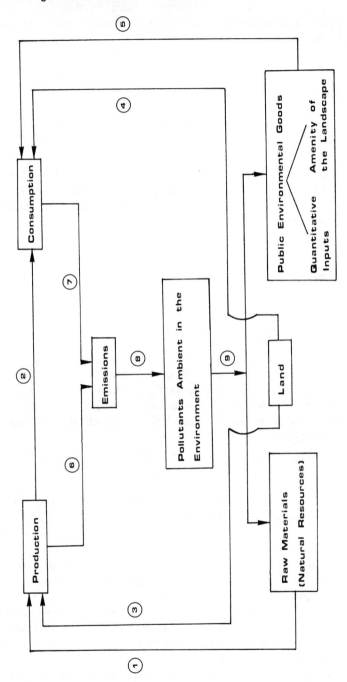

Figure 2–1. Interaction between the Environment and the Economy

the result of inputs to consumption, to which the environment contributes in a quantitative as well as a qualitative way.

Supplier of Resources

The environment provides resources that are used as inputs in production activities, for example, water, sun, minerals, oxygen for combustion processes, and so on (arrow 1 in figure 2-1). The commodities generated by the resources are supplied for consumption (arrow 2). In figure 2-1 the economic system is characterized by production, consumption, and emissions; the environmental system is distinguished by raw materials, land, public environmental goods, and pollutants ambient in the environment.

Receptacle of Wastes

The joint products (arrows 6 and 7) of the production and consumption activities which have no further utility are emitted into the environment. Joint products exist when several goods are produced at the same time. Often the joint product cannot be used; for example, carbon oxide and sulfur dioxide arising from burning fossil fuels and carbon monoxide as well as nitrogen oxides produced by our cars are undesirable by-products. For instance, in West Germany, three million tons of sulfur dioxide were produced per year in the early eighties, mostly from electricity generation, and 3,1 million tons of nitrogen oxides, mostly from transportation.

The reception of emissions, that is, of joint products no longer utilizable, is the third function which the environment fulfills for the economic system (arrows 6 and 7).

The emitted pollutants are absorbed by different environmental media: atmosphere, land, and water. Then the pollutants are partly decomposed, accumulated, transported to other areas, or transformed. Emissions, therefore, are not identical with pollutants ambient in the environment. Emissions are the undesired joint outputs of production and consumption activities. Pollutants are ambient in a certain environmental medium at a certain time. Emissions are changed into pollutants by diffusion or transformation processes in the environment (arrow 8). The distinction between emissions and pollutants ambient in the environment is important. One must always refer to pollutants when defining the target variable—environmental quality. However, economic policy must be directed against the emissions.

The pollutants ambient in the environment at any certain time influence the quality of the environmental services, namely, the public-consumption goods and raw materials. This relationship results from the fact that pollutants can affect the characteristics of environmental systems. Thus, pollutants influence air quality; or they may negatively affect a beautiful landscape by reducing visibility, as is the case in the southwest United States. The behavior of ecosystems or meteorological systems may be changed. For instance, air pollution may reduce the growth rate of trees or may even lead to their destruction. We define this relationship by a damage function (arrow 9).

Note that at first glance this function may be interpreted as an index function since, in our simple approach, pollutants both influence and define environmental quality (for instance, in parts per million). However, environmental quality may also be measured in terms of characteristics other than pollutants, such as the height of trees, longevity of plants, abundance of wildlife, and so on. Then the damage function can no longer be understood as an index function. The damage function is understood here in a technical sense; damages are measured in physical units or in qualitative terms, but they are not yet evaluated in money terms.

In the literature, the damage function has been interpreted in a broader sense. Pollutants may not only have an impact on environmental quality as a public-consumption good or raw materials (that is, nature), but also influence production processes [for instance, air pollution may lead to a quicker corrosion of railway tracks or building facades or result in a lower production output (Siebert and Antal 1979*b*)] .

Location Space

Finally, the environment which is defined over space provides space for location for the economic system, namely, land for industrial and residential locations, agricultural land, and land for infrastructure. This function is similar to the provision for raw materials.

Material Flows between the Environment and the Economic System

To the extent that the interdependence between the environment and the economic system is not of a qualitative nature, the interrelationship can be described in an input-output table (Leontief 1970). Figure 2-2 illustrates such a simplified table. While regarding the economy as a set of sectors which produces for final demand (consumption, capital investment, export, and governmental demand), square 1 in figure 2-2 denotes the interdependence between the sectors and final demand. An additional split of square 1 would include, for example, those quantities which sector i provides for sector j (intermediate demand) or for

Inputs / Outputs	Economy	Environment
Economy	1	3
Environment	2	4

Figure 2-2. Input-Output System of the Economy and the Environment

final demand. The output of a sector would be listed in the rows, and its inputs in the columns (Førsund 1985).

Square 2 contains the outputs of the environmental system which are used as inputs in the different economic sectors (raw materials, water, and oxygen) or which go directly to final demand (oxygen) without having been used in a production process. Square 3 comprises the output of the economic system into the environment, namely, the emissions occurring in the production and consumption activities. If one imagines the economy being sectorally disaggregated, squares 2 and 3 indicate the environmental inputs by sectors and the sectoral sources of emissions. A disaggregation of the environment, that is, in ground, water, and air systems, shows from which environmental system natural resources come and to which sectors of the environment emissions go. Finally, square 4 indicates flows among the branches of the environment.

The interdependencies of quantitative supply between the environment and the economy (listed in figure 2-2) are of such a nature that the mass withdrawn from the environment must flow back to it. Because of the mass-balance concept, mass cannot be lost (Kneese, Ayres, and d'Arge 1970). Note, however, that mass must not flow back to the environment during the period in which it was withdrawn. With capital formation, durable consumer goods, and recycling, it is possible that masses taken from the environment today are emitted into the environment in later periods.[3]

Appendix 2A represents the input-output approach for calculating the quantity of pollutants (in tons) which are generated per $1 million of final demand for a product (pollutant loading of a product). Moreover, other applications are indicated.

Competing Uses

The four functions of the environment (public good for consumption, supplier of raw materials, reception medium for pollutants, and space locations) described are competing with one another if the demand for the environmental service cannot be met at a given environmental endowment. The fact that the environment can be utilized for different purposes is one of the chief reasons for the environ-mental problem. In the following analysis, these competing uses are examined more closely.

Congestion of Public Goods

I consider a single use of an environmental medium and ask to what extent its quality is negatively affected by the number of users. Pure public goods can be used by all individuals to the same extent owing to the nonexistence of an exclu-sion technology. Let U_l^A denote the quality U of the public good l used by indi-vidual A. Then we have for the pure public good

$$U_l^A = U_l^B = \cdots = U_l^Z = U_l \tag{2.2}$$

The congestion problem, on the other hand, is characterized by the fact that environmental goods have a capacity limit. As soon as the intensity of use sur-passes capacity, the quality of the public good is negatively affected. Let N de-note the quantity of users and $\bar{N}$ the capacity limit. An additional user $N > \bar{N}$ affects the quality of the public good negatively (for example, the quality of a national park inundated by a great number of visitors). Thus

$$\frac{dU_l^A}{dN} = \frac{dU_l^B}{dN} = \cdots = \frac{dU_l^Z}{dN} = \frac{dU_l}{dN} \begin{cases} < 0 & \text{for } N > \bar{N} \\ = 0 & \text{for } N \leqslant \bar{N} \end{cases} \tag{2.3}$$

For congestion, the definition that a public good can or should be used by every-body simultaneously still applies. However, the public good that is to be used has changed in its quality. The problem, therefore, is determined by a qualitative scarcity restriction. Beyond the capacity limit, an additional user unfavorably affects the quality of the public good available for other users.

The problem of congestion of public goods can be related to spatially limited environmental goods (say, national parks) or to the entire human living space. In this global interpretation, the environmental question can be under-stood as a congestion problem as described by Boulding's (1971*b*) paradigm of the spaceship earth: the growth of the world's population affects the quality of the human living space when the economic system has negative impacts on the environment, when space is limited, when the given raw materials are depletable, and when the regeneration functions of renewable raw materials are limited. Two components are constitutive in order for this global congestion problem to arise: First, the demand for the globally interpreted good "environment" must increase as a result of population growth, economic development (if the income elasticity of the demand for environment is greater than 1), or a change of preferences in favor of the public good "environment" as a result of development processes. Second, the supply of the good "environment" must be limited.

In the following analysis, the environmental question as a global congestion problem is explained by a more detailed consideration of some (quantitative and partly qualitative) constraints, that is, competing uses. These competing uses have to be considered against the background of a rising demand for environmental goods. Moreover, the congestion of environmental goods has to be considered as one reason for the global congestion problem.

Conservation

There is a competitive use between the role of the environment as a public-consumption good (for example, aesthetic values of nature and landscape) and its function as a location for economic activities. Krutilla (1972), influenced by the conservation movement, illustrates this problem with the Hells Canyon case where a natural amenity may be given away for the mining of raw materials. Also, it cannot be excluded that competing uses occur within the basic function "public-consumption good" itself (for example, a lake used as a drinking-water reservoir or for motorboats).

Let U_l denote the quality of environmental good l, for example, of a national park. Note that the quality of a public good also implies a minimal spatial extension. Let M_k denote the amount of land for location of the type k, let R_h describe the quantity of a resource R_h, and let U_L represent another environmental good L. Then the competitive use can be written as

$$U_l \geqslant \bar{U}_l \Rightarrow \begin{matrix} M_k = 0 \\ R_h = 0 \\ U_L = 0 \end{matrix} \qquad (2.4)$$

That is, the supply of a certain quality $U_l \geqslant \bar{U}_l$ excludes the simultaneous use of land for location, as mining ground, and the supply of another public good L. This competing use is binary in the sense of an "alternative" and exclusive character. Equation 2.4 can also be formulated as a quantitative restriction of land use expressed in square meters. One specific aspect of these competing uses is mainly that a minimum quantity of the public good must be used since the public good is not divisible.

Another qualitative aspect of this restriction is that allocation decisions can be unilaterally or reciprocally irreversible. The mining of raw materials in Hell's Canyon today will preclude its later use as a national park; in contrast, however, its use as a national park will not prevent (technically) the mining of raw materials at some future date. This (intertemporal) irreversibility has to be considered when decisions are made about resource allocations.

Raw-Material Problem

The demand to preserve natural systems for the future can compete with the raw-material supply function of the environment for the present generation. This happens, for instance, when the raw materials withdrawn from the environment are not renewable. Then the question arises as to which alternative uses the scarce raw materials should be allocated. In this regard, the static conflict is not as interesting as the competing alternative uses of raw materials over time. In the case of raw materials, an additive restriction of the form

$$\sum_i R_{hi} \leqslant R_h \tag{2.5}$$

can be given. The withdrawals of nonrenewable materials have to be summed over time, with R_h denoting the total usable resource for all periods. For renewable resources, R_h has to be explained by a regeneration function.

Use of Space

The factor land can be considered to be a special case of resources that cannot be regenerated. A number of different economic allocations compete for the factor land, for example, land for the location of agriculture, industry, residential areas, mining, and infrastructure. If j denotes the different allocation possibilities of land of type k, the additive (that is, quantitative) restriction is

$$\sum_k \sum_j M_{kj} \leqslant M \tag{2.6}$$

Within this additive restriction, irreversibilities also arise because the structure of an area can be interpreted as an embodiment of past locational decisions or as ossified decisions of the past. The given spatial structure influences the topical choice of location. Therefore, restriction 2.6 should also be interpreted with reference to time.

Pollution

This case of competing uses is characterized by the fact that the environment can be used as not only a public-consumption good, but also a receptive medium for pollutants. The damage function in figure 2-1 expresses this competing use.

The concepts of competing uses and negative externalities reflect the same empirical phenomenon but from a different point of view. The concept of competing uses begins with environmental goods and examines alternative purposes for which an environmental good may be used. The concept of negative externalities, however, starts out from an economic activity and encompasses the effects of externalities on other activities. In both approaches the environmental system represents a technological link between two economic activities. We can summarize: Competing uses are one reason for externalities; negative externalities in the environment are the consequences of unsolved competitive uses. Both formulations are attempts to explain the same problem, namely, the problem of environmental disruption.

Zero Price of Environmental Use

The environmental problem is one of competing uses and is, therefore, a question of scarcity. Thus using the environment presents itself as an allocation problem to the economist. The question is how the environment should be allocated to the various competing uses.

In the following discussion, the congestion problem, the conservation issue, and the question of land use are not examined. We concentrate on the question of environmental pollution.

In the past (and today to some extent), the environment was often used as a receptive medium for pollutants at a negligible price. The institutional arrangement for the use of nature's resources did not put a price on the environment. The environment was used like the commons in the Middle Ages; it was regarded as a common-property resource (Kneese 1977). The term *common-property resource* is referred to here as an institutional arrangement which defines the use of natural resources in a specific historical setting. These goods were treated as free goods with no price being attached to them.

Common-property resources may or may not be identical to public goods. The pure public good is defined from the point of view of nonexisting exclusion technologies or the undesirability of exclusion. Common-property resources are defined with respect to a prevailing institutional framework of pricing environmental services. If natural goods are treated as common-property resources because no exclusion technologies exist, they are also public goods (compare chapters 5 and 6).

What is the consequence of a zero price for a natural resource? Such an institutional arrangement of environmental use produces a discrepancy between private and social costs and a suboptimal allocation of the environment as well as of the production factors, labor and capital. Costs are the evaluated inputs of factors of production. *Opportunity costs* are defined as the utility loss of a forgone opportunity. The opportunity costs of resources used in the production of good A consist of forgone opportunities of producing good B (next best opportunity). With a zero price for environmental use, the opportunity costs, then, are not fully appreciated. Suppose that water is used as a receptive medium for pollutants by the pulp and paper industry. Then the opportunity costs may be given, for example, by those utilities forgone in the use of the water for the production of beer or, if the water can be processed, by those costs associated with the processing. Alternatively, if the water is to be used for drinking purposes, the alternative costs lie in the forgone consumption of drinking water. The opportunity costs of a phosphate open-pit mine are the decreases in productivity of the agricultural fields nearby. To cite another example, the alternative costs of air as a receptive medium for pollutants consist of health damage resulting from pollutants.

If the opportunity costs of environmental use are not considered in private decisions, there will be a discrepancy between social and private costs relating to an individual business. Private costs denote factor inputs evaluated from a single activity's point of view. Social costs comprise all costs of an economic activity. Therefore, social costs include not only the value of production factors used by an individual business, but also negative externalities in other units of the economy. In the case of environmental disruption, social costs also include the impairment of environmental quality.

A zero price does not solve the problem of competing uses. Its effect is that private costs and social costs diverge from each other. The accounts of single economic units consider only private costs, not those costs caused by negative externalities in other economic units.

The discrepancy between private and social costs is significant because the prices of goods do not always include all social costs that come about during production. This means that the prices of goods which are produced with a high pollution intensity do not reflect their environmental nuisance. Further, it signifies that the costs of these goods are calculated at a price that is too low. What are the consequences of this cost omission? Consider two products, one being produced with a high proportion of pollution and the other being produced with less pollution. If no price is demanded for the damage done to the environment, the price of the detrimental product does not include the social opportunity costs of the environmental damage. The price of the product that damages the environment is too low. Therefore, the demand and the production of the pollution-intensive good are too high. We have, then, two different allocation effects:

First, the use of the environment at a zero price leads to an overproduction of ecologically harmful products. This means that too many resources are employed in the pollution-intensive sector and too few in the environmentally favorable sector. The distortion of the relative prices thus causes a systematic distortion of production in favor of the ecologically damaging products. A zero price for environmental use, then, can be understood to be an artificial production benefit for the pollution-intensive sector.

Second, the common-property resource is overused since no price is charged for it. The consequence is environmental degradation.

With a zero price for environmental use, the economic system does not include automatic control mechanisms that check an overuse of the environment and a distortion of the sectoral structure. The economic system does not provide incentives to reduce pollution. On the contrary, it systematically favors the products which damage the environment. From the previous analysis it follows that a zero price cannot bring about an optimal allocation of the environment among competing uses. A solution to the environmental problem can be achieved only be deciding which of the competing demands on the environment is of primary importance. Scarcity calls for the introduction of prices. In the following analysis, we examine the institutional arrangements through which prices can be determined so that polluters are forced to take into account the negative externalities caused by them. Thus, our question is: How can we best implement the "polluter pays" principle?

Environmental Effects of Government Decisions

In addition to the effects of economic decisions in the private sector, government activities also influence the quality of the environment. A large part of today's energy supply is provided by government-influenced enterprises. Since the generation of energy is one of the critical factors responsible for the development of pollutants ambient in the air, the government can play an important part in determining environmental quality. Furthermore, government instruments that have direct and indirect impacts on space, for example, in regional planning, influence environmental quality. Other measures, such as stabilization policies, which at first glance hardly seem to affect the environment can also have an impact on environmental quality. In the past, environmental effects were not taken into consideration in government decisions. The government, as well as the private sector, had not included the environment in its calculations and so had put the environment at a zero price for its purposes. Consequently, one of the reasons for environmental degradation has been due to government activity.

How Much Environmental Quality?

If a scarcity price has to be determined for the environment, how should this price be set? Can the market establish such a price? As a first answer, economists tend to conclude not since the environment is a public good, that is, it seems property rights for the environment cannot be clearly defined. A more detailed analysis, however, suggests that property rights to use the environment as a receptacle of wastes can be established. The assignment of such property rights may be accomplished by private bargaining or by the government restructuring the institutional framework of the market economy. One way of doing this is through the introduction of emission taxes, that is, effluent charges. In this context, we have to consider the question of which environmental quality we should set. The strength of an emission tax clearly depends on the level of environmental quality being sought. Since reaching a specific environmental quality level will imply costs, the benefits and costs of environmental policy should be considered. Also, the political processes through which the target variable "environmental quality" is determined is of interest in our analysis.

A Taxonomy of the Environmental Problem

Theoretical models always abstract from real aspects of a problem. Therefore, it is worthwhile to survey the main components of a problem even if some aspects are not analyzed later. The environmental problem, then, should take into account the following aspects.

Environmental media. Air, water, land, and natural ecological systems are the environmental media mentioned most often. Depending on the medium to be considered, specific problems are to be dealt with. For instance, the diffusion function differs among environmental media. It may be easier to find solutions to the environmental problems of smaller systems, such as a pond in a local neighborhood, than for larger systems, such as the ozone layer of the world. Purification may be possible after emissions have entered one medium (water) but not another (air).

Spatial extent of environmental media. Environmental media may be local, regional, national, international, or global.

Form of appearance of pollutants. Pollutants may arise as joint outputs of consumption or production. This is the case with which I concern myself mostly in this book. Pollutants may also be found in consumption goods such as DDT in agricultural products. Then they are not joint outputs, but rather joint inputs, for instance, in consumption processes. Pollutants may also be found in new products that enter the market, such as chemicals.

Type of pollutants. Pollutants may differ with respect to their properties (organic wastes, chemical properties). They may be poisonous, damaging in the long run, or neutral.

Origin of pollutants. Pollutants may stem from raw materials or from energy. They may come from stationary or mobile sources.

Time pattern of generation. Pollutants may occur in a continuous or discontinuous fashion. Examples are emissions from smoke stacks and technical accidents, respectively.

Longevity of pollutants. Pollutants may be easily absorbed by environmental media, such as organic wastes in water, or they may take longer, as is the case with DDT with respect to the food chains in nature. Consequently, we may distinguish between short-, intermediate-, and long-term problems.

Notes

1. Th. Veblen, *The Theory of the Leisure Class* (London: Allen and Unwin, 1925).

2. Compare K. Lancaster, "Change and Innovation in the Technology of Consumption," in *The American Economic Review* (Menaska, Wis.: American Economic Association, 1966), pp. 14–23.

3. The implications of the transformation of mass into energy in the mass-balance concept are not discussed. Also compare the problem of entropy, see Faber et al. (1983).

4. In the following text, we use the term environmental quality for simplifying purposes, although the public good environment definitively has a quantitative characteristics for instance pounds of oxygen consumed.

Appendix 2A:
Input-Output Analysis and the Environment

Leontief (1970) uses input-output analysis to analyze relationships between the economic system and the environment. Assume a linear function between the quantity of waste product h and the output level of sector K to be

$$W_h = d_{hK} X_K$$

where X_K can be defined in physical as well as in value terms. The vector of the wastes w is given by $w = Dx$, where D denotes the matrix of the coefficients d_{hK}. For a given final demand y, in reference to the function $x = (I - A)^{-1}y$, the vector of the pollutants is given by $w = D(I - A)^{-1}y$.

In this manner, the vector w of the waste products in determined by a secondary calculation (Leontief and Ford 1972). It is also possible to determine the vector of the waste products endogenously by introducing w into the model. In this case, the matrix A is extended by the matrix D. The resulting matrix $\begin{bmatrix} A \\ D \end{bmatrix}$ is not quadratic and so it is not applicable to input-output analysis. Nevertheless, it is applicable to problems of linear programming. However, if the assumption is made that the activities w can abate waste products, then a quadratic matrix is given. The problem is

$$\begin{bmatrix} I-A & -B \\ D & -I+S \end{bmatrix} \begin{bmatrix} x \\ w \end{bmatrix} = \begin{bmatrix} c \\ c^+ \end{bmatrix}$$

with $A = [a_{kK}] = \left[\dfrac{X_{kK}}{X_K}\right]$ input-output coefficient

$D = [d_{hK}] = \left[\dfrac{W_{hK}}{X_K}\right]$ Quantity of emission $h = 1 \ldots l$ per output unit (joint product)

$B = [b_{kH}] = \left[\dfrac{x_{kH}}{W_k}\right]$ input of activity $H = 1 \ldots l$ per unit of abated emissions provided by sector k

$\Sigma = [\sigma_{hH}] = \left[\dfrac{W_h}{W_H}\right]$ waste product $h = 1 \ldots l$ caused per output unit W_H with $H = 1 \ldots l$

Here σ_{hH} denotes the quantity of wastes h generated in the abatement of a unit of waste product H. If the d_{hK} coefficients are negative, then they denote the use of a waste product as an input. Finally, c is final demand of tolerated emissions.

The level of emissions can be determined, given levels of c and c^+. It is given by the vector w:

$$\begin{bmatrix} x \\ w \end{bmatrix} = \begin{bmatrix} I - A & -B \\ \hline D & -I - \Sigma \end{bmatrix} \begin{bmatrix} c \\ c^+ \end{bmatrix}$$

Assuming that not only production but also consumption brings about wastes, the wastes are determined by $w^+ = D^+ c^+$, where $D^+ = d_{hK}^+$ denotes emission h occurring per unit of final demand k. Then the total emission vector w of production and consumption may be written as

$$\overline{w} = [D \mid \Sigma] \begin{bmatrix} x \\ w \end{bmatrix} + D^+ c$$

Using this approach, Førsund (1985) estimates the emissions of the Norwegian economy. The sum of the columns depicts the interdependency between product prices and value added. For a given value added, the price of the products can be calculated. This also applies to the calculation of prices of abatement activities. Assume that the producers have to abate part of a total waste. If one transforms the waste products which appear as joint products into a value factor, then the price change of the goods resulting from this political measure can be determined.

Let t_{hK} denote the part of the pollutant h that is caused by industry K and that also has to be abated by it. Then we have

$$\begin{bmatrix} I - A' & -D't \\ \hline -B' & I - \Sigma't \end{bmatrix} \begin{bmatrix} p_1 \\ p_2 \end{bmatrix} = \begin{bmatrix} \omega_1 \\ \omega_2 \end{bmatrix}$$

with p_1 and p_2 as price vectors of the activities x and w and ω_1 and ω_2 as the added values of these activities.

Leontief comes to the conclusion that waste-abatement sectors contribute to the production of waste products by their demand for inputs from other sectors and through the stimulation of demand itself. Here is how we evaluate this multiplier of pollution abatement. Assume that the vector of the waste products w that is connected with a given output vector X is given. If the costs per unit of alternative waste-abating processes are known, then the minimal costs of the waste abatement can be calculated in a programming model.

Let l represent the abatement costs without considering the generation of pollutants in abatement. Let l' represent abatement costs that also take into account the fact that pollutants are generated in abatement. Then the expression l'/l is the desired multiplier. Also, a waste-income multiplier can be calculated. This multiplier denotes the quantity of waste products per dollar income of a sector (not as in Leontief's study, where it is per unit of final demand). Such a multiplier could be relevant with respect to studies of industrialization.

Another application of the input-output approach is to study the impact of an emission tax or of other policy instruments on the price vector of an economy (Conrad 1985), to explicitly include abatement capital (Conrad and Morrison 1986), to specify the discharges of emissions into different media and their sectorial sources or to indicate the macroeconomic impacts of abatement activities (Førsund 1985).

The input-output approach when used to analyze the interrelation of the economy with the environment has met with considerable critism. The linearization of the ecological system, as is suggested by Isard (1972), is particularly doubtful.

The yield of waste products does not say anything about the quantity of pollutants remaining in the environment. Thus, the transformation of waste products to pollutants should be determined by a diffusion function.

Adjustment processes for reducing pollutants are not fully taken into account. Substitution processes, such as recycling, take place which change the coefficients.

The data of the four-digit SIC number depend on a sector's definition with regard to the type of product. They give little information as to materials, production processes, or the relationship between processes and products.

Part II
Static Allocation Aspect

3

Production Theory and Transformation Space

In the following four chapters, the static allocation aspect is analyzed. We study production theory, assuming emissions as joint outputs of production and treating environmental quality as a variable in the production set (chapter 3). After defining the production possibilities, we study which prices should be set in order to reach optimal results with respect to a welfare criterion. Also, we analyze whether optimality can be attained in a competitive equilibrium when environmental quality is taken into consideration (chapter 4). In chapter 5, we present the public-goods approach to environmental allocation. Benefit/cost analysis, the Lindahl solution, and institutional mechanisms which reveal individual preferences are discussed. Whereas the public-goods approach starts from the assumption that environmental quality cannot be attributed to individuals, the property-rights discussion stresses the point that the introduction of property rights may solve the allocation problem (chapter 6).

Production Theory

We consider a simplified two-sector economy characterized by pollutants which are generated as joint products of output and then emitted into the environment (emissions). For simplifying purposes, we assume that there is only one type of pollutant generated by the two sectors:[1]

$$S_i^p \geqslant H_i(Q_i) \qquad H_i' > 0, H_i'' \geqslant 0 \text{ for } i = 1, 2 \tag{3.1}$$

This emission function assumes that at a given technology the quantity of pollutants S_i^p increases proportionally or progressively with output Q_i, but excludes the case in which the quantity of pollutants increases regressively. Figure 3-1a depicts the emission function for the cases $H_i'' = 0$ (linear curve) and $H_i'' > 0$ (strictly convex curve).

The production function is characterized by a declining marginal productivity and does not distinguish among different production factors. Rather, for simplicity, we assume only one type of resource R (compare figure 3-1b):

$$Q_i \leqslant F_i(R_i) \qquad F_i' > 0, F_i'' < 0 \tag{3.2}$$

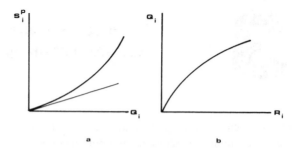

Figure 3-1. Emission and Production Functions

From equations 3.1 and 3.2 a function results which shows the emissions to be dependent on the resource input:

$$S_i^p = H_i[F_i(R_i)] = Z_i(R_i) \quad Z_i' > 0, Z_i'' \gtreqless 0 \tag{3.1a}$$

This function shows that the pollutants in this approach can also be understood to be joint products of the input. Obviously, a model could be formulated in which equation 3.1a, instead of 3.1, could be used. Note that $Z_i' = H_i'F_i' > 0$.

If one applies the mass-balance concept to the production function, then a concave production function implies a convex emission function. This is explained as follows. Let α and β designate the quantitative content of resources in commodity 1, and let S_1^p be the joint product. Then we have,

$$\alpha Q_1 + \beta S_1^p = R_1$$

so that

$$S_1^p = \frac{1}{\beta}(R_1 - \alpha Q_1) = \frac{1}{\beta}[R_1 - \alpha F_1(R_1)] = Z_1(R_1)$$

Because the function F is concave, the emission function Z has to be convex. Thus, the mass-balance concept and a concave production function imply $Z_i'' > 0$. Such a convex emission function is assumed in the following analysis. Note that $Z_i'' = H_i''F_i'^2 + H_i'F_i''$, so that $Z_i'' > 0$ implies that $H_i'' > 0$.

The pollution-abatement function tells us that pollutants can be reduced by an input of resources in abatement R_i^r, where S_i^r denotes the abated quantities of the pollutants. As with the production function, here a declining marginal productivity is assumed to prevail. The abatement function is specific to each sector, as is the emission function.[2]

$$S_i^r \leqslant F_i^r(R_i^r) \quad F_i^{r\prime} > 0, F_i^{r\prime\prime} < 0 \tag{3.3}$$

In reality, pollutants can be abated by different processes. First, pollutants can be reduced by new production technologies. Here I assume a given technology. Second, pollutants can be reduced by filtering and withholding procedures before they actually enter the environmental media. Therefore, one can start from the fact that the abatement technologies are sector-specific. This case is assumed here. Finally, pollutants can be abated even when they are already ambient in the environmental media (water).

The diffusion function in equation 3.4 explains the relationship between emissions S_i^p and the quantity of pollutants ambient in the environmental media S.[3] A more precise formulation of the diffusion function should take into consideration the assimilative capacity of the environmental system, that is, its capacity to receive pollutants and reduce them without changing the quality of the environment. The determination of this assimilative capacity (in a river system, for example, the current speed, percentage of oxygen, temperature, and quantity of pollutants) and its temporal variation can be influenced by resource inputs (for example, in-stream aeration of a river system and afforestation). This purification of media (for example, water management) could be introduced into the model by an abatement function which is not specific to a sector (for example, the purification function of a water cooperative). Anyway, since the diffusion problem is not considered further, equation 3.4 is utilized solely as an equation for defining pollutants ambient in the environment. In this model, the diffusion function degenerates to a definition; pollutants ambient in the environment are identical to the total quantity of emissions. In the following, the concepts of total emissions and pollutants ambient in the environment are used synonymously because of the nonconsideration of the diffusion problem.

$$S = \sum_i S_i^p - \sum_i S_i^r \qquad (3.4)$$

The damage function in equation 3.5 specifies how pollutants S have an effect on environmental quality. Here the damage function is a physical relationship and does not evaluate environmental quality in monetary terms. In a simple interpretation, equation 3.5 may be understood as an index function which defines an index of environmental quality in terms of pollutants. Alternatively, environmental quality may be defined independently of pollutants (for example, amenity of the landscape and stability of ecological systems). Then equation 3.5 defines a physical relationship rather than an index function. Besides damage to the public-consumption-good environment, one can imagine other damage functions: Pollutants influence the quality of inputs in production processes, the production processes themselves, almost finished goods (financial losses), and so on. The damage function, shown in figure 3–2, considers only environmental damages.

$$U \leqslant G(S) \qquad G' < 0, G'' < 0 \qquad (3.5)$$

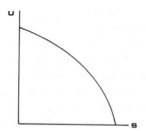

Figure 3-2. Damage Function

A resource restriction limits the production and abatement possibilities of the economy considered:

$$\sum R_i + \sum R_i' \leqslant \bar{R} \tag{3.6}$$

Transformation Space with Environmental Quality

Equations 3.1 through 3.6 describe the production possibilities of the economy; if one wants to produce more at a given technology with resources being fully utilized, then emissions will increase and the quality of the environment will be reduced. This is due to the fact that, according to the emission function, emissions rise with increasing output. Also, in order to increase production, resources must be withdrawn from abatement. Environmental quality then declines for two reasons: more emissions from increased production and reduced abatement. In contrast, an improvement of environmental quality at a given technology with full utilization of the resources is possible only if more resources are used in abatement and the production of the commodities is reduced. It becomes clear that the central competitive use in the case of environmental pollution exists between the environment as a public-consumption good and as a receptive medium for pollutants.

Figure 3-3 represents graphically the restrictions described in equations 3.1 through 3.6 for a two-commodity economy. The transformation space in figure 3-3 illustrates the maximum production possibilities for commodities 1 and 2 and the public good, environmental quality. Restrictions 3.1 through 3.6 may also be expressed by the equation $U = \phi(Q_1, Q_2)$. An important question then, is: What characteristics does the transformation space have? That is, is the function $U = \phi(Q_1, Q_2)$ concave or not (compare Appendix 3A)?

The following intuitive considerations serve to determine more precisely the form of the transformation space. A more formal treatment is given in Appendix 3A. For simplicity, it is assumed here that only one type of abatement activity exists, and R_3 denotes the resource input in abatement. Moreover, it is assumed

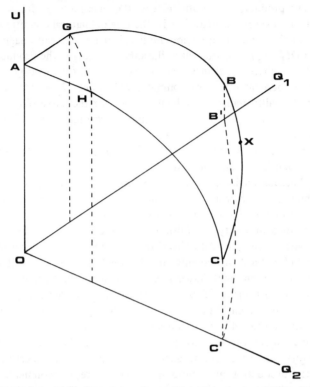

Figure 3-3. Transformation Space with Environmental Quality

that commodity 1 is the pollution-intensive commodity. This can be expressed as

$$H_1'F_1' > H_2'F_2' \qquad (3.7)$$

Condition 3.7 can be interpreted with the help of equation (3.1a), for $H_i'F_i'$ is the first derivative of the Z function. The term

$$Z_i' = H_i'F_i' = \frac{\partial S_i^p}{\partial Q_i} \frac{\partial Q_i}{\partial R_i}$$

denotes what quantity of emissions occurs if a resource is used in sector i. Thus $H_i'F_i'$ can be interpreted as the marginal propensity of the resource input to pollute. Condition 3.7 states that the marginal propensity of the resource input to pollute in sector 1 is higher than in sector 2. Sector 1 is the pollution-intensive sector. For a more detailed interpretation of equation 3.7, compare Siebert et al. (1980, p. 24).

At zero production in both sectors, the maximum environmental quality (OA in figure 3-3) is reached, that is, the original natural condition. Let $Q_2 = 0$ and expand the production of commodity 1. Then one can imagine a resource allocation (R_1, R_3) such that all pollutants occurring in the production of commodity 1 are abated (distance AG in figure 3-3). Analogously, AH indicates those production quantities of commodity 2, when $Q_1 = 0$, at which the environmental quality remains maximal. Except for the curve GH, the horizontal roof represents a situation with maximum environmental quality and underemployment.

Expand the production of commodity 1 at point G for $Q_2 = 0$ by 1 unit. Then the quantity of emissions increases progressively owing to the fact that $H_1'' > 0$. Because environmental quality decreases overproportionally with increased emissions, environmental quality has to fall overproportionally as a consequence of the increase in production of commodity 1. With an increase in production of commodity 1, additional resources are used in production. Since these resources must be withdrawn from abatement, the quantity of abated emissions falls (and environmental quality declines). We know that as a result of each unit of input withdrawn from abatement, the unabated emissions increase overproportionally. This is explained by the decreasing marginal productivity in abatement. Finally, according to the law of declining marginal returns, each additional unit of commodity 1 produced required an increasingly greater input of resources. Consequently, for a shift from G to B, the quantity of pollutants has to increase progressively as inputs are reallocated from abatement to the production of commodity 1. Therefore, environmental quality has to decrease progressively. The curve GB is concave. The concavity of curve GB can also be shown formally (Appendix 3A).

The distance BB' denotes that quality of the environment which results from a total specialization in the production of commodity 1, given full employment and no abatement. The distance CC' represents that quality of the environment which corresponds to a total specialization in commodity 2 with no abatement. And $CC' > BB'$ reminds us that commodity 1 is the pollution-intensive commodity.[4]

Define $\alpha = Q_1/Q_2$ and hold α constant. Consider a point on the curve GH. A unit of resources is withdrawn from abatement and put into the production of commodities 1 and 2 with the quantitative relation α of both commodities remaining constant. The quantity of emissions rises progressively in both sectors; in abatement, the quantity of unabated emissions decreases progressively, since the marginal productivity of disposal activities increases with a lower factor input. A reallocation of the resources in favor of production, given a constant proportion of commodities α, thus causes the emissions to rise progressively. At the same time, marginal productivity increases underproportionally in production. The curve of the transformation space, for α held constant, is concave (compare equation 3A.12).

Curve BC represents the transformation problem for the case of resources not being used in abatement ($R_3 = 0$). The projection of curve BC into the $Q_1 Q_2$ plane, that is, the curve $B'C'$, is the traditional transformation curve. In a situation without environmental policy, the economy is located on curve BC. Point X on the transformation curve, that is, the vector of goods and thus the factor allocation $\{R_1, R_2\}$, is determined by the relative price p_2/p_1.

This intuitive reasoning and formal analysis show that the transformation space is concave. There is a tradeoff between the production of commodities and the provision of environmental quality. If one wants a higher output, the quality of the environment must be reduced. And if one wants the quality of the environment to be improved, output has to be reduced.

Variables Affecting the Transformation Space

This analysis suggests that the form of the transformation space is affected by the following variables: resource endowment of the economy, pollution intensity of the two sectors, and productivity in production and abatement.

In figure 3–4a a case is presented in which sector 1 is pollution-intensive whereas sector 2 produces no pollutants at all. In this case, sector 2 can produce without negatively affecting environmental quality. Point C depicts a situation in which all resources are used in the production of commodity 2 and no environmental degradation occurs.

In figure 3–4b we have assumed that curve GB shifts outward to GB''. This can be due to technical progress in the production of commodity 1, in the emission function (reduced emissions), or in abatement of sector 1. It is conceivable

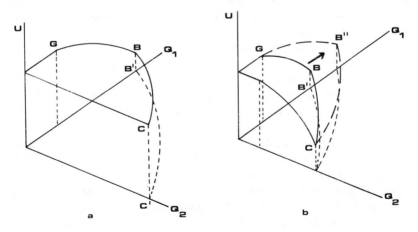

Figure 3–4. Specific Cases of the Transformation Space

that, because of technical progress, sector 1 is no longer the pollution-intensive sector. Another condition not depicted in figure 3-4 is an increase in resource endowment. In such a case, the whole transformation space shifts outward, including curve GH in figure 3-3.

In reality, we may also observe that pollutants have a negative impact on production. For example, particulates from mining may reduce the productivity of nearby citrus trees. Then the production function shown in 3.2 has to be redefined as

$$Q_i = F_i(R_i, S) \quad \text{with } F_{iS} < 0, F_{iSS} < 0 \tag{3.8}$$

Here $F_S < 0$ indicates that pollutants affect production negatively; that is, pollutants have a negative productivity effect. And $F_{iSS} = dF_{iS}/dS < 0$ says that the negative productivity will become smaller in absolute terms. If equation 3.8 holds true, increased production means not only a decline in the quality of the environment, but also a reduction of output since pollutants will have a negative impact on output. With a larger stock of pollutants, the transformation space may tend to contract (curve GB'' in figure 3-5). From equation 3B.4 we have

$$\frac{\partial U}{\partial Q_i} \lessgtr 0 \Leftrightarrow \phi_{1S} + \phi_{2S} \gtrless \frac{1}{F_3'} \tag{3.9}$$

By defining an inverse to the production function 3.8 we get

$$R_i = \phi_i(Q_i, S)$$

Then ϕ_{iS} indicates the inputs required to compensate for the effect of negative productivity caused by one unit of pollutant, if output in sector i is to be kept constant. The term $\phi_{1S} + \phi_{2S}$ denotes total inputs required to keep output constant in both sectors. The right side of inquality 3.9 denotes resources used for abating one unit of pollutant. If the inputs required to compensate for the negative-productivity effect caused by one unit of pollutant are smaller than those required for abating one unit of pollutant, then $\partial U/\partial Q_i < 0$, that is, curve GKB'' in figure 3-5 has a negative slope. If more resources are needed in order to compensate for the negative-productivity effect caused by one unit of pollutant than those required for its abatement, curve GKB'' will have a positive slope. When S rises, the absolute value of ϕ_S^i rises. Also, F_3' will fall and $1/F_3'$ will rise.

Compare the transformation space $AGB''C''H$, in which negative externalities in production exist (equation 3.8), with the case $AGBCH$, in which no negative externalities in production exist (equation 3.2). One can expect that negative externalities in production will shift the transformation space inward. Also, the transformation space may not be concave in the case of negative externalities.

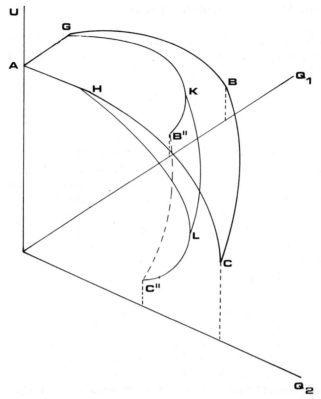

Figure 3-5. Transformation Space with Negative Externalities

This may raise serious theoretical questions since normally one assumes the concavity of the transformation space when analyzing the existence of equilibrium or the properties of optimality in a state of competitive equilibrium.[5] Note that points G and H are identical in figures 3-3 and 3-5 since there is no negative-productivity effect at maximal environmental quality.

The properties of the transformation space are affected by the intensity of the negative-productivity effect of pollutants. If the negative productivity is small or negligible, then the transformation space will not curve inward. If sector 1 is strongly affected by pollutants, then the inward bend will be stronger for sector 1 than for sector 2.

Note that $\partial U / \partial Q_i > 0$ holds true in section $C''B''KL$. This means that environmental quality has positive opportunity costs. One can increase environmental quality and production at the same time. There is no tradeoff between environmental quality and private outputs.

An Alternative Approach of Production Theory

An alternative approach in the description of the production properties of an economy is to integrate equations 3.1, 3.2, and 3.3 into a production function (Pethig 1979)

$$Q_i = F_i(\tilde{R}_i, \tilde{S}_i) \tag{3.10}$$

In equation 3.10, resource input $\tilde{R}_i$ is defined as $\tilde{R}_i = R_i + R_i^r$; that is, it indicates total resources used by sector 1 without distinguishing between resources used for production and those used for abatement. Similarly, $\tilde{S}_i$ is defined as $\tilde{S}_i = S_i^p$ - S_i^r, that is, net emissions. In equation 3.10, net emissions are interpreted as a factor of production with $F_{iS} \geqslant 0$. And $\tilde{S}_i$ can be interpreted as being an assimilative service which the environment provides for use by firms. Equation 3.10 does not tell anything about which quantities of resources are used for production or for abatement. Also, there is no information about gross emissions S_i^p or the abated emissions S_i^r. The concept underlying equation 3.10 assumes that production, emission, and abatement technologies can be described as technological relationships allowing substitution between the resource inputs $\tilde{R}_i$ and $\tilde{S}_i$. Note that $\tilde{R}_i$ can be interpreted as a vector for different types of inputs, such as labor and capital. Also, observe that $\tilde{S}_i$ in equation 3.10 indicates net emissions of sector i, not the stock of pollutants in the environment. Equation 3.10 can easily be extended in order to allow for a negative-productivity effect emanating from a pool of pollutants by introducing a variable S with $F_S < 0$.

The law of conservation of matter represents a restriction for equation 3.10. In terms of weight, the sum of regular output and net emissions cannot surpass the input. Consequently, net emissions must be restricted. For instance, a montonic function φ_i may restrict net possible emissions:

$$\tilde{S}_i \leqslant \varphi_i(\tilde{R}_i) \tag{3.11}$$

Equation 3.11 specifies the input space of the production function. Assume that equation 3.11 is linear. Then the production technology in 3.10 and 3.11 can be described as in figure 3.6. Note that $F_{iS} > 0$ is assumed for $\tilde{S}_i < \varphi_i(\tilde{R}_i)$ and $F_{iS} = 0$ for $\tilde{S}_i = \varphi_i(\tilde{R}_i)$; that is, the assimilative capacity of the environment has a zero productivity if the maximum amount of net possible emissions is used. In figure 3-6 the isoquants indicate the possibilities for substitution between the inputs $\tilde{R}_i$ and $\tilde{S}_i$.

Although in this approach one does not explicitly consider abatement activities, it has the advantage of lending itself to traditional production theory. For instance, once a price for pollutants is introduced, traditional microeconomic results can be reinterpreted with respect to environmental problems.

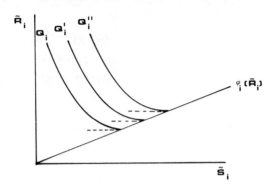

Figure 3-6. Production Function with Emissions as Input

Notes

1. The inequality sign allows for the case where the generation of pollutants is inefficient in the sense that more pollutants are generated than necessary. Note, however, that because of the mass-balance concept, emissions are restricted.

2. I do not consider the mass-balance concept in abatement. Note that declining marginal productivities in abatement imply residuals of abatement activities.

3. It is assumed here that pollutants ambient in the environment die away at the end of the period. In chapter 12 this assumption of the immediate decay of the pollutants is removed.

4. Note that the pollution intensity of sectors is defined in terms of marginal propensities. On the relation of marginal and average pollution intensities, compare Siebert et al. (1980).

5. A more detailed analysis is given in Siebert (1982g).

Appendix 3A:
Properties of the
Transformation Space

The transformation space $U = \phi(Q_1, Q_2)$ is concave if $d^2U < 0$, that is, if the Hessian matrix H is negative definite:

$$H = \begin{bmatrix} \dfrac{\partial^2 U}{\partial Q_1^2} & \dfrac{\partial^2 U}{\partial Q_1 \, \partial Q_2} \\[2mm] \dfrac{\partial^2 U}{\partial Q_2 \, \partial Q_1} & \dfrac{\partial^2 U}{\partial Q_2^2} \end{bmatrix} \tag{3A.1}$$

The Hessian matrix is negative definite if $|H_1| = \partial^2 U / \partial Q_1^2 < 0$ and if $|H_2| = |H| > 0$.

In order to analyze the concavity of the transformation space, I assume, for simplicity, that only one abatement activity exists. Then the problem is defined by

$$\begin{aligned} S &= H_1(Q_1) + H_2(Q_2) - S^r \\ Q_i &= F_i(R_i) \quad \text{or} \quad R_i = F_i^{-1}(Q_i) \\ S^r &= F_3(R_3) \\ \bar{R} &= R_1 + R_2 + R_3 \end{aligned} \tag{3A.2}$$

Substitution yields

$$U = G[H_1(Q_1) + H_2(Q_2) - F_3(\bar{R} - R_1 - R_2)] \tag{3A.3}$$

Now, we have[1]

$$\begin{aligned} \frac{\partial U}{\partial Q_1} &= G' \left(H_1' - F_3' \frac{dR_3}{dQ_1} \right) = G' \left(H_1' - F_3' \frac{dR_3}{dR_1} \frac{1}{F_1'} \right) \\ &= G' \left(H_1' + \frac{F_3'}{F_1'} \right) < 0 \end{aligned} \tag{3A.4}$$

and

$$
\begin{aligned}
\frac{\partial^2 U}{\partial Q_1^2} &= G'' \frac{dS}{dQ_1}\left(H_1' + \frac{F_3'}{F_1'}\right) + G'\left[H_1'' + \frac{F_1'(dF_3'/dQ_1) - F_3'(dF_1'/dQ_1)}{F_1'^2}\right] \\
&= G''\left(H_1' + \frac{F_3'}{F_1'}\right)^2 + G'\left[H_1'' + \frac{1}{F_1'^2}\left(-F_3'' - \frac{F_3'F_1''}{F_1'}\right)\right] < 0
\end{aligned}
\tag{3A.5}
$$

Define $A_i = H_i' + F_3'/F_i' > 0$, $E_i = G'(H_i'' - F_3'F_i''/F_i'^3) < 0$, and $D = G'F_3''/(F_1'F_2') > 0$. Then equation 3A.5 becomes

$$
\frac{\partial^2 U}{\partial Q_1^2} = G''A_1^2 + E_1 - \frac{DF_2'}{F_1'}
\tag{3A.6}
$$

The minor H_1 is negative. It follows from equation 3A.6 that curve GB in figure 3–3 is strictly concave. Analogously, we obtain $\partial U/\partial Q_2 < 0$ and $\partial^2 U/\partial Q_2^2 < 0$.

We have (for constant Q_1 and constant R_1)

$$
\begin{aligned}
\frac{\partial^2 U}{\partial Q_1 \partial Q_2} &= \frac{\partial[G'[S](H_1' + F_3'/F_1')]}{\partial Q_2} \\
&= G'' \frac{dS}{dQ_2}\left(H_1' + \frac{F_3'}{F_1'}\right) + \frac{G'}{F_1'}\frac{dF_3'}{dR_3}\frac{dR_3}{dR_2}\frac{dR_2}{dQ_2} \\
&= G''\left(H_2' + \frac{F_3'}{F_2'}\right)\left(H_1' + \frac{F_3'}{F_1'}\right) - \frac{G'}{F_1'}\frac{F_3''}{F_2'} \\
&= G''A_1A_2 - D < 0
\end{aligned}
\tag{3A.7}
$$

Equations 3A.6 and 3A.7 are not yet sufficient to establish that $H_2 > 0$ as defined in equation 3A.1. The first term of H_2 is positive, the second is negative. Only if the product of the cross derivatives as defined in equation 3A.7 is smaller than the product of the derivatives as defined in equation 3A.6, will the transformation function be concave.

The Arrow-Enthoven theorem makes less stringent demands for the existence of a global maximum. If the target function is concave, then the quasi-convexity of every restriction is sufficient (thus quasi-concavity, too).[2] The production, abatement, and damage functions are concave and thereby quasi-concave too. The emission function is a monotonic function of a variable and thereby quasi-concave as well as quasi-convex. The resource restriction is linear. Consequently, the Arrow-Enthoven conditions are fulfilled. Thus the condition of concavity is more restrictive than the condition for a quasi-concavity.

An alternative (more intuitive) approach for verifying the concavity of $U = \phi(Q_1, Q_2)$ runs as follows. The transformation space $U = \phi(Q_1, Q_2)$ is concave if every restriction is concave. The production, abatement, and damage functions are concave. The resource restriction is linear and hence concave (and convex). The emission function is linear for $H_i'' = 0$ (and thus concave and convex). If we assume that $H_i'' = 0$, the transformation space $U = \phi(Q_1, Q_2)$ is concave because all single restrictions which define it are concave.

The concavity of the transformation space implies that a cut through the transformation space for a given U, that is, a given level of pollutants S, will also be concave. We have

$$\bar{S} = H_1(Q_1) + H_2(Q_2) - F_3(R_3)$$

$$d\bar{S} = 0 = H_1'dQ_1 + H_2'dQ_2 - F_3'(-dR_1 - dR_2)$$

$$0 = H_1'dQ_1 + H_2'dQ_2 + \frac{F_3'}{F_1'}dQ_1 + \frac{F_3'}{F_2'}dQ_2$$

$$\frac{dQ_1}{dQ_2} = -\frac{H_2' + F_3'/F_2'}{H_1' + F_3'/F_1'} = -\frac{A_2}{A_1} < 0 \tag{3A.8}$$

so that the rate of transformation corresponds to the relation of marginal costs (including costs of abatement):

$$\frac{d^2Q_1}{dQ_2^2} = -\frac{1}{A_1^2}\left\{ A_1\left[H_2'' + \frac{1}{(F_2')^2}\left(F_2'\frac{dF_3'}{dQ_2} - F_3'\frac{dF_2'}{dQ_2}\right)\right]\left[\frac{dH_1'}{dQ_2}\right] \right.$$

$$\left. + \frac{1}{(F_1')^2}\left(F_1'\frac{dF_3'}{dQ_2} - F_3'\frac{dF_1'}{dQ_2}\right)\right]\right\} \tag{3A.9}$$

We have[3]

$$\frac{d^2Q_1}{dQ_2^2} = -\frac{1}{A_1^2}\left\{ A_1\left[H_2'' + \frac{1}{(F_2')^2}\left(-F_3''\frac{F_3'F_2''}{F_2'}\right)\right]\right.$$

$$- A_2\left[\frac{dH_1'}{dQ_1}\frac{dQ_1}{dQ_2} + \frac{1}{(F_1')^2}\left(-\frac{F_3''F_1'}{F_2'} - \frac{F_3'F_1''}{F_2'}\frac{dR_1}{dR_2}\right)\right]$$

$$\left. - A_1F_3''\frac{1}{(F_2')^2}\frac{dR_1}{dR_2} + A_2F_3''\frac{1}{F_1'F_2'}\frac{dR_1}{dR_2}\right\} \tag{3A.10}$$

This implies

$$\frac{d^2Q_1}{dQ_2^2} < 0: \quad -A_1\frac{F_3''}{F_2'} + A_2\frac{F_3''}{F_1'} - A_1\frac{F_3''}{F_2'}\frac{dR_1}{dR_2} + A_2\frac{F_3''}{F_1'}\frac{dR_1}{dR_2} > 0$$

$$\frac{d^2Q_1}{dQ_2^2} < 0: \quad -\left(1+\frac{dR_1}{dR_2}\right)\frac{F_3''}{F_1'F_2'^2}(H_1'F_1' - H_2'F_2') > 0$$

$$\frac{d^2Q_1}{dQ_2^2} < 0: \quad H_1'F_1' \gtreqless H_2'F_2' \qquad\qquad (3A.11a)$$

$$1+\frac{dR_1}{dR_2} \gtreqless 0 \qquad\qquad (3A.11b)$$

Assume that sector 1 is the pollution-intensive sector, that is, $H_1'F_1' > H_2'F_2'$. Then $dR_1/dR_2 < -1$ implies that the use of one additional unit of resource in the less pollution-intensive sector will not require that sector 1 lose one unit of resource. This is due to the fact that a shift toward the less pollution-intensive sector, for given S, requires less resources in abatement. This reduction in abatement enables more resources to be made available for sector 2. If sector 2 is assumed to be the pollution-intensive sector, one additional unit of output by sector 2 requires that sector 1 lose more than one unit of resource. This follows because additional resources have to be put into abatement in order to keep a given level of pollution S.

Define a constant relation $\alpha = Q_1/Q_2$. Then equation 3A.3 simplifies to

$$U = G[H_1(\alpha Q_2) + H_2(Q_2) - F_3(\bar{R} - R_1 - R_2)] \qquad\qquad (3A.12)$$

It can easily be shown that this curve is concave.[4]

Notes

1. $\dfrac{dF_3'}{dQ_1} = \dfrac{dF_3'}{dR_3}\dfrac{dR_3}{dR_1}\dfrac{dR_1}{dQ_1} = -F_3''\dfrac{1}{F_1'} > 0$ and $\dfrac{dF_1'}{dQ_1} = \dfrac{dF_1'}{dR_1}\dfrac{dR_1}{dQ_1} = F_1''\dfrac{1}{F_1'}$
< 0

2. A.C. Chiang, *Fundamental Methods of Mathematical Economics* (New York: McGraw-Hill, 1974), p. 730.

3. $\dfrac{dF_3'}{dQ_2} = \dfrac{dF_3'}{dR_3}\dfrac{dR_3}{dR_2}\dfrac{dR_2}{dQ_2} = F_3''\dfrac{dR_3}{dR_2}\dfrac{1}{F_2'} = F_3''\dfrac{1}{F_2'}\left(-\dfrac{dR_1}{dR_2} - 1\right)$

$\dfrac{dH_1'}{dQ_2} = \dfrac{dH_1'}{dQ_1}\dfrac{dQ_1}{dQ_2} = H_1''\dfrac{dQ_1}{dQ_2} < 0$ and $\dfrac{dF_2'}{dQ_2} = F_2''\dfrac{1}{F_2'}$

and $\dfrac{dF_1'}{dQ_2} = \dfrac{dF_1'}{dR_1}\dfrac{dR_1}{dR_2}\dfrac{dR_2}{dQ_2} = \dfrac{F_1''}{F_2'}\dfrac{dR_1}{dR_2}$

4. Compare H. Siebert (1978b, p. 55).

Appendix 3B:
Transformation Space
with Negative-Productivity
Effect

Assume a production function

$$Q_i = F_i(R_i, S) \quad \text{with } F_{iS} < 0, F_{iSS} < 0 \tag{3B.1}$$

The inverse defines the input requirements

$$R_i = \phi(Q_i, S) \tag{3B.2}$$

where the properties of the inverse are determined by the assumption on the production function. Substituting equation 3B.2 into the system of equations 3.1 and 3.3 through 3.6, we have

$$U = G \left\{ \sum H_i(Q_i) - F_3 \left[\bar{R} - \sum \phi_i(Q_i, G^{-1}(U)) \right] \right\} \tag{3B.3}$$

Equation 3B.3 implicitly defines a function between U and Q_i; that is, it defines the transformation space. Equation 3B.3 should be compared with equation 3A.3 which defines the transformation space for the traditional production function. From 3B.3 we have

$$\frac{\partial U}{\partial Q_i} \leq 0: \quad \phi_{1S} + \phi_{2S} \leq \frac{1}{F_3'} \tag{3B.4}$$

The concavity of the transformation space for this case is not analyzed here further. However, compare Siebert (1982g).

4 Optimal Environmental Use

The transformation space analyzed in chapter 3 describes the production possibilities of two private goods and the public good "environmental quality." All combinations of the transformation space can be attained. But which set of outputs should be sought? In order to answer this question, we must introduce value judgments that eventually allow us to determine the desired set of outputs.

Criteria for Optimality

For our purposes it is sufficient to review briefly the three most often used optimality criteria.[1]

Koopmans Efficiency

An output is Koopmans-efficient if, with given technology and given resources, the ith output cannot be increased for given quantities of all other commodities j. For our problem, this means that an allocation is not efficient if, for a given output Q_1 and Q_2, environmental quality can be increased. Similarly, an allocation is not Koopmans-efficient if, for a given environmental quality, the output of one of the commodities can be increased without having to decrease the output of the other. Inefficient allocations lie inside the transformation space in figure 3-3. Koopmans efficiency requires that we produce on the transformation space in order not to waste resources.

Social-Welfare Function

It is assumed that society has a welfare function

$$W = W(C_1, C_2, U) \tag{4.1}$$

or that a politician knows the welfare function of the society. In such a welfare function, environmental quality is an argument variable. In figure 3-3, one can imagine such a welfare function being represented by a three-dimensional indifference lid. Higher indifference lids represent higher levels of welfare. The optimizing problem consists of finding the highest indifference level for a given transformation space. The optimal point will be reached where an indifference lid is tangential to the transformation space. Mathematically, the properties of the optimum can be determined by maximizing equation 4.1 subject to constraints 3.1 through 3.6, which define the transformation space.

Pareto Optimality

The Pareto criterion does not start from a social-welfare function; rather, it assumes individual utility functions in which utility is defined by an ordinal measure, that is, the utility function is a utility index function. A situation is Pareto-optimal if, for constant utility of all individuals except j, the utility of individual j cannot be increased. A situation is not Pareto-optimal if, for constant utility of all individuals except j, the utility of individual j can be increased.

To simplify the problem of environmental allocation, we assume an economy consisting of two individuals, 1 and 2. The utility of both individuals depends on the quantities consumed of the two private goods and on environmental quality. Variable C_i^j denotes the quantity of commodity i consumed by individual j. Note that, unlike the consumption quantities of the private goods i, U does not have a personalized superscript; environmental quality is a public good:[2]

$$W^j = W^j(C_1^j, C_2^j, U) \tag{4.2}$$

Other variables may also enter into the utility function (or the social-welfare function) such as employment, price-level stability, and equity. In this chapter, we use the Pareto criterion as a guideline for optimal allocation. In chapter 5 we see that the choice of the value criterion also has important institutional aspects. For instance, the question arises by which mechanism a social-welfare function can be aggregated from individual preferences or by which institutional arrangement individual evaluations can be revealed.

Optimization Problem

For simplicity, assume an economy consisting of two individuals. Apply the Pareto criterion and maximize the utility of individual 1, subject to the utility of individual 2 remaining constant (equation 4.2). The utility that can be obtained by individual 1 is restricted not only by the condition that the utility of individual 2 has to remain constant but also by the constraint posed by the transformation space (equations 3.1 through 3.6). Finally, the quantity demanded by the two individuals equals total demand

$$C_i = \sum_j c_i^j \tag{4.3}$$

and total demand for a commodity cannot exceed output:

$$C_i \leq Q_i \tag{4.4}$$

The reader not familiar with optimization is referred to Appendix 4A. The problem[3] consists of maximizing the Lagrangean function

$$L = W^1(C_1^1, C_2^1, U) - \sum_i \lambda_{S_i^p}[H_i(Q_i) - S_i^p]$$

$$- \sum_i \lambda_{Q_i}[Q_i - F_i(R_i)]$$

$$- \sum_i \lambda_{S_i^r}[S_i^r - F_i^r(R_i^r)]$$

$$- \lambda_S \left[\sum S_i^p - \sum S_i^r - S\right]$$

$$- \lambda_U[U - G(S)]$$

$$- \lambda_R \left[\sum R_i + \sum R_i^r - \bar{R}\right]$$

$$- \lambda^2[\overline{W^2} - W^2(C_1^2, C_2^2, U)]$$

$$- \sum_i \lambda_i \left[\sum_j c_i^j - Q_i\right] \tag{4.5}$$

Note that the restraints in equation 4.5 are the emission function, the production function, the abatement function, the diffusion function, the damage function, and the resource restraint. These restraints define the transformation space. Also, the restraints require the constancy of utility of individual 2, the identity of total demand and the sum of individual demand, and the limitation of total demand to feasible output. The necessary conditions for an optimum of equation 4.5 are given in Appendix 4B. The reader is urged to derive the implications for himself in order to acquire an understanding of the mechanics of the model.

A Shadow Price for Pollutants

From Appendix 4B we have the following results. Note that all shadow prices and all variables relate to the optimum. Normally, shadow prices are denoted by an asterisk, which we omit for simplifying purposes:

$$\lambda_U = W_U^{1'} + \lambda^2 W_U^{2'} \tag{4.6a}$$

The evaluation of one unit of environmental quality results from the aggregation of individual utilities (compare the Lindahl solution in chapter 5). Now, $W_U^{j'}(C_1^{j*}, C_2^{j*}, U^*)$ represents the marginal evaluation of the environment by individual j. If, however, we assume a social-welfare function in the maximization problem, we would have $\lambda_U = W_U'$, that is, the shadow price of environmental quality would be determined by the "social" evaluation

$$\lambda_S = \lambda_{S_i^P} = \lambda_{S_i^r} = -G'\lambda_U \tag{4.6b}$$

The shadow price of pollutants ambient in the environment, emissions, and abated emissions is equal to the physical marginal damage of one unit of the emission multiplied by the social evaluation of the environment. Thus we already have one condition for the determination of an emission tax rate. The shadow price for emissions has to be set in such a way that it is equal to the prevented marginal damage of a unit of emission. Note that equation 4.6b requires the same shadow price for pollutants ambient in the environment, for emissions, and for abated emissions. This is due to the fact that we have used a simplified form of a diffusion function (equation 3.4).

$$\lambda_S = \frac{\lambda_R}{F_i^{r'}} \tag{4.6c}$$

The shadow price for pollutants (emissions) has to be set in such a way that it is equal to marginal abatement costs, $\lambda_R / F_i^{r'}$. The inverse function to the abatement function 3.3, $R_i^r = \phi_i(S_i^r)$, is an input requirement function. The first derivative

$$\frac{dR_i^r}{dS_i^r} = \frac{1}{dF_i^r/dS_i^r} = \frac{1}{F_i^{r'}}$$

indicates the factor input necessary to reduce one unit of pollution. If this expression is multiplied by the resource price λ_R, we obtain the marginal abatement costs.

Thus, we have two conditions for the shadow price of one unit of emission. These conditions are explained in figure 4-1. In figure 4-1a, O_1S_1 denotes the quantity of emissions of sector 1, or, starting from S_1, the abated emissions. The curve AS_1 denotes the marginal costs of pollution abatement in sector 1. With a concave abatement function, marginal costs of abatement rise progressively. Similarly, O_2S_2 in figure 4-1b denotes emissions of sector 2, and BS_2 indicates the marginal abatement costs in sector 2. If both curves are aggregated horizontally, CS^0 (figure 4-1c) represents the curve of total marginal abatement costs with OS^0 denoting the quantity of emissions in the economy in a given initial situation. The emission tax is determined by the curve CS^0. Observe that in figure 4-1 we have assumed that λ_R is given. Consequently, the curve CS^0, depicting marginal costs of abatement, will shift if λ_R changes. Stated differently, λ_R has been assumed to be the shadow price of the optimal solution. Similarly, the cost curve will shift if the volume of emissions changes. Therefore, figure 4-1 represents a partial equilibrium analysis if one assumes optimal values for a set of variables.

Curve DD in figure 4-1c specifies the evaluated marginal environmental damage of emissions (pollutants). It follows from the damage function 3.5 that marginal damage increases progressively (at a constant λ_U) with increasing emissions. When we read curve DD from S^0 to O, the curve represents the prevented marginal damage. Note that λ_U has been assumed to be the optimal shadow price.

The shadow price for emissions should be set in such a way that prevented marginal damage and marginal costs of abatement are equal. Now, OT is the optimal level of the shadow price for emissions, S^0S' is the quantity of the emissions to be abated, and OS' is the quantity of emissions that is tolerated. Figure 4-1 shows the tradeoff between the improvement of the environmental quality and the costs connected with it. If one intends to improve environmental quality by abating more pollutants, then abatement costs arise, that is, resources have to be put into abatement and have to be withdrawn from the production activities. The opportunity costs of a better environment thus consist of the forgone resources used in production. Note that the interpretation of figure 4-1 is consistent with the analysis of chapter 3, where we have established $\partial U/\partial Q_i < 0$. This implies that there are opportunity costs of production in terms of environmental losses or that environmental improvement implies a loss of output.

Figure 4-1c contains the basic message of economics concerning the environmental issue. If an environmental problem exists, there must be a scarcity price for using the environment. This price is determined by the marginal benefit received from environmental quality and by the costs of achieving this target. The reader will notice that other approaches such as benefit/cost analysis or the bargaining solution will lead to the same diagram.

In equation 4.6c, the costs of environmental policy are expressed by re-

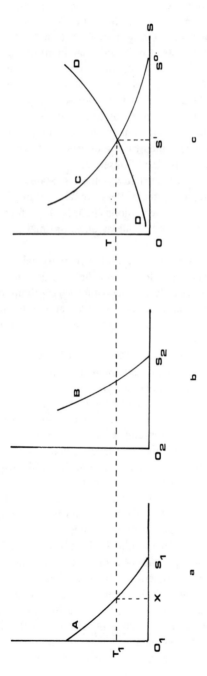

Marginal damage
Marginal cost of abatement

Figure 4-1. Determination of the Emission Tax

sources withdrawn from production. Assume that individual utility functions contain such variables as full employment, price-level stability, balance-of-payments equilibrium, or equity; then environmental policy may negatively affect these variables. If this is the case, the prevented damage of abatement is reduced, and curve DD in figure 4-1 will shift downward. Thus, if there are additional costs of environmental quality, more pollutants will be tolerated. Since we have to abate a smaller quantity of emissions, the scarcity price for pollutants will be lower.

Implications for the Shadow-Price System of the Economy

Setting a price for emissions implies that the price system of the economy will be affected. What are the implications of a scarcity price for the environment on the price vector of the economy?

$$\lambda_i = W_i^{1'} = \lambda^2 W_i^{2'} \tag{4.6d}$$

The Lagrangean multiplier λ_i denotes the shadow price of commodities from the consumers' point of view (evaluation by the consumer). Note that λ^2 is a multiplier that allows us to transform one unit of utility of individual 1 to one unit of utility of individual 2:

$$\frac{\lambda_1}{\lambda_2} = \frac{W_1^{1'}}{W_2^{1'}} = \frac{W_1^{2'}}{W_2^{2'}} \tag{4.6e}$$

The relative shadow price of the two commodities corresponds to the relation of their marginal utilities for each individual. We can also say that the relative utilities among individuals must be equal. This is a well-known result from traditional consumer theory. While the formal conditions for the household optimum are not changed when a zero shadow price is assessed for the environment, the shadow price of the pollution-intensive commodity may be affected. Its consumption may be lower.

$$\lambda_{Q_i} = W_i^{1'} - \lambda_{S_i} p H_i' = \lambda^2 W_i^{2'} - \lambda_{S_i} p H_i' \tag{4.6f}$$

Whereas λ_i indicates the marginal evaluation of a commodity by consumers, λ_{Q_i} denotes the shadow price for producers (producers' price). The producers' price is determined by the evaluation of consumers minus the social costs of production. The social costs of production are expressed by the pollution per unit of output H_i' and the shadow price of pollutants. Equation 4.6f indicates that the incentive for producers is corrected. The net price of the pollution-intensive commodity for producers is lowered; thus, the incentive to produce the pollution-intensive commodity is reduced:

$$\frac{\lambda_{Q_1}}{\lambda_{Q_2}} = \frac{W_1^{1'} - H_1' \lambda_S}{W_2^{1'} - H_2' \lambda_S} = \frac{\lambda^2 W_1^{2'} - H_1' \lambda_S}{\lambda^2 W_2^{2'} - H_2' \lambda_S} \qquad (4.6g)$$

With a zero price charged for environmental use ($\lambda_S = 0$), relative prices are distorted for producers in the sense that not all social costs of production are attributed to individual producers. If there is a shadow price for pollutants, relative producers' price will be changed. Assume that commodity 1 is the pollution-intensive commodity, that is, $H_1' F_1' > H_2' F_2'$. Then the relative price will be changed in favor of the non-pollution-intensive commodity if an environmental policy is pursued. We can expect that the pollution-intensive sector will be restricted by the environmental policy.

$$\lambda_R = \lambda_{Q_i} F_i' \qquad (4.6h)$$

The resource has to be used in private production in such a way that the resource price is equal to the marginal-value product (the marginal productivity of the resource multiplied by the shadow price of the commodity[4]). When this result is written as

$$\lambda_{Q_i} = \frac{\lambda_R}{F_i'}$$

it indicates that the shadow price of a good has to be equal to its marginal production costs. The inverse to the production function is the input requirement function $R_1 = F_i^{-1}(Q_i)$. For the first derivative of this function, we have

$$\frac{dR_i}{dQ_i} = \frac{1}{F_i'}$$

If the resource input for one additional unit of output is multiplied by the resource price, we obtain the marginal production costs of the commodity.

Conditions 4.6f and 4.6h require that the producers' price of a commodity (net price) be identical to the marginal evaluation by consumers minus the social costs of production.

Optimum and Competitive Equilibrium

In the previous sections of this chapter, I analyzed the implications of a Pareto optimum when environmental problems exist. Two basic propositions of welfare economics relate optimal allocation and a competitive equilibrium to each other (Quirk and Saposnik 1968). These two propositions are as follows: A competitive equilibrium provides an optimal allocation of resources. For a given endowment of individuals, an optimal allocation can be obtained through a competitive equilibrium if an appropriate transfer is used. Do these two propositions also hold in the case of environmental disruption? In order to develop our argument, we first characterize the competitive equilibrium. In a second step, we have to relate optimal allocation to competitive equilibrium.[5]

Competitive Equilibrium

A competitive equilibrium is defined as an allocation A and a price vector P so that for $[A,P]$

1. All markets are cleared.
2. Each consumer maximizes his utility subject to the budget restraint.
3. Each producer maximizes his profit subject to the production function.

Consumers

It is assumed that each consumer maximizes his utility for given prices $(\tilde{p}_i, \tilde{r})$, where $\tilde{p}_i$ are market prices for commodities and $\tilde{r}$ is the resource price. The government levies an emission tax $\tilde{z}$. Government receipts from emission taxes are transferred to the households. Profits of the production sector are also transferred to the households according to a given distribution parameter (profit shares). With given factor prices and a given distribution parameter, the income Y^j is given for the individual household. Household j maximizes the Lagrangean expression

$$L = W^j(C_1^j, C_2^j, U) - \lambda_Y^j(\tilde{p}_1 C_1^j + \tilde{p}_2 C_2^j - Y^j)$$

Environmental quality is given for the individual household. The necessary conditions for the household optimum are

$$W_i^{j'} - \lambda_Y^j \tilde{p}_i \leq 0$$

and   (4.7)

$$\sum_i \tilde{p}_i C_i^j - Y^j \leq 0$$

Note that λ_Y^j is the shadow price of a unit of income (or money) of individual j. Since marginal utilities are measured in utils and prices in money, λ_Y^j is a conversion factor which transforms units of money into utils.

Producers

It is assumed that each producer maximizes his profit for given prices $\tilde{p}_i, \tilde{r}, \tilde{z}$

$$G_i = \tilde{p}_i Q_i - \tilde{r}(R_i + R_i^r) - \tilde{z} S_i$$

subject to

$$Q_i - F_i(R_i) \leqslant 0 \qquad S_i^r - F_i^r(R_i^r) \leqslant 0$$
$$H_i(Q_i) - S_i^p \leqslant 0 \qquad -S_i + S_i^p - S_i^r = 0 \tag{4.8}$$

From Appendix 4C we have

$$\tilde{r} \geqslant (\tilde{p}_1 - \tilde{z}H_1') F_1'(R_1) = \tilde{p}_1^* F_1' \tag{4.9a}$$
$$\tilde{r} \geqslant (\tilde{p}_2 - \tilde{z}H_2') F_2'(R_2) = \tilde{p}_2^* F_2'$$
$$\tilde{r} \geqslant \tilde{z}F_i^{r\prime}(R_i^r) \tag{4.9b}$$

Assume $R_i > 0$. Then equations 4.9a and 4.9b specify that the producer will use resources in production up to a point where the marginal-value product of a resource is equal to the price of the resource. Note that the marginal-value product in this case is defined with respect to the producers' price or net price $\tilde{p}_i^*$, that is, market price $\tilde{p}_i$ minus emission tax $\tilde{z}$ per unit of output $\tilde{z}H_i'$. Condition 4.9a indicates that an emission tax sets a new price signal for production. *Ceteris paribus*, the net price of a pollution-intensive commodity will be lower because of a higher emission tax per unit of output. Thus, the incentive to produce the pollution-intensive commodity will be reduced.

Equation 4.9b requires that, for $R_i^r > 0$, the marginal-value product of a resource in abatement $\tilde{z}F_r^{i\prime}$ be equal to the resource price. Assume that $\tilde{r}$ and $\tilde{z}$ are given; then we have an incentive to use resources for abatement. If, *ceteris paribus*, $\tilde{z}$ is increased, $F_i^{r\prime}$ must fall and R_i^r must rise.

In table 4-1 the conditions for Pareto optimality, for a utility maximum of the household, and for a profit maximum of the firm are reproduced. Intuitively, the reader can see that the conditions for the Pareto optimum and perfect competition are very similar.

Table 4-1
Pareto Optimum and Competitive Equilibrium

Pareto Optimum		Competitive Equilibrium[a]	
$W_i^{1\prime} - \lambda_i^1 \leq 0$	(1)	$W_i^{j\prime} - \lambda_Y^j \tilde{p}_i \leq 0$	(1)
$\lambda^2 W_i^{2\prime} - \lambda_i^2 \leq 0$	(1a)		
$(\lambda_i - \lambda_{S_i^p} H_i')F_i' - \lambda_R \leq 0$	(2)	$(\tilde{p}_i - \tilde{z}H_i')F_i' - \tilde{r} \leq 0$	(2)
$\lambda_{S_i^r} F_i^{r\prime} - \lambda_R \leq 0$	(3)	$\tilde{z}F_i^{r\prime} - \tilde{r} \leq 0$	(3)
$\sum_j C_i^j - Q_i = 0$	(4)	$\sum_j C_i^j - Q_i = 0$	(4)
$\bar{R} - \sum_i R_i - \sum_i R_i^r = 0$	(5)	$\bar{R} - \sum_i R_i - \sum_i R_i^r = 0$	(5)

[a]It is assumed that $S_i > 0$ so that from equation 4C.4 $\tilde{z} = \lambda_{S_i}$. Then since $\lambda_{S_i} \leq \lambda_{S_i^r}$, the term $-r + \lambda_{S_i^r} F_i^{r\prime} \leq 0$ can be written as $-r + \tilde{z}F_i^{r\prime} \leq 0$.

Optimal Environmental Allocation in a Competitive Economy

We can now establish the two propositions of welfare economics for an economy with environmental disruption.

Proposition 1. Let $[A, P]$ denote a competitive equilibrium with allocation A and price vector $\mathbf{P} = (\tilde{p}_1, \tilde{p}_2, \tilde{r}, \tilde{z})$. Let prices be

$$\tilde{p}_i = \frac{\lambda_i}{\lambda_Y^1} = \frac{\lambda_i}{\lambda^2 \lambda_Y^2} \qquad \text{with } \lambda_Y^1 = \lambda^2 \lambda_Y^2$$

$$\tilde{r} = \frac{\lambda_R}{\lambda_Y^1}$$

$$\tilde{z} = \frac{\lambda_{S_i^p}}{\lambda_Y^1} = \frac{-(W_U^{1\prime} + \lambda^2 w_U^{2\prime})G'}{\lambda_Y^1}$$

Then A is Pareto-optimal.

Proof. Now, A is a competitive equilibrium. Consequently, the price vector $\mathbf{P}$ satisfies the conditions in column 2 of table 4-1. The market equilibrium conditions 4 and 5 are given. They are identical to the restraints 4 and 5 of the optimum. By setting $\tilde{z}$ equal to $- (W_u^{1'} + \lambda^2 W_u^{2'}) G'/\lambda_Y^1$, and with the other prices as indicated above, and then substituting these prices into the conditions of a competitive equilibrium (second column), we obtain the conditions of the optimum. Therefore, the allocation A is optimal.

Proposition 2. Let A^* be a Pareto-optimal allocation so that the conditions of column 1 in table 4-1 hold. Then a price vector $\mathbf{P}^*$ including emission taxes exists such that $[A^*, P^*]$ constitutes a competitive equilibrium.

Proof. Let prices be defined as in proposition 1. Then, after substituting these definitions into column 1, we obtain the conditions of column 2. These conditions together with the constraints are identical to those of a competitive equilibrium. Consequently, A^* is a competitive equilibrium.

Requirements for an Emission-Tax Solution

In this chapter we show that a maximization model yields shadow prices for environmental use. If we view the implications of an optimization model as a guideline for economic policy, then our model indicates the informational requirements for the setting of an emission tax. These requirements are:

1. The policymaker needs information on the quantity of emissions. The emissions must be measurable with reasonable costs.
2. The policymaker needs information on the level of abatement costs for alternative states of the environment.
3. The policymaker must be able to determine (and to evaluate) prevented damage.
4. The diffusion function between emissions and pollutants ambient in the environment must be known.

In chapters 7 and 8 we analyze some of the problems that arise when an emission tax is implemented.

Notes

1. On welfare criteria, compare Quirk and Saposnik (1968). The "maximin" criterion suggested by Rawls (1971) has received considerable attention in the analysis of resource use, especially in an intertemporal context. Compare Fisher (1981) p. 71. On ethical issues also compare Kneese and Schulze (1985).

2. Alternatively, we could define U^j as the environmental quality used by individual j. Then we would have to observe the restraint $U^1 = U^2 = U$.

3. For a model with an explicit diffusion function and negative externalities, compare Siebert (1975a).

4. Rewrite equation 4.6g as

$$\frac{\lambda_{Q_1} F_1'}{\lambda_{Q_2} F_2'} = \frac{W_1^{j'} F_1' + H_1' F_1' \lambda_S}{W_2^{j'} F_2' + H_2' F_2' \lambda_S}$$

5. On a general equilibrium with explicit consideration of the environment also compare Dudenhöffer (1983), Mäler (1985) and Pethig (1979).

Appendix 4A:
Nonlinear Optimization

Let $f(x) = f(x_1, x_2, \ldots, x_n)$ denote a differentiable concave function that has to be maximized. Let the vector

$$g(x) = \begin{bmatrix} g_1(x) \\ g_2(x) \\ \vdots \\ g_m(x) \end{bmatrix} \geq 0$$

be a differentiable and concave function that has to be regarded as a restriction. Then the optimizing problem is to find a vector x^* which maximizes $f(x)$ under the constraints $g(x) \geq 0$ and $x \geq 0$. The procedure is to form the Lagrangean function

$$L(x, \lambda) = f(x) + \lambda' g(x)$$

where

$$\lambda = \begin{bmatrix} \lambda_1 \\ \lambda_2 \\ \vdots \\ \lambda_m \end{bmatrix} \geq 0$$

is the Lagrangean multiplier λ and where λ' denotes the row vector of λ. Here x^* is the optimal solution of the maximization problem if a vector $\lambda^* \geq 0$ exists and if

$$L_x(x^*, \lambda^*) \leq 0 \qquad x^* L_x(x^*, \lambda^*) = 0 \qquad x^* \geq 0$$
$$L_\lambda(x^*, \lambda^*) \geq 0 \qquad \lambda^* L_\lambda(x^*, \lambda^*) = 0 \qquad \lambda^* \geq 0$$

is fulfilled for $L(x, \lambda)$. If the qualification of the Slater-secondary condition is fulfilled, the aforementioned conditions are necessary and sufficient for a global maximum.

Observe that if $g(x)$ is convex, then the constraint is expressed as $g(x) \leq 0$.[1]

Note

1. On the technique of nonlinear optimization, compare A.C. Chiang, *Fundamental Methods of Mathematical Economics* (New York: McGraw-Hill, 1974), chap. 4; M.D. Intriligator, *Mathematical Optimization and Economic Theory* (Englewood Cliffs, N.J.: Prentice-Hall, 1971), chap. 4; A. Takayama, *Mathematical Economics* (New York: The Dryden Press, 1974), chap. 1.

Appendix 4B:
Implications of the
Allocation Problem

The Kuhn-Tucker conditions for equation 4.5 are

$$\frac{\partial L}{\partial C_i^1} = W_i^{1'} - \lambda_i \leqslant 0 \qquad\qquad C_i^1 \geqslant 0 \qquad C_i^1 \frac{\partial L}{\partial C_i^1} = 0 \qquad (4B.1)$$

$$\frac{\partial L}{\partial U} = W_U^{1'} - \lambda_U + \lambda^2 W_U^{2'} \leqslant 0 \qquad U \geqslant 0 \qquad U \frac{\partial L}{\partial U} = 0 \qquad (4B.2)$$

$$\frac{\partial L}{\partial R_i} = \lambda_{Q_i} F_i' - \lambda_R \leqslant 0 \qquad\qquad R_i \geqslant 0 \qquad R_i \frac{\partial L}{\partial R_i} = 0 \qquad (4B.3)$$

$$\frac{\partial L}{\partial R_i^r} = \lambda_{S_i^r} F_i^{r'} - \lambda_R \leqslant 0 \qquad\qquad R_i^r \geqslant 0 \qquad R_i^r \frac{\partial L}{\partial R_i^r} = 0 \qquad (4B.4)$$

$$\frac{\partial L}{\partial S_i^p} = \lambda_{S_i^p} - \lambda_S \leqslant 0 \qquad\qquad S_i^p \geqslant 0 \qquad S_i^p \frac{\partial L}{\partial S_i^p} = 0 \qquad (4B.5)$$

$$\frac{\partial L}{\partial S_i^r} = -\lambda_{S_i^r} + \lambda_S \leqslant 0 \qquad\qquad S_i^r \geqslant 0 \qquad S_i^r \frac{\partial L}{\partial S_i^r} = 0 \qquad (4B.6)$$

$$\frac{\partial L}{\partial S} = \lambda_S + \lambda_U G' \leqslant 0 \qquad\qquad S \geqslant 0 \qquad S \frac{\partial L}{\partial S} = 0 \qquad (4B.7)$$

$$\frac{\partial L}{\partial C_i^2} = \lambda^2 W_i^{2'} - \lambda_i \leqslant 0 \qquad\qquad C_i^2 \geqslant 0 \qquad C_i \frac{\partial L}{\partial C_i^2} = 0 \qquad (4B.8)$$

$$\frac{\partial L}{\partial Q_i} = -\lambda_{S_i^p} H_i' - \lambda_{Q_i} + \lambda_i \leqslant 0 \qquad Q_i \geqslant 0 \qquad Q_i \frac{\partial L}{\partial Q_i} = 0 \qquad (4B.9)$$

$$\frac{\partial L}{\partial \lambda} \geqslant 0 \qquad\qquad \lambda \geqslant 0 \qquad \lambda \frac{\partial L}{\partial \lambda} = 0 \qquad (4B.10)$$

where λ denotes the vector of Lagrangean multipliers. Note that equation 3.4 requires the strict equality. In this case, we can write equation 3.4 as two different types of inqualities (greater than or equal to zero and less than or equal to zero), thereby implying equality.

The Lagrangean multipliers are interpreted as follows: First, consider a constraint which restricts the variable by an absolute value such as $\bar{R}$. Then a parametric change in $\bar{R}$, that is, $dL/d\bar{R} = \lambda_R$, indicates how the value of the Lagrangean function is changed if $\bar{R}$ is marginally varied. For instance, λ_R denotes the value of one unit of the resource for the goal function. So λ_R can be interpreted as the shadow price of the resource. Second, now consider the case in which the variable is not restricted by an absolute value but, rather, by a function, as in $Q \leqslant F(R)$. Then we can find an interpretation of the Lagrangean multiplier by introducing a disposal activity (slack variable). Such a fictive activity disposes of one unit of a variable. Define D as quantities of output removed from the system, so that the constraint can be written as $Q + D = F(R)$. Then the constraint is transformed to $-\lambda_Q[Q + D - F(R)]$. The expression $\partial L/\partial D = -\lambda_Q$ indicates how the value of the goal function is changed when one unit of output is eliminated from the system, and λ_Q is the shadow price of output.

All other Lagrangean multipliers can be interpreted similarly. In equation 4.5 we have already characterized the Lagrangean multiplier by the appropriate indices.

The interpretation of our optimization problem is made easier by some reasonable assumptions. Since $R_i > 0$ or $R_3 > 0$, $\lambda_R > 0$. Also assume that both sectors produce, so that $R_i, Q_i, S_i^p > 0$. Let some environmental quality exist so that $U > 0$. Let both individuals demand positive quantities of the two commodities. Finally, if $\lambda_{S_i^r} > 0$ (this is an implicit price for pollutants), then $R_i^r > 0$. Under these assumptions, the conditions in 4B.1 to 4B.10 are all equalities.

Appendix 4C:
Implications of the Profit Maximum

The Lagrangean function of the problem in 4.8 is

$$L_i = \tilde{p}_i Q_i - \tilde{r}(R_i + R_i^r) - \tilde{z} S_i - \lambda_{S_i^p} [H_i(Q_i) - S_i^p]$$
$$- \lambda_{Q_i} [Q_i - F_i(R_i)]$$
$$- \lambda_{S_i^r} [S_i^r - F_i^r(R_i^r)]$$
$$- \lambda_{S_i} [S_i^p - S_i^r - S_i]$$

The necessary conditions for the maximum of the problem in 4.8 are

$$\frac{\partial L}{\partial Q_i} = \tilde{p}_i - \lambda_{Q_i} - \lambda_{S_i^p} H_i' \leqslant 0 \qquad Q_i \geqslant 0 \qquad Q_i \frac{\partial L}{\partial Q_i} = 0 \qquad (4C.1)$$

$$\frac{\partial L}{\partial R_i} = -\tilde{r} + \lambda_{Q_i} F_i' \leqslant 0 \qquad R_i \geqslant 0 \qquad R_i \frac{\partial L}{\partial R_i} = 0 \qquad (4C.2)$$

$$\frac{\partial L}{\partial R_i^r} = -\tilde{r} + \lambda_{S_i^r} F_i^{r'} \leqslant 0 \qquad R_i^r \geqslant 0 \qquad R_i^r \frac{\partial L}{\partial R_i^r} = 0 \qquad (4C.3)$$

$$\frac{\partial L}{\partial S_i} = -\tilde{z} + \lambda_{S_i} \leqslant 0 \qquad S_i \geqslant 0 \qquad S_i \frac{\partial L}{\partial S_i} = 0 \qquad (4C.4)$$

$$\frac{\partial L}{\partial S_i^r} = -\lambda_{S_i^r} + \lambda_{S_i} \leqslant 0 \qquad S_i^r \geqslant 0 \qquad S_i^r \frac{\partial L}{\partial S_i^r} = 0 \qquad (4C.5)$$

$$\frac{\partial L}{\partial S_i^p} = \lambda_{S_i^p} - \lambda_{S_i} \leqslant 0 \qquad S_i^p \geqslant 0 \qquad S_i^p \frac{\partial L}{\partial S_i^p} = 0 \qquad (4C.6)$$

$$\frac{\partial L}{\partial \lambda} \geqslant 0 \qquad \lambda \geqslant 0 \qquad \lambda \frac{\partial L}{\partial \lambda} = 0 \qquad (4C.7)$$

5 Environmental Quality as a Public Good

In this chapter we analyze the public-goods approach to the environmental problem. Environmental quality is considered to be a public good that must be consumed in equal amounts by all. This approach starts from the premise that private property rights cannot be defined for environmental quality (or if technically feasible, that private property rights should not be defined). Then the market cannot allocate the environment, and government intervention becomes necessary. How does the government determine the desired environmental quality? One approach is to assume a social-welfare function which allows us to specify the benefits and costs of environmental quality. In a similar way, benefit/cost analysis implicitly presupposes a social-welfare function as a guideline for evaluation. Another approach is to base the evaluation of environmental quality on individual preferences. A Pareto-optimal allocation requires individualized prices of environmental quality to be assessed according to the individual's willingness to pay. If individuals are not inclined to reveal their true willingness to pay, we have to look into institutional arrangements that may reveal and aggregate individual preferences.

Characteristics of a Public Good

It is useful to distinguish between the polar cases of private and public goods. A private good can be attributed to a specific individual. Individuals compete against each other in using the good, and potential users can be excluded. There is rivalry in use and private property rights exist. The concept of competing uses can be expressed as

$$C^1 + C^2 + \cdots + C^n = Q \tag{5.1}$$

where C denotes quantities of a good and the superscripts indicate individuals.

A pure public good is consumed in equal amounts by all (Samuelson 1954); the pure public good cannot be parceled out to individuals. The use by one individual does not subtract from any other individual's use. There is no rivalry in use. Individuals cannot be excluded from using the public good; that is, in contrast to a private good, property rights cannot be attributed to individuals. Consequently, a public good U is characterized by

$$U^1 = U^2 = \cdots = U^n = U \tag{5.2}$$

The difference between the polar cases of private and public goods is illustrated in figure 5-1. Total demand for a private good of an economy is summed horizontally; that is, we add quantities. In figure 5-1a curves BC and AD indicate the marginal willingness to pay, that is to give up income, of two different individuals. Marginal willingness to pay decreases with the quantity according to the usual property of demand functions. Curve BEF denotes the marginal willingness of both individuals or the willingness to pay signaled in the market. In the case of a public good, quantities cannot be added; rather, we add vertically, that is, we sum the individual evaluations (on public goods, compare Head 1974; Milleron 1972; and Loehr and Sandler 1978). Again, curves BC and AD denote the willingness to pay of both individuals. Since the public good must be used in equal amounts by all, the willingness to pay of both individuals, e.g. curve HGD, is found by aggregating vertically.

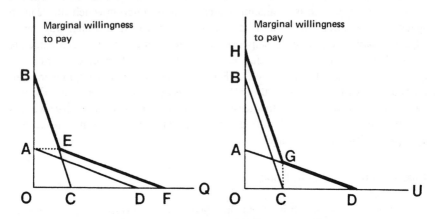

Figure 5-1. Aggregation of Willingness to Pay

A public good is characterized by the technical property that the commodity is to be used in equal amounts by all. Actually, this property depends on the given exclusion technology. For instance, the lighthouse—the prototype of a public good— may well be considered to be a private good if a device is necessary to receive signals from the lighthouse. Indeed, we may conceive of exclusion technologies in many cases so that property rights can be attributed, and public goods are changed into private ones. However, even if an exclusion technology exists, we may judge the good so meritorious that the exclusion technology should not be applied. In this case we speak of merit good (Musgrave and Musgrave 1976). Also, the exclusion technology may not be acceptable under normative constraints.

The merit good is on the border line between a private and a pure public good. Exclusion is technically feasible, for instance by excluding someone from

Table 5-1. Classification of Goods

Characteristics of good	Institutional arrangement	Exclusive property rights	Non-exclusive property rights
Rivalry in use		Private good	Common property resource
			————— Merit good —————
Non-rivalry in use			Pure public good

a school system, and there is some rivalry in use, for instance by an additional student reducing the quality of a school. Rivalry in use may give rise to congestion problems. Thus, between the polar cases of pure private and pure public goods we have many intermediate forms. Note that on this border line, the two characteristics used in Table 5-1 may not be independent from each other; the institutional setting of property rights also defines the characteristics of goods.

In yet another intermediate form, a public good may be limited by membership (theory of clubs), by space (local public goods), or by time. In this case, there is no rivalry for those who can use the good, but some form of exclusion exists.

In Table 5-1 the two criteria of the institutional arrangement of exclusive property rights and the characteristics of the good with respect to rivalry or non-rivalry are used to classify goods.

The terms *public good* and *common-property resource* are often used synonymously. However, they should be clearly distinguished. A common-property resource is a good for which exclusive property rights are not defined and where rivalry in use prevails. The non-existence of exclusive property rights means that access to the good is not limited or not severely limited. Consequently, the users compete with each other eventually affecting the quantity available or the quality (congestion). In contrast to merit goods where access is not limited for normative reasons and where a deliberate decision is taken not to limit access, in the case of common-property resources, property rights are not clearly defined because of historical conditions, although exclusion mechanisms are possible. It is mainly for historical reasons that common-property resources are used as free goods. In the past, many goods were free goods and common-property resources simultaneously; today, because of increased scarcity and the more comprehensive definition of property rights, they have become private goods. For instance, fish as a protein source have been used as a common-property resource in the world's oceans because no property rights were assigned. Today, some forms of property rights such as the 200 mile zone and limitations on economic harvesting begin to emerge.

How is the environment related to the public-goods concept? In chapter 2 we discuss the functions of the environment for the economic system; not all these functions define characteristics of a public good. For instance, in its role as a receptacle of wastes, the environment can be interpreted as a common-property resource, but not as a public good. Similarly, the provision of natural resources such as water does not fall under the heading of a public good. In ancient times water may have been used as a free good because of its bounty. This abundance rendered competing uses and rivalry and hence the installation of a property rights system meaningless whatever service water did provide. Water was used as a common-property resource. But eventually, as water became scarce, a system of modified property rights was developed for the different services water did provide. Property rights for other national resources such as land, oil, and wood are well established. It is only with respect to the role of the environment as a supplier of public-consumption goods (such as beautiful landscapes, air to breathe, or other life-supporting systems) that the public-goods approach becomes relevant.

For this discussion of this topic, the following aspects should be clearly distinguished:

1. If the environment is used as a common-property resource (receptacle of wastes, provider of natural resources such as water and fish) and if this resource becomes scarce, the characteristic of the common-property resource has to be changed by introducing scarcity prices or other allocation mechanisms.

2. Some functions of the environment (provision of life support systems, amenities, and so on) constitute a public good. In the following analysis, we summarize these functions through use of the term *environmental quality*. We know that the definition of a public good depends on existing exclusion technologies and value judgments. Consequently, the problem arises as to whether, for specific uses of the environment, the public good can be changed into a private one. In this chapter, we analyze the public-goods problem within the context of the environmental issue. In chapter 6, the attribution of property rights is studied.

Allocation of Public Goods

The existence of a public good implies that an individual can take the position of a free rider. Once the public good exists or once it is produced, an individual may use the public good, but he may not be willing to contribute to its costs of production. If the individual is asked to indicate his willingness to pay for the public good, he may give false answers. For instance, if he expects that his answer will serve to calculate his share of costs for the public good, he may understate his preference for the public good (including the extreme case of a zero willingness to pay), expecting that those with a higher willingness to pay will guarantee that the good will be provided. If the individual does not anticipate having to contribute to the costs of production, he may overstate his preference for the public good.

In the case of private goods, the individual cannot take the position of a free rider. If he wants a specific good, he has to give up income for it. His willingness to pay is indicated by the market price. Since his income could be used for other goods, the individual's willingness to pay also indicates his opportunity costs. Thus, the market process reveals the willingness to pay. This demand-revealing process does not operate in the case of public goods since they cannot be attributed to individuals.

The consequence is that public goods should not be allocated through the market mechanism, in order to prevent a misallocation of resources. Public goods require government activity. Actually, there are a wide range of potential government activities. If the public good "environmental quality" cannot be allocated through the market mechanism, three problems arise as to what quantity of the public good "environmental quality" should be provided, by which procedures this target is determined, and by which mechanism the fulfillment of the target can best be reached.

With respect to the determination of the target variable, we can assume that the government will determine the desired environmental quality. Either the government knows what the people want, or it does not take individual preferences into consideration. Western constitutional democracy, having developed over centuries, stresses that individual value judgments should ultimately determine the targets of government activity. But how can individual preferences be revealed if the individual can take the position of the free rider? With this background, the following approaches to the problem of environmental allocation can be distinguished:

1. A social-welfare function is given to the policymakers, including environmental quality as an argument variable. Environmental quality is determined by maximizing this function.
2. Through a more pragmatic approach, the government studies the benefits and costs of environmental policy and uses this information to determine the desired environmental quality.
3. The government tries to base its target values on individual preferences and assigns individualized prices for environmental quality (Lindahl solution).
4. Since the Lindahl solution does not guarantee that individual preferences are truly revealed, other mechanisms of social choice are sought.

Social-Welfare Function

Assume a given social-welfare function of the policymaker in which private goods C_i and environmental quality U are argument variables. Also, other policy variables such as the employment level E, price-level stability P, and the balance-of-payments situation B are included in the welfare function

$$W = W(C_1, C_2, U, E, P, B) \tag{5.3}$$

Then the allocation problem consists of maximizing equation 5.3 subject to the transformation space, that is, the constraints discussed in chapters 3 and 4.

An important implication of this approach is similar to that found in the optimization model (equation 4.6a).

$$\lambda_S = \frac{\lambda_R}{F_i^{r'}} = -G'\lambda_U \tag{5.4}$$

The shadow price for pollutants has to be set in such a way that the marginal costs of abatement are equal to the prevented marginal environmental damage. Here G' denotes marginal damage in physical terms (per unit of pollutant), and λ_U indicates the evaluation of one unit of the environment by the policymaker. The minus sign on the right-hand side of equation 5.4 can be interpreted as prevented damage.

The implication of this approach is explained in figure 5-2 where OS^0 denotes emissions and, if viewed from S^0 toward O, emissions abated. Curve S^0C represents marginal abatement costs; these costs can be interpreted as opportunity costs, that is, costs of a forgone opportunity. In terms of the transformation space, these opportunity costs mean less commodities. Curve OD represents the marginal damage of pollutants. Read from S^0, curve OD can be interpreted as prevented damage. Also OS' is the optimal level of pollution, that

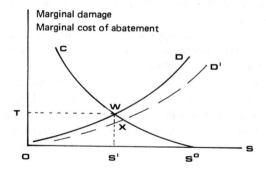

Figure 5-2. Optimal Environmental Quality

is, the target value, and $S^0 S'$ represents the quantity of pollutants to be abated. And OT is the shadow price per unit of emission. Note that figure 5-2 is interpreted in the same way as figure 4-1c.

In addition to forgone income (bypassed production opportunities), environmental policy may negatively affect other target variables of economic policy such as full employment or price-level stability. If this is the case, curve OD shifts downward to OD', and fewer pollutants have to be abated (point X). The losses in terms of economic-policy variables reduce the desired level of environmental quality.

The problem of this approach lies in the assumption that a social-welfare function—"the economist's most favorable fiction"[1]—exists. For instance, we may assume that there is a superman or a dictator who knows what is good for the people. If, however, the social-welfare function is to be aggregated from individual preferences, we may encounter problems. Assume that we postulate the following: the social-welfare ranking must be complete, transitive, and reflexive (universality condition); it must change if one individual changes his ranking, given the indifference of all other individuals; it must be independent of irrelevant alternatives; it must not be imposed by someone (nonimposition condition) and should not be dictatorial (nondictatorship condition) (Arrow 1951; Quirk and Saposnik 1968). It can be shown that no social ranking exists that satisfies these five conditions [Arrow's (im)possibility theorem].

Benefit/Cost Analysis

The pragmatic analogue to the approach of the social-welfare function in environmental policy is benefit/cost analysis. This approach was first used in public-investment projects such as irrigation systems and reservoir dams. The benefits and costs of alternative projects were analyzed, and for given investment funds, the project providing the maximum net benefit was given priority. Benefit/cost analysis has also been applied in cases where a target level had to be determined. Thus, benefit/cost analysis can be used to determine the benefits and costs of environmental quality. Assume that gross benefits B and costs C are continuous functions of environmental quality U, and let $N(U)$ denote net benefits. Then the problem of determining the optimal environmental quality is given by maximizing

$$N(U) = B(U) - C(U) \tag{5.5}$$

The maximum net benefit is reached when

$$\frac{dB}{dU} = \frac{dC}{dU} \tag{5.6}$$

Equation 5.6 states that the marginal benefits of environmental quality are equal to its marginal costs. This condition is identical to the condition stated in equations 4.6b and c. Marginal benefits can be interpreted as prevented damages, and costs are identical to abatement costs and forgone target values. Equation 5.6 can be explained by figure 5-2 where CS^0 indicates abatement costs and OD signifies prevented damage. Benefit/cost analysis obtains the same result as the maximization of a social-welfare function. This is not surprising since the benefit/ cost approach presupposes that benefits can be determined, that is, that the evaluation of damages is possible. Implicitly, a welfare function is assumed to exist. Thus, the benefit/cost approach can be regarded as a rudimentary optimality model determining optimal environmental quality.

In the following analysis, we look into the problem of whether, in a pragmatic approach, benefits and costs of environmental policy can be determined. Even in this practical approach we must confront some of the theoretical problems already discussed, such as the free-rider dilemma. Since it is easier to specify the costs of environmental policy, we begin with this factor.

Costs of Environmental Quality

There are two types of costs of environmental quality: resource costs and target losses for economic policy.[2] Resource costs arise because improving environmental quality requires resources. A firm being forced to reduce its emissions by a given percentage has to use resources to abate pollutants. Or assume that the firm has to pay a tax per unit of emissions. Then the firm will abate pollutants as long as abatement is more profitable than paying taxes. Many studies indicate that abatement costs rise progressively.[3] Figure 5-3 shows such a cost curve for some sectors of the West German economy.[4]

If we sum the abatement costs over all firms (and other abatement activities), we obtain total resource costs for the economy. These can also be explained by the transformation space (figure 3-3). Assume environmental quality is to be improved, that is, we move up the transformation space. Then the quantity of commodities is reduced. At a given production technology, there is a tradeoff between environmental quality and the availability of other goods. Resource costs are opportunity costs since resources used for abatement are lost for production purposes. In figure 3-3, opportunity costs are indicated by the slope dQ_1/dU of the transformation space for a given quantity 2. This marginal rate of transformation tells us which quantity of commodity 1 we have to give up for one additional unit of environmental quality.

The resource costs of environmental policy have been estimated empirically. According to the 1984 Annual Report of the U.S. Council on Environmental Quality (Table A-19), 62.7 bill US $ were spent on pollution control costs in 1983. This amounts to 1.9 percent of the US gross national product. As a rule,

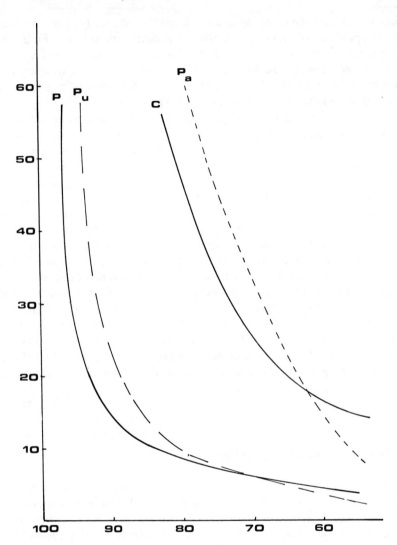

The vertical axis measures marginal costs in the German marks per unit of pollution abatement. The horizontal axis indicates pollutants abated in percent. Here C is chemical industry, P is paper, P_a is public abatement, and P_u is pulp.

Figure 5-3. Abatement Costs

resource costs for the economy as a whole are the range of 1-2 percent of gross national product. Additional information on pollution control costs, for instance with respect to environmental media and industry, is given in tables A-19 and A-20 of the 1984 Annual Report. Pollution control costs for specific sectors were studied by the OECD (1972a, 1977a, b). On other costs estimates compare Maloney and Yandle (1984) and Conrad (1985).

The second category of costs is target losses. To what extent will the improvement of environmental quality affect employment, price-level stability, economic growth, and the balance-of-payments equilibrium? For instance, the Organization for Economic Cooperation and Development (OECD) (1977b) estimated the macroeconomic effects of pollution-control programs in Japan, Italy, the Netherlands, and the United States. The results do not allow uniform statements for each country. In general, one can expect higher price levels resulting from environmental policy (OECD 1978b, p. 10). This is also confirmed by the U.S. Council on Environmental Quality (1979). Also pollution control can be expected to reduce productivity growth (US Council of on Environmental Quality 1980), increase energy prices and may affect the balance of payment situation. In some studies, the stimulating effect of pollution abatement on new abatement technologies is stressed, and as another positive effect, higher levels of employment are forecasted. The same result is reached by some studies for West Germany (Meissner and Hödl 1977; Sprenger 1979). It is questionable whether the net increase in employment can be expected; after all, environmental policy implies a restructuring of the economy to the disadvantage of the pollution-intensive sectors.

Evaluation of Environmental Quality

In this section we discuss some approaches that have been offered for the determination of the benefits of environmental policy. We focus on the evaluation problem. Other questions such as technical information on the extent of physical damages (damage function) are not discussed here (Freeman 1985, Mäler 1985).

Market Prices

The usual method of evaluating commodities starts from their market prices. Market prices tell us how much an individual is willing to pay for a commodity or, from a different perspective, the opportunity costs that he is willing to forgo for a good. If market prices categorize individual preferences, then one can assess the value of a commodity through the consumers' purchase and demand behavior. Because environmental quality is a public good, market prices do not exist for emissions. Market prices, therefore, can be used only to a limited extent, namely, in those cases where markets provide goods similar to environmental quality, such as "private botanic gardens" (entrance fee; compare cost evaluation below).

Willingness to Pay

The willingness-to-pay analysis tries to determine how many dollars one is willing to pay for an improvement in environmental quality. By asking for the willingness to pay for varying levels of environmental quality, we obtain a relation between the environmental quality wanted and the individual's willingness to pay. We can assume that the willingness-to-pay function is downward-sloping. By summing the willingness to pay of all individuals, we obtain the total value of a given environmental quality for society.

The willingness to pay of an individual depends on a set of factors such as his attitude toward society, the level of applicable information available, spatial extent of the public good, frequency and intensity of use, and income. For instance, the level of information about the effects of environmental pollution plays an essential role. It can be expected that an individual who is better informed about environmental damages, *ceteris paribus,* has a higher willingness to pay. In this context, it is clear that a precondition for effectively utilizing the individual willingness-to-pay approach is that the respective individuals must know the damage function. He has to know what kind of damages are caused by a given quantity of pollutants: injuries to health and the ecology, influences on the consumption good "environment," on production, and on property values. Furthermore, the willingness to pay is different depending on the type of the considered commodity. Several public goods are bound spatially; some pollution can be limited to a single area. The smaller the space occupied by a public good, the easier it is to obtain individual contributions to support it. In this case, the public good is a group good. A dump at the outskirts of a village can easily be removed by sharing the operation costs; however, the willingness to pay in order to prevent a deterioration in the atmosphere will be relatively small. If this thesis is correct, it can be expected that global public goods, such as the atmosphere, will be undervalued.

The willingness to pay also depends on the type of use and the intensity of the needs. Which person living upstream is willing to pay for the purification of wastewater when he does not use it as drinking water anymore? One can also imagine some groups for whom it is more important to have a certain environmental quality than others. Heart and tuberculosis patients, or people suffering from bronchitis, will assign a higher priority to air containing a smaller sulfur dioxide content than will healthy people who are not so blatantly affected by the quality of the surrounding air.

The willingness to pay also differs with income and wealth. On the one hand, one can hold the thesis that high-income recipients can compensate for worse environmental quality through private goods. For example, empirical research shows that in New York, recipients of lower incomes have to tolerate a worse environmental quality (Zupan 1973). On the other hand, one can expect that persons with higher income will deem the good "environment" more important than lower-income groups. Furthermore, the possibility of substituting private goods for poor environmental quality is limited.

The central problem of the willingness-to-pay approach is the fact that individuals can intentionally distort their answers because environmental quality is a public good. Individuals can take the position of the free rider. The interviewee can intentionally falsify his answers. For example, he can state a value which is too low when he fears that the poll may be the basis for later charges or, conversely, indicate a too high value in order to emphasize a certain program. If one does not succeed in discovering the actual evaluation of the individuals, the validity of the willingness-to-pay approach is doubtful indeed.

The intensity of the above distortion depends on several previously mentioned factors such as attitudes toward society and the spatial expansion of the environmental good. It is also influenced by the method by which the supply of environmental quality is financed; for example, whether funds for financing environmental policy are raised by general taxes or according to the individual's willingness-to-pay statement. This point is raised again in the analysis of social choice mechanisms (see below).

Evaluation of Costs

Another measure of the evaluation of environmental quality is obtained by determining those costs which a person will tolerate in order to gain a better environmental quality. For example, environmental quality may influence migration behavior. As a rule, the income level in metropolitan areas with high industrialization and low environmental quality is higher than in less environmentally damaged areas. The person who emigrates from a low-environmentally-quality area "votes" against it as a living place. If one is able to isolate environmental quality as a determinant of regional mobility from other factors causing migration (such as regional wage differences and group adherence), then it is possible to evaluate environmental quality. Forgone wages and removal expenses are indicators of the sum that someone is willing to pay for better environmental quality. If data are available for several areas, one can correlate different levels of environmental quality to the corresponding income levels and reach a conclusion as to what the evaluation for environmental services is.

A cost evaluation can also be performed for public-consumption goods such as national parks; for example, one can determine which journey and overnight accommodation costs individuals are willing to pay in order to enjoy a national park. Also, prices for land and buildings can be interpreted as indicators of environmental quality. Within a town with areas of different environmental quality, it can be expected that purchasers prefer areas with a higher environmental quality. This preference should be expressed by an increasing demand for this land and by higher land prices. Of course, as with migration, we must ensure that environmental quality can be sufficiently isolated as a factor of influence for the land and building values, that is, that the influence of variables such as the type, age, and social status of the housing areas can be evaluated. These studies, however, encounter considerable problems. On the one hand, since land and buildings are not often sold, market prices are seldom available. Thus, one must resort to approximate values, for example, tax values. On the other hand, this procedure presumes that the price actually includes an evaluation of environmental pollution by the purchasers, and that the purchasers consider air pollution to be an essential element in their purchase decision.

Cost evaluation has also been proposed for cases where one's health is endangered. Assume that the damage function shows a relationship between pollutants and days of illness, or illness probabilities. In this case, the social costs of the illness can be approximated by doctors' fees, medical costs, hospital costs, as well as lost income. These costs are interpreted as the lowest value attributable to the health damage. In a similar way, when death is caused by environmental damage, such cases are deemed to represent forgone income. The reader may judge for himself whether this position is tenable.

Note that in the case of migration and land or building values, environmental quality is implicitly evaluated by individual decisions. If cost estimates for the restoration of environmental quality are based on targets set by the government, as in the case of emission norms for firms, these restoration costs cannot be considered to be the accurate indicator of environmental-quality evaluation. The reason is simple. We cannot fix a target, specify its opportunity costs, interpret these costs as an evaluation, and then use benefit/cost analysis to determine the target.

On a formal treatment of the problem how the observation of demand of a private consumption good (and a private input of production) can be used to estimate the willingness to pay for a public good compare Mäler (1985). Mäler shows that very specific assumptions are needed to measure the demand for the public good from data on demand for the private good. If the private and the public good are perfect substitutes in a consumption process of the household, we have such a case where the demand for the public good can be measured in terms of cost savings for the private inputs (Mäler 1985, p. 58). On modelling the estimation of benefits also compare Freeman (1985).

Individual Preferences and the Pareto-Optimal Provision
of Environmental Quality

In the previous four sections we assume that the policymaker has an explicit or implicit social-welfare function with which he can determine the desired environmental quality. The existence of such a welfare function can be doubted once we require certain properties. Benefit/cost analysis also poses considerable evaluation problems. In the following analysis, we want to base environmental policy on individual preferences, not on the preference function of an omnipotent policymaker. Given individual preferences, what is the optimal environmental quality? In a first step, we assume that individual preferences can be revealed. Later, we ascertain which institutional arrangements enable this to be accomplished.

If we base the determination of optimal environmental quality on individual preferences, we can return to equation 4.5. There the maximization problem in the case of Pareto optimality is discussed. We use the optimality conditions stated in Appendix 4B. Divide equation 4.6a by $W_1^{1'} = \lambda^2 W_1^{2'}$. Then we have[5]

$$\frac{\lambda_U}{W_1^{1'}} = \frac{W_U^{1'}}{W_1^{1'}} + \frac{W_U^{2'}}{W_1^{2'}}$$

Using equations 4B.2 to 4B.4 and 4B.9,[6] we have

$$\frac{1}{-G'(H_1' + F_1^r/F_1')} = \frac{W_U^{1'}}{W_1^{1'}} + \frac{W_U^{2'}}{W_1^{2'}} \tag{5.7}$$

Equation 5.7 describes a property of optimal allocation. The term on the left side defines the marginal rate of transformation $\mathrm{MRT}_{Q_1 U}$ (dQ_1/dU) for the case when sector 2 does not produce. This follows from equation 3A.4. The right side is the sum of the marginal rates of substitution for the two individuals between environmental quality and the private good, $\mathrm{MRS}_{Q_1 U}^j$ (dQ_1^j/dU). Note that for an indifference curve we have $dW^j = 0$, that is, $dQ_1^j/dU = W_U^{j'}/W_1^{j'}$. Consequently, equation 5.7 can be expressed as

$$\mathrm{MRT}_{Q_1 U} = \mathrm{MRS}_{Q_1 U}^1 + \mathrm{MRS}_{Q_1 U}^2 \tag{5.8}$$

The marginal rate of transformation indicates the opportunity costs of one unit of environmental quality in terms of commodity 1. An additional unit of environmental quality implies some loss of private goods. The marginal rate of substitution indicates which marginal utility from good 1 the individual can give up for marginal utility from environmental quality, given a constant utility level. The marginal rate of substitution denotes the willingness to pay of the individual according to his (truly revealed) preferences. A Pareto optimum of environmental allocation requires that the opportunity costs of one unit of environmental quality be equal to the aggregated willingness to pay of the individuals of a society. Equation 5.8 is Samuelson's well-known summation condition for public goods (Samuelson 1954).

In figure 5–4, the Pareto-optimal provision of environmental quality is illustrated. We assume that only one private good, commodity 1, is produced and consumed so that the transformation space of figure 3–3 is reduced to curve $AGBB'$ in figure 5–4a. This curve results from a cut through the transformation space for R_2, $R'_2 = 0$. In figure 5–4b, curve b denotes an indifference curve of individual 2. In figure 5–4b, curve b represents an indifference curve of individual 2. Pareto optimality requires that individual 2 remain on an arbitrarily chosen indifference level. We plot curve b in figure 5–4a. Then the lense above (and on) the indifference curve b and below (and on) the transformation curve represents the feasible consumption space for individual 1. This feasible consumption space is shown by curve RR' in figure 5–4c. Observe that if we let individual 2 obtain his indifference level b, the range of environmental quality which will be provided is given by RR'. Pareto optimality requires that, for a given indifference level b of individual 2, the utility of individual 1 be maximized. This is the case at point L where the consumption space feasible for individual 1 reaches the highest indifference curve of individual 1.

In figure 5–4a, the marginal rate of transformation $MRT_{Q_1 U} = dQ_1/dU$ is measured by $tg\alpha$. Similarly, angles have to be drawn for the marginal rates of substitution; they are, however, not shown in order not to overload the diagram. The slope of curve RLR' is given by $MRT_{Q_1 U} - MRS^2_{Q_1 U}$. This follows from the construction of curve RLR'. In point L we have

$$MRT_{Q_1 U} - MRS^2_{Q_1 U} = MRS^1_{Q_1 U}$$

which is equivalent to equation 5.8.

In the Pareto optimum, both individuals use the same environmental quality as a public good; $O^1 X$ denotes the quantity of the private good used by individual 2, and $O^2 Y$ indicates the quantity used by individual 1. Figure 5–4 is an illustration of the problem stated in equation 4.5 along with some of its implications.

From welfare economics we know that the Pareto criterion results in only a partial ranking of economic situations. Assume, for instance, that we begin with a lower indifference curve $b' < b$ for individual 2. Then the consumption space RR' feasible to individual 1 would be larger and the Pareto-optimal point L' would be situated northeast of L. We can imagine a set of Pareto-optimal situations that can be defined as the utility frontier.

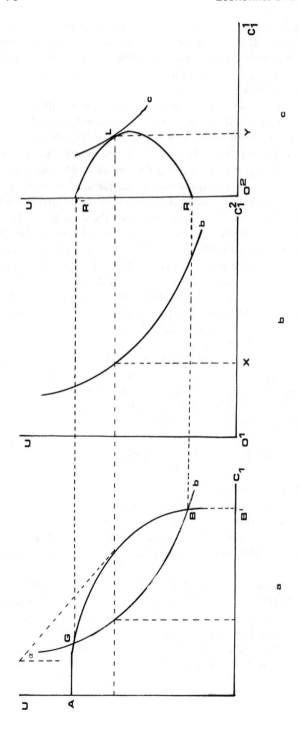

Figure 5-4. Pareto Optimum of Environmental Allocation

Thesis of Market Failure

A Pareto-optimal provision of environmental quality requires that the aggregated willingness to pay be equal to the opportunity costs of environmental quality. Equation 5.8 can be expressed in terms of prices. The marginal rate of transformation MRT is identical to the relationship of marginal costs MC; the marginal rates of substitution are identical to the relative prices, so that we have

$$\frac{MC_U}{MC_{Q_1}} = \frac{P_U^1}{P_{Q_1}} + \frac{P_U^2}{P_{Q_1}} = \frac{P_U^1 + P_U^2}{P_{Q_1}} \tag{5.9}$$

We know that in a competitive equilibrium the price for private good 1 is identical for all individuals and equal to marginal costs. Then equation 5.9 requires that prices for the public good "environmental quality" be differentiated among individuals. The sum of individual prices (individual evaluations) must equal the marginal costs of production of the public good. The same conditions follow from equation 4.6 or 4.10.

It is obvious that the market cannot find a set of differential prices for environmental quality. This is because environmental quality is a public good. Once a unit of this good is provided for one individual, it is also available to another individual. Therefore, it is impossible to exclude the other individual. For instance, consider figure 5-4. Once a range RR' of the public good is provided for individual 2, it is also available for individual 1.

Lindahl Solution

The Lindahl solution (Head 1974; Lindahl 1919; Roberts 1974) assumes that personalized prices for the public good "environmental quality" can be established. Individuals truly reveal their preferences, and either an environmental agency or an auctioneer sets personalized prices for each individual according to the individual's willingness to pay. Each individual contributes to the costs of the public good according to his marginal utility multiplied by the quantity of environmental quality used.

Alternative Implementations

There are three ways to interpret the Lindahl solution in an environmental context:[7]

1. Consumers pay individualized prices p_U^i for environmental quality; the receipts are used to pay a subsidy to firms per unit of abated emissions.

2. Consumers pay individualized prices p_U^j. The receipts are used for pollution abatement by public agencies such as water cooperatives.
3. Firms pay an emission tax per unit of pollution according to the "polluter pays" principle. Tax receipts are used to pay individualized compensations. Then prices p_U^j are negative.

In our approach, this last interpretation is used. Our application is consistent with chapter 4 where we assume that tax receipts are transferred to households. Here we specify the rules according to which compensation takes place.

Decision of Consumers

We assume that consumers are compensated for environmental degradation. Let U^j indicate the actual environmental quality desired (used) by individual j. So $U^{max} = G(S)$ for $S = 0$ defines the maximal environmental quality, that is, ecological paradise. Then

$$U^{Pj} = U^{max} - U^j \qquad (5.10)$$

indicates the environmental degradation tolerated by individual j. Let $p_U^j \leqslant 0$ indicate the individualized price per unit of pollution. Then the decision of the household is to maximize utility subject to the budget constraint with given prices, including $p_U^j \leqslant 0$:

$$\max W^j(C_1^j, C_2^j, U^j)$$

such that

$$\sum_i \tilde{p}_i C_i^j \leqslant Y^j - p_U^j U^{Pj} = Y^T$$

$$Y^j = \tilde{r} R^j + \sum_i \theta_i^j G_i \qquad (5.11)$$

Now, R^j is the initial resource endowment of household j, and θ_i^j represents given profit shares of household j with respect to firm i. For a given price vector, income Y^j is given. In the budget constraint, the term $-p_U^j U^{Pj}$ represents compensation payments to individual j. It is an addition to income Y^j. And Y^T is total household income including compensation.

Substituting equation 5.10 into the budget constraint and assuming, for simplifying purposes, only one commodity, we find that the budget constraint is

$$U^j \leqslant \frac{\tilde{P}_1}{p_U^j} C_1 - \frac{Y^j}{p_U^j} + U^{max} \qquad (5.12)$$

The budget constraint is illustrated in figure 5-5a. The budget constraint has a negative slope $\tilde{p}_1/p_U^j$. We have

$$C_1 = 0 \quad \Rightarrow \quad U^j = U^{\max} - \frac{Y^j}{p_U^j}$$

$$U^j = 0 \quad \Rightarrow \quad C_1 = \frac{Y^j}{\tilde{p}_1} - \frac{p_U^j}{\tilde{p}_1} U^{\max}$$

We know that $U^j \leqslant U^{\max}$, so that a section of the budget constraint is not relevant. If a higher compensation is paid, that is, if p_U^j rises in absolute terms, then the slope becomes lower and C_1 becomes larger (for $U^j = 0$). The budget constraint turns around point P as indicated in figure 5-5a. Observe that for $U^j = U^{\max}$, the budget constraint passes through point P since we have $C_1^j = Y^j/\tilde{p}_1$ independent of the compensation rate.

In figure 5-5b the willingness-to-pay function of the household is derived. For a given compensation rate, point A in quadrant I represents a household optimum. If compensation is increased, the new optimum point is C. We know that the change in demand can be split into a substitution effect AB and an income effect BC. Whereas the substitution effect always implies a reduction in demand for environmental quality, with increased compensation the income effect may work the other way. Increased compensation means a higher total income Y^T, and higher income may result in a higher demand for environmental quality. We assume here that the income effect does not outweigh the substitution effect. Then we have this: An increase in the compensation rate implies that a household tolerates more degradation U^P or that the desired environmental quality decreases. The relationship

$$U^j = \psi(p_U^j) \quad \text{with} \quad \frac{dU^j}{d|p_U^j|} < 0 \tag{5.13}$$

is the willingness-to-pay function shown in quadrant II of figure 5-5b. So far, we have interpreted equation 5.13 by starting from $U^{\max}$ and asking for the tolerated degradation. We can also start from zero environmental quality and ask for the household's willingness to pay with respect to environmental improvement. The willingness to pay is high for a low environmental quality, and it becomes smaller as environmental quality improves.

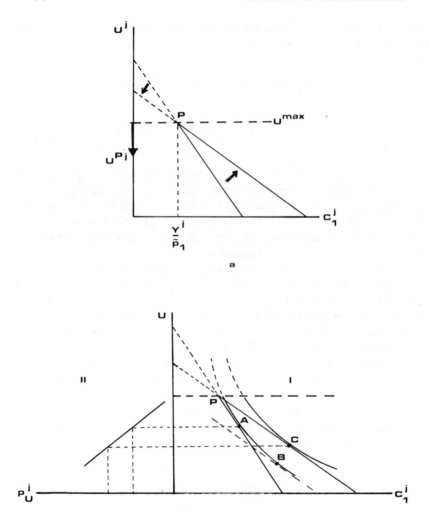

Figure 5-5. Household Optimum

Definition of the Lindahl Equilibrium

An allocation A and a price vector P are a Lindahl equilibrium if (1) (C_1^j, C_2^j, U^j) is a solution to the maximization problem of households as described in equation 5.10, (2) (Q_i, R_i, R_i^r, S) is a solution to the maximization problem of firms as stated in equation 4.8, and (3) the following conditions hold:

$$Q_i = \sum_j c_i^j$$

$$\bar{R} = \sum_i R_i + \sum_i R_i^r$$

$$U^1 = U^2 = U \qquad\qquad\qquad (5.14)$$

$$S = \sum_i S_i = \sum_i S_i^p - \sum_i S_i^r$$

$$-p_U^1 U^1 - p_U^2 U^2 = -(p_U^1 + p_U^2)U = z \sum_i S_i \quad \text{with } U = G(S)$$

Assume that an auctioneer sets prices z, p_U^j for the economy. Condition 3 indicates the constraints that the auctioneer has to observe. The first two conditions are the usual equilibrium conditions for the commodity markets and the resource markets, respectively, and $U^1 = U^2 = U$ requires that prices be set in such a way that both individuals use the same environmental quality. This is the public-good constraint relevant for the auctioneer. Since U determines S, that is, the tolerable quantity of emissions, it is required that the supply of emission "rights" be identical to the demand of polluters. Finally, the budget must be balanced. The contribution of both individuals must be equal to the costs of producing the public good. Prices for the public good are personalized.

Graphical Illustration

In figure 5-6, we illustrate the basic idea of the Lindahl solution.[8] In quadrant III of figure 5-6a, the willingness-to-pay functions for environmental quality U of individual 1 (curve TT') and individual 2 (curve VV') are shown. Curve $V'PW$ denotes the aggregated willingness to pay for alternative environmental qualities. Quadrant IV shows the damage function $U = G(S)$, as explained in equation 3.5. As a result of this function, willingness to pay can also be related to emissions S. Quadrant II serves to transform the price p_U to an emissions tax z, with $tg\alpha = z/p_U$ (compare Pethig 1980). Let e_S indicate a unit (pound) of pollutants, and let e_U indicate a unit of environmental quality. Then $tg\alpha$ has the dimension

$$\frac{\$/e_S}{\$/e_U} = \frac{e_U}{e_S}$$

Thus, $tg\alpha$ is merely a conversion factor.

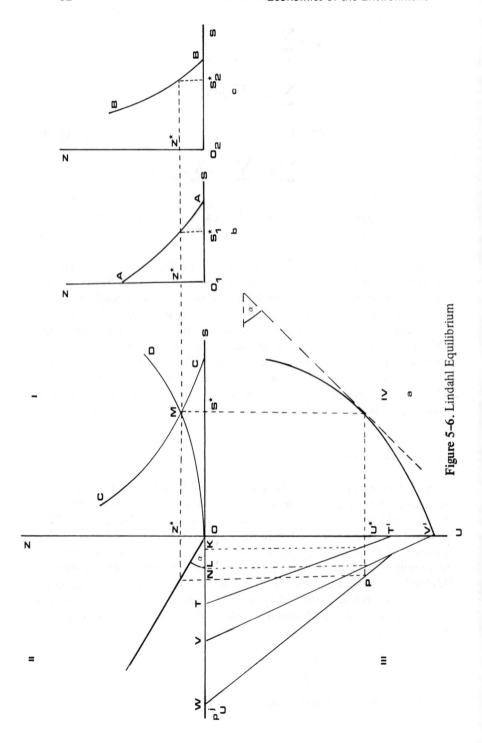

Figure 5-6. Lindahl Equilibrium

Curve OD denotes the marginal evaluation of pollutants by both individuals.[9] There is a relatively high willingness to pay for an improvement in environmental quality if environmental quality is low, for example, if many pollutants exist. The willingness to pay becomes smaller for higher levels of environmental quality (lower levels of pollution). If we interpret the S axis in quadrant I from point C toward point O, the S axis indicates abated pollutants; consequently, curve DO can also be interpreted in terms of prevented damage.

Curve CC in quadrant I denotes the marginal costs of abatement (compare figure 4-1). This curve is aggregated horizontally from the cost curves AA of firm 1 (figure 5-6b) and BB of firm 2 (figure 5-6c).

The optimum is found where marginal costs of abatement are identical to marginal prevented damage. Here S^* is the optimal level of pollution, and U^* represents optimal environmental quality with both individuals using the same environmental quality, that is, $U^1 = U^2 = U$. The individualized prices are $p_U^{1*} = OK$ and $p_U^{2*} = OL$. We see that these prices differ if the willingness-to-pay curves are different. Only if both individuals have identical curves of willingness to pay will we have an identical price for environmental quality.

Whereas the price for environmental quality is differentiated among consumers, the price z for pollutants or emissions is identical for all polluters. The curves of marginal abatement costs of firm 1 (figure 5-6b) and firm 2 (figure 5-6c) are given. By aggregating both cost curves, we obtain curve CC which can be interpreted as the marginal-cost curve of abatement for the economy. The optimal level of pollution is determined where marginal costs of abatement and marginal prevented damage are equal. The optimal emission tax is z^*.

Because of the construction of the aggregated curve of marginal abatement costs, we know that $S_1^* + S_2^* = S^*$. Also we know that total tax receipts z^*S^* are identical to the sum of individual tax payments by firms $z^*S_1^* + z^*S_2^*$. The budget constraint requires that total tax receipts z^*S^* (quadrangle OS^*Mz^*) be identical to total compensation payments OU^*PN.

The auctioneer has to set prices according to the conditions in equation 5.14. The individuals must truly reveal their willingness to pay. Also the first quadrant of figure 5-6a and figure 5-6b and c can be interpreted as illustrating a pseudo-market of emissions or emission rights. The supply of emission rights OS^* is determined by the political process. The demand ($O_1 S_1^*$ and $O_2 S_2^*$) is determined by decisions of the firm. In a Lindahl equilibrium, the supply and demand of emissions rights are equal.

Figure 5-6 attempts a graphical representation of a general equilibrium. However, the reader should be aware of the fact that some of the curves are drawn for equilibrium variables. These curves can shift if specific variables change. For instance, the marginal-cost curves of abatement assume a given resource price; if this price changes, then the curves will shift. The willingness-to-pay curves of both individuals depend on income that is ultimately determined in a general equilibrium. Also $tg\alpha = dU/dS$ in quadrant II is given by the equilibrium value $G'(S^*)$.

Mechanisms of Social Choice

The Lindahl solution for the public-good problem presupposes that individuals truly reveal their preferences; that is, the free-rider problem is neglected. If we explicitly consider the problem of how individual preferences can be revealed, we have to study the institutional arrangements for the aggregation of individual preferences. These mechanisms are discussed in detail in public-choice theory (Mueller 1979, Schwartz 1986; Sen 1970; Slutsky 1977; Tulkens 1978).

Majority Voting

Voting can be interpreted as an institutional arrangement in which policy targets are determined by aggregating individual preferences. An example is the simple majority rule which states that out of two alternatives, x is preferred to y by society, if the majority prefers x to y.

The problem is whether the voting rule succeeds in transforming individual preferences into an overall preference of society, that is whether the voting rule is reasonable (Schwartz 1986, p. 176) or whether it may lead to contradictions in the aggregation.

Consider the following four requirements:

1. Individual preferences are not restricted (unrestricted domain).
2. The decision is independent of who among the voters has a specific preference (anonymity).
3. The decision is independent of the description of the alternatives (neutrality).
4. If the ranking of alternatives x and y by an individual is reversed, the ranking of society should be reversed if the society was indifferent before (positive reaction or sensitivity).

Majority voting satisfies these requirements (Schwartz 1986, p. 26, 38, 39; Frey 1978, p. 77). These requirements are special cases of Arrow's (1951) four postulates on the aggregation process (Frey 1978, p. 70). Thus, according to Arrow's Impossibility Theorem, aggregation by majority rule may not be possible in a consistent way. For instance, cycling cannot be excluded. Cycling means that the outcome of voting varies with the sequence of voting procedures.

In order to establish consistency of aggregation, some of Arrow's postulates may be partly released and weaker assumptions may be introduced. One approach is to losen the postulate of unrestricted domain of individual preferences and to introduce more a priori homogeneity into the preference orderings of individuals. For instance, it can be assumed that individual preference functions have a single peak. This condition can be perceived as a property of homogeneity of a ranking rule (Mueller 1979). If this condition is given, the median voter

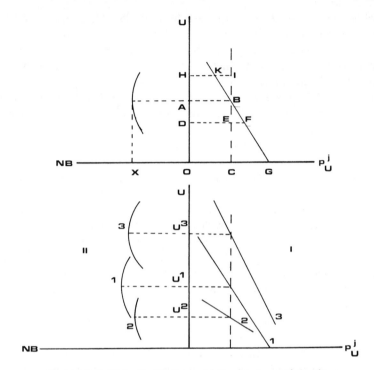

Figure 5-7. Majority Voting and Environmental Quality

plays a decisive role. He determines the outcome of the voting process because he turns a minority into a majority. Another approach is to give a up the postulate of the Independence of irrelevant alternatives, especially the comparison of two alternatives only (Frey 1978, p. 75).

How can we envision an institutional context in which majority voting is used to decide on environmental quality (Dudenhoeffer 1983). In figure 5-7 the determination of environmental quality with majority voting is illustrated. We assume that the voter has to pay a price $p^j_U \geqslant 0$. This price is illustrated by OC in figure 5-7a. Define the net benefit of the individual voter as his willingness to pay minus the costs borne by him. With an environmental quality OA, his costs are given by the quadrangle $OABC$ and his willingness to pay is given by $OABG$. His net benefit is given by triangle BGC or by OX. Note that the net benefit is interpreted here as a consumer surplus.

Assume now that the government charges the same price OC and provides a lower environmental quality OD. Then the net benefit of the consumer is reduced by triangle BFE. This means that for a lower environmental quality OD, the net benefit of the consumer is lower. If, in contrast, the government provides a higher environmental quality, such as OH, with the same price OC, then the household has to pay *OHIC*, but it loses benefits indicated by triangle *KIB*. The net benefits will be lower for environmental quality *OH* relative to *OA*. Consequently, the net-benefit curve of the household will have the form indicated in quadrant II of figure 5-7a. The net-benefit curve is derived for a given price *OC*; it will shift if the price is changed.

In figure 5-7b three different voters are considered with different willingness-to-pay curves (quadrant I). Their net-benefit curves are shown in quadrant II. Individual 1 will prefer U^1, individual 2 will prefer U^2, and individual 3 will prefer U^3. The votes must be given pairwise; that is, the voter must choose between different alternatives. If the decision is to be made between U^1 and U^2, voter 2 will vote for U^2; the other two voters will vote for U^1. If the decision is to be made between U^1 and U^3, voter 3 will vote for U^3; the two others will vote for U^1. If the decision is to be made between U^2 and U^3, both alternatives will receive at least one vote; individual 1 will vote for that alternative which is preferable to him, so that either U^2 or U^3 may be the result. Assume that he votes for U^3. Then a new vote has to be taken between alternatives U^1 and U^3; individuals 1 and 2 will vote for U^1, and individual 3 will vote for U^3. So U^1 will get the majority of the votes. The median voter has determined the result of the voting process.

In figure 5-7 we have assumed that the price p_U is exogenously given to the voter so that figure 5-7 represents a partial-equilibrium illustration of the decision problem of a voter. In a general equilibrium approach, markets must be cleared, and the budget of the environmental agency receiving payments from consumers and giving subsidies to firms for emission abatement (or vice versa) must be balanced. Consequently, as long as these conditions of market clearing and balance of the budget are not satisfied, the price for environmental quality will change. Then the net-benefit curves in quadrant II will shift with a change in price. After environmental quality is determined by the median voter, the costs of producing the public good are given. Since costs and receipts from payments by consumers must balance, a new price must be set if the balance does not exist. Then new net-benefit curves must be constructed. This may cause another voter to become the median voter. We can conceive of a *tâtonnement* process by which the sum of prices eventually equals marginal costs of the environmental quality. Note that the willingness-to-pay curve may shift in the *tâtonnement* process with such variables as allocation, prices, and income. Dudenhoeffer (1983) has established a general equilibrium model in which majority voting determines environmental quality and in which all the above mentioned feed backs are included.[10]

Although the single-peakedness condition guarantees a consistent decision of society, we cannot establish that voting will lead to a Pareto-optimal allocation, as was the case with the Lindahl equilibrium. Moreover, problems of individual rationality arise. Also we do not analyze whether majority voting will guarantee that preferences are truly revealed (Mueller 1979, p. 68).

Other Forms of Voting

Simple majority voting is just one specific voting rule. Many other forms of voting exist such as qualified majority (for instance for changes in the constitution) or more generalized forms of majority voting being extended from the two-alternative to the multialternative case. Other rules are the plurality rule where the alternative favored by the largest number is chosen, possibly with a runoff, preferential voting with voters ranking alternatives, or even unanimity rules. Voting may take place under different institutional settings. For instance, a referendum concerns one specific issue and, as practised in the United States or in Switzerland, a definite public good is voted upon; very often the costs of the public good are indicated, including the apportioned cost per citizen. For example, in the city of Davos in Switzerland, voters were asked whether they supported a new water-purification facility with costs being attributed to houseowners. In such cases the voter can only say yes or no; the political fight among different groups for a yes or no vote may be considered as a way of revealing preferences.

Logrolling or vote trading means that alternatives are no longer independent of one another. A group of voters forms a coalition with another group, and they trade votes, one group lending votes to the other on one issue and receiving support on another issue in return.

Voting may also be studied in the context of political parties attemtping to maximize votes and competing with each other with bureaucracy and interest groups playing an important role. The reader is referred to the literature of public choice.

Finally, the legal system is instrumental in revealing preferences of a society, for instance in protecting the views of specific groups and minorities.

Demand-Revealing Processes

New institutional mechanisms of aggregating individual preferences have been proposed which explicitly attempt to reveal the willingness to pay of each person. One such proposal is the Clarke tax (Clarke 1971; Tideman and Tullock 1976). The Clarke tax can be described as follows. One regards two alternatives, A and B. Every voter is asked to state his willingness to pay for the options. Let S_A denote the sum of the willingness to pay of all optionholders who prefer A to B, and S_B denotes the sum of the willingness to pay of all optionholders who prefer B to A. The society chooses A if $S_A > S_B$; thus the willingness to pay for A is higher than for B. In order to ensure that individuals do not distort their preferences, a Clarke tax is levied. An optionholder has to pay this tax when his vote influences the result; namely, he pays the difference $S_A - S_B$ where S_A and S_B are calculated without his willingness to pay.

Therefore, every optionholder has the option either to leave the result as it would have been without his vote or to change the result by the price of the net loss to the others. A distorted answer would not be favorable to the optionholder. If the optionholder prefers a value which is lower than the net value for others, then the optionholder would prefer to leave the result as it is without his vote. Hence there would be no reason to falsify his preference. However, when this value is greater to the optionholder than the net value is for others, then the optionholder would want to influence the results and would have no reason to conceal his preference. Thus, the Clarke tax presents a social choice mechanism which urges the individual not to distort his preference.

The Clarke tax is a process for revealing public-goods demand; it burdens the optionholder whose willingness to pay reverses public decisions. It is, as Tideman and Tullock (1976) believe, immune to individual maneuvers. At the same time, it avoids the impossibility (stressed by Arrow) of a consistent, transitive, and nondictatorial aggregation of individual desires. However, the optionholders have to fulfill higher requirements: It is not sufficient to vote yes or no (that is, to have only an order of alternatives); rather, it is necessary to evaluate these alternatives too. On the other hand, if the optionholders form coalitions, they can evade this new social mechanism. Moreover, the budget is not balanced with regard to the Clarke tax (surplus). Therefore, the question arises as to whether the budget surplus should be withdrawn from circulation and whether a redistribution of this surplus influences the relevant incentives.

Pethig (1979) applied the Groves-Ledyard mechanism to the preference disclosure for environmental goods. This mechanism is related to the Clarke tax: Economic subjects inform the environmental agency about their desired environmental quality, but they do not evaluate it. The environmental agency employs a compensation scheme (positive or negative). If an individual deviates from the average reply of all other individuals by demanding a better environmental quality, then he is assessed accordingly through tax mechanisms, that is, he gets burdened. This assessment will lead to a modification of his desires. The communication process between the environmental agency and individuals runs iteratively, eventually resulting in a condition where all individuals want the same environmental quality. While elections, referenda, and the Clarke tax do not result in a situation where all individuals desire the same quantity of a public good (in elections, for example, 50.01 percent decide), the compensation function of the Groves-Ledyard mechanism is strict enough that a harmonization of desires is achieved.[11]

An Example: Ambient Air Quality Standards

In practical environmental policy, sufficient information on prevented damage in monetary terms very often is not available. Standards for minimum quality of

Table 5-2. U.S. National Ambient Air Quality Standards

Pollutant	Primary (Health Related)		Secondary (Welfare Related)	
	Averaging Time	Concen-tration	Averaging Time	Concen-tration
Total suspended particulates	Annual Geometric Mean	75 ug/m^3	Annual Geometric Mean	60 ug/m^3
	24-hour	260 ug/m^3	24-hour	150 ug/m^3
SO$_2$	Annual Arithmetic Mean	(0.03 ppm) 80 ug/m^3	3-hour	(0.50 ppm) 1300 ug/m^3
	24-hour	(0.14 ppm) 365 ug/m^3		
CO	8-hour	(9 ppm) 10 mg/m^3	Same as Primary	
	1-hour	(35 ppm) 40 mg/m^3	Same as Primary	
NO$_2$	Annual Arithmetic Mean	(0.053 ppm) 100 ug/m^3	Same as Primary	
O$_3$	Maximum Daily 1-hour Average	0.12 ppm (235 ug/m^3)	Same as Primary	
Pb	Maximum Quarterly Average	1.5 ug/m^3	Same as Primary	

environmental media then are often established on ad hoc basis taking into account information available in the different scientific disciplines on the impact of pollutants on health or on the natural environment. For instance, a minimum air quality may be specified for a metropolitan area, or quality standards for a river system or for groundwater may be set. It is reasonable to view these standards as fixed targets or as normative restrictions to other policy decisions. (Compare also the standard-price approach discussed in chapter 7).

As an example of quality standards, Table 5-2 shows the national ambient air quality standards in the US for different pollutants.[12] Primary standards are intended to protect health, secondary standards protect public welfare, as measured by effects of pollutant on vegetation, materials and visibility.

Notes

1. J. Tumlir, *National Interest and International Order* (London: Trade Policy Research Center, 1978), p. 10.

2. This distinction is not clear-cut since resource costs can also be interpreted as a target loss, namely, as a decline of national income.

3. Compare, for instance, U.S. Council of Environmental Quality, *Annual Report* (Washington, 1971), p. 119; Kneese and Bower 1979, chap. 4; OECD (1977*a*, *b*) with respect to the aluminum, fertilizer, metal industry.

4. On data compare Der Rat von Sachverständigen für Umweltfragen (1978, p. 115).

5. An inner solution is assumed.

6. Note that $W_1^{1'} = \lambda_1 = \lambda_S H_1' + \lambda_{Q_1} = \lambda_S H_1' + \dfrac{\lambda_R}{F_1'} = \lambda_S \left(H_1' + \dfrac{F_1^{r'}}{F_1'} \right)$

7. On the Lindahl solution in an environmental context, compare Pethig (1979, 1980).

8. An alternative graphical illustration is the Kolm-Edgeworth box (Malinvaud 1971; Pethig 1979). Also compare Mäler (1985).

9. Curve *OD* starts at point *O* for two reasons. First, the curve $U = G(S)$ in quadrant IV has to be drawn in such a way that for $S = 0$ we have $U = U^{max}$. Second, we can expect that the aggregated willingness to pay is zero for U^{max}.

10. Besides single-peakedness, Dudenhoeffer (1983) needs a strong assumption on the homogeneity of preferences. The majority of consumers have the same characteristics (p. 73).

11. The same result is reached in a Lindahl equilibrium. On the practicability of the Groves-Ledyard mechanism compare Mäler (1985), p. 47.

12. Compare Council on Environmental Quality, 15th Annual Report, 1984, p. 12.

Property-Rights Approach to the Environmental Problem

The public-goods approach to the environmental problem discussed in chapter 5 represents the basic argument for government intervention. The property-rights idea can be considered as a counterposition. The property-rights approach suggests that if exclusive property rights are adequately defined, the public-good environmental quality can be transformed into a private good, and optimal environmental allocation will be reached. Government intervention, if necessary, is needed only in assigning environmental property titles. With property rights adequately defined, the market will find the correct allocation. Both approaches agree that actually property rights are not adequately defined for the environment as a receptacle of wastes. To change the environment as a common-property resource in its role as a receptacle of waste into a private good by assigning property rights for emissions is consistent with both approaches. Whereas the public-goods approach suggests that, because of the nature of public goods, property rights cannot be specified, the property-rights approach is more optimistic.

Property-Rights Approach

A *property right* can be defined as a set of rules specifying the use of scarce resources and goods (Furobotn and Pejovich 1972). The set of rules includes obligations and rights; the rules may be codified by law, or they may be institutionalized by other mechanisms such as social norms together with a pattern of sanctions. Property rights may be defined over a wide range of specific resource uses. Dales (1968) distinguishes four types of property rights:

First, *exclusive* property rights cover the right of disposal and the right to destroy the resource, notably the right of sale. But even this extensive form of ownership is controlled by a set of rules which protect other individuals or maintain economic values. For instance, a homeowner may not destroy his house. In cities we are not allowed to burn garbage on our property. If there is a mineral well near the lot you own, you may not be permitted to build a factory on your property. City zoning and criminal law are examples of restrictions on exclusive property rights.

Second, *status* or *functional ownership* refers to a set of rights accorded to some individuals, but not to others. In this case the right to use an object or to receive a service is very often not transferable. Examples of this type of right include licenses to drive a taxi or notarize documents, and, during the Middle Ages, the right of admission into a guild.

Third, *rights to use a public utility* (merit good such as a highway) or a public good (a national park) relate to a specific purpose.

Fourth, *common-property resources* represent de facto a nonproperty because nearly no exclusion is defined.[1]

Property rights may be transferable, or they may be limited to a specific person or status (such as functional ownership). Property rights may be defined with respect to the right to use the resource directly, or they may be defined such that use is allowed only in a very remote way. For instance, the right to vote in an election represents a property right in a general interpretation.

The property-rights approach represents a very interesting and powerful line of economic reasoning since it permits us to integrate economics with law and other social sciences. The property-rights approach can be interpreted as a contribution to the theory of institutions, where an *institution* is defined as a set of rules that specifies how things are done in a society. In terms of the property-rights approach, the basic question of economics can be posed: How are property rights to be defined so that the economic system generates "optimal" results? The word *optimal* may mean quite a few criteria, such as freedom of the individual, incentives to produce, to find new technologies, and to supply resources (for example, capital and labor). Also we may ask whether property rights can be defined in such a way that externalities are internalized.

Property-Rights and Environmental Allocation

What are the implications of the property-rights approach for the environmental problem? As we have seen, historically property rights have not been defined for the use of the environment. Under such conditions, markets cannot fulfill the allocation function, and the resulting structure of production is distorted. For instance, the fish of the oceans are treated as a common-property resource; consequently, this resource is overused. Burton points out that the growing desert of the Sahel region in Africa is due to the nonexistence of property rights.[2] As a result of heavy fighting among migrating tribes over many years, a complex system of using the land as a common property has emerged that has not contained elements for the conservation of natural resources. Parts of northern Africa were the granary of the Roman Empire; after property rights were changed into a common-property pasture system by the Arabs in the sixth century, the conservation of the land degenerated.

This message of the property-rights approach is consistent with our analysis so far. The environment as a receptacle of wastes, if used at a zero price, can be interpreted as a common-property resource. This implies, as is pointed out in chapter 2, an overuse of the environment and a distortion of sector structure in favor of the pollution-intensive sector. The property-rights approach requires that the property-rights (or constraints) for using the environment should be more clearly defined, that is, that the character of common property be changed. The same implication follows from allocation analysis. The environment should no longer be used as a free good for receiving wastes; rather, a scarcity price should be charged. One way of introducing a price and redefining property rights is to introduce an emission tax. Another way would be to auction pollution licenses. Finally, the government could specify maximum emissions per firm (permits) which would implicitly set a price on pollutants. In all these cases, the environment, as a receptacle of wastes, would be transformed into a private resource with a positive price by defining a new set of rules.

There may be a second implication of the property-rights approach: Is it possible to define property rights in such a way that the public good "environmental quality" can also be transformed into a private good? Can we imagine such an exclusion technology whereby the characteristics of the public good "environmental quality" are changed? Exclusion technologies not only are determined by technical properties; they also depend on institutional arrangements, normative considerations, and the costs of exclusion. If exclusion is practicable, completely different policy implications result: The public-goods approach to environmental problems motivates government intervention since the market does not provide public goods. The property-rights approach maintains that in many cases involving public goods, private property rights can be defined. Further, this approach asserts that more imagination is needed in order to find the correct institutional arrangements, and that government activity should be limited to cases where a definition of private property rights is not possible. In the following analysis, we proceed in two steps. First, we assume that property rights can be defined; then we ask how the attribution of property rights will affect environmental allocation. Later we look into the problem of whether property rights can be defined.

Coase Theorem

One of the basic results of the property-rights approach to environmental allocation has been proposed by Coase (1960).[3] The Coase theorem states:

> Let exclusive property titles to the environment be defined, and let them be transferable. Let there be no transaction costs. Let individuals maximize their utilities, and let them be nonaltruistic. Then a bargaining solution among different users of the environment will result in a Pareto-optimal allocation of the environment. The resulting allocation is independent of the initial distribution of property titles.

The Coase theorem can be illustrated with figure 5-2. For simplicity it is assumed that we consider two individuals, a polluter and a pollutee. We distinguish two cases.

Case 1. Assume the exclusive property right to the environment is given to the pollutee (consumer). The damage per unit of pollutants for the pollutee is indicated by curve OD. The damaged person will be willing to tolerate a certain degree of emissions if he is adequately compensated. The sufferer will agree to environmental impairment as long as the compensation per additional emission unit lies above his marginal-damage curve. The bargaining position of the sufferer thus moves along the marginal-damage curve OD in figure 5-2. On the other hand, the polluter is willing to offer compensation for the use of the environment as long as the compensation per unit of pollution is lower than his marginal abatement costs. Thus, the position of the polluter is determined by the curve S^0C of the marginal abatement costs. The result of this bargaining process is found at point W. Optimal environmental quality will be OS', and the required abated emissions will be S^0S'. The polluter will pay a compensation per unit of emission to the owner of the environment.

Case 2. Assume that the polluter owns the exclusive right to use the environment. In this case, the pollutee has to pay compensation so that the polluter avoids emissions. The willingness to pay of the sufferer is determined according to his marginal prevented damage; that is, his bargaining position is determined by curve OD. The polluter is willing to abate pollutants only if he receives a compensation greater than his marginal-cost curve of abatement S^0C. The solution is found again at point W. The same environmental quality results as was determined in case 1. Also the same quantity of emissions has to be abated.

The Coase theorem shows that optimal environmental allocation is independent of the initial distribution of property titles. This is a powerful result of the property-rights approach. The reader may see that figure 5-2 describes three different solutions to environmental allocation, namely, the optimization approach of chapter 4 (Pareto optimum), the benefit/cost approach, and the bargaining solution. All three approaches require the equality of marginal benefits (that is, marginal prevented damage) and marginal costs of abatement.

Whereas the allocation is independent of the definition of property rights, the distribution of income is not. Since income distribution may have a feedback on the marginal evaluation of environmental quality and on marginal costs (via demand, commodity, and factor prices), we must specify that, as an additional condition of the Coase theorem, income distribution does not affect these variables (at least not significantly), although we know that there is feedback.

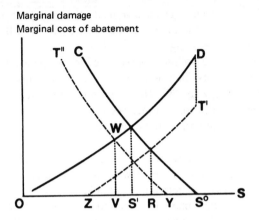

Figure 6-1. Coase Solution with Transaction Costs

Coase Theorem and Transaction Costs

The impact of transaction costs on environmental allocation is shown in figure 6-1. In figure 6-1 curve OD denotes marginal prevented damage, and curve S^0C indicates marginal abatement costs. Assume, now, that transaction costs arise and that they are carried by the party who tries to induce the owner of the environment to agree to a different use. Also assume for simplifying purposes that transaction costs can be defined per unit of emissions so that in this interpretation we can talk of marginal transaction costs. It is assumed that marginal transaction costs are constant.

Let us again distinguish between the two different cases of property titles.

Case 1. If the pollutee owns the environment, the polluter is willing to compensate the pollutee according to the polluter's marginal-cost curve CS^0. In this case, however, the polluter also has to carry the marginal transaction costs; the net transfer according to the pollutee who is endowed with the exclusive property right, therefore is given by the marginal abatement cost minus transaction costs. Relative to the situation without transaction costs, the compensation offered to the pollutee is reduced; the polluter's bargaining curve shifts downward from S^0C (in figure 6-1) to YT'' with the vertical distance between the curves representing the transaction costs per unit. Note that the curve shifts in a parallel fashion, that is marginal transaction costs are assumed to be constant.

With transaction costs, instead of point S', the new solution is at point V, so that more pollutants are abated (S^0V instead of S^0S', and a higher environmental quality is obtained. This result is intuively clear. Transaction costs raise the price of the right to pollute for the firm, so that the firm has an incentive to abate more.[4]

Case 2. If the polluter owns the environment, the pollutee's upper limit to compensate the polluter is the prevented damage (curve OD). But the pollutee will also have to carry the marginal costs of transactions so that he can only offer a compensation to the polluter consisting of the marginal prevented damage minus the transaction costs. In this case, the bargaining curve of the pollutee shifts downward from OD to ZT'. This implies there is a reduced incentive to abate pollutants because the polluter receives a smaller transfer payment. Instead of S^0S', only S^0R pollutants will be abated; environmental quality will be lower.

As a result we have. When transaction costs exist, the environmental quality reached in a bargaining process varies with the institutional arrangement of property rights. The Coase theorem no longer holds.

In figure 6-1, constant marginal transaction costs have been assumed. If some fixed cost element in the bargaining process is involved, the determination of environmental quality will become more complicated. Fixed bargaining costs will have to be allocated to emissions abated in the bargaining process. It has also been pointed out that the pollutee may have higher transaction costs than the polluter. This may be due to the fact that the pollutees are many, or that they have to ensure participation of many in identifying the damages.

The Coase theorem has been criticized on many grounds, including the existence of differences in bargaining positions, relevance of transaction costs, insufficient analysis of the bargaining process, and equity considerations. The crucial factor, however, is that, in reality, we have more than one person in each bargaining party. Consequently, environmental quality is a public good for the consumer with non-rivalry in use, and the aforementioned free-rider problem arises. By assuming only one pollutee, the Coase theorem has assumed away the existence of public goods.

Can Property Rights Be Specified?

With respect to the definition of property rights, two levels of discussion have to be distinguished. Is exclusion technically feasible? And if so, is it normatively acceptable?

First, property rights for using the environment as a receptacle of wastes can be defined so as to include even difficult cases such as the fluorocarbons from spray cans which affect the ozone layer. We can envision international treaties banning or reducing the production of fluorocarbons. In the case of regional or national environmental problems, property rights may also be established.

Second, property rights can be defined for using natural resources such as fish in the ocean. Via international negotiations, fishing permits may be introduced and allocated to different nations by means of auctions or political bargaining.

In the examples given above, however, even with property rights defined, there remains the public-goods problem. The ozone layer is a public good, and from a policy point of view we have to determine how much of the ozone layer ought to remain pollution-free. In solving this question, we meet the free-rider issue again; the willingness to pay of different individuals (or, more realistically, of nations) may not be truly revealed. The same problem arises in the oceans when the existence of a species such as whales is interpreted as being a public good to be enjoyed by all.

Whereas in the case of global or international environmental goods, such as the ozone layer or the Mediterranean Sea, the public good remains, more local types of environmental quality may lose their public-good character through exclusions. For instance, the cleanliness of a village in the German Odenwald may be a concern for the villagers, and this may be a group good. The village may develop social mechanisms in order to maintain this public good, and in this sense, property rights may be defined. Exclusion exists for national parks, for instance, when limits are placed on the number of overnight permits granted in order to reduce congestion. It is also conceivable to limit access by an entrance fee, that is, to exclude those not willing to pay a given price. In other instances, the price of land or houses denotes an implicit evaluation of a beautiful location and serves as a mechanism of exclusion and of revealing willingness to pay. Finally, we can envision a setting where the exclusive property right for the environment, such as the air quality of a region, is given to an individual (or a government agency), and the owner charges a price for providing this environmental quality. Those not willing to pay the price have to leave the region, while others willing to pay could move into the area. In all these examples, Samuelson's criterion that the public good is consumed in equal amounts by all no longer holds.

An advantage of the property-rights approach is that it has stimulated imagination with respect to the question of whether property rights can be specified. For instance, a hundred years ago people would not have believed that it would be possible to sell the airspace above one's house. This, however, happened in Manhattan as a result of new zoning laws. It is probable that today we are unable to conceive of all possible exclusion technologies which may eventually arise.

The definition of property rights has been a historical process. If we look at human development since Adam and Eve left paradise, the increasing scarcity of resources required the definition of property rights. When land was in ample supply, property titles for land were not necessary. When people competed for the scarce good "land," property titles became relevant. Similarly, water once was a free good, but today property titles for water are well accepted. The continuing endangerment of wildlife species or fish induces institutional arrangements for conserving these resources. And the increasing scarcity of energy or raw materials leads to property rights for the sea. Even in the case of the orchards and the bees, the prototype of examples of externalities discussed by Meade[5], Cheung (1973) has shown that property rights have developed. It is interesting to note that some property rights have developed via private bargaining.

There are people who project this historical development into the future and who are confident that an adequate definition of property rights can be left to individual bargaining with only an initial stimulus provided by the government (Wegehenkel 1980). I take the position that it is worthwhile to give additional thought to the question of how new property rights can be defined.

In this endeavor, however, the problem arises as to whether technically possible exclusion mechanisms are morally acceptable. It is a value judgment that access to natural amenities such as a national park should be open to everyone under reasonable conditions. The idea of giving the exclusion right of the environment to an individual or a government agency and forcing those not willing to pay to leave the area is not acceptable in a culture which has experienced the *cujus regio, ejus religio* principle.[6] Further, such an exclusion right would impede the citizens' freedom of movement. Thus, basic values of a society limit the range of possibilities in which property rights may be defined. We cannot exclude that values will change over time, so that the property-rights approach and the public-goods approach to economic problems will remain interesting counterpositions in the future.

Notes

1. It is recommended to take a second look at some common properties. For instance, the village forest in the Swiss Alps may, at first glance, be interpreted as being a common property. A closer analysis often shows that there is a set of rules regulating its use. Thus, the forest may serve as a protection against avalanches, and withdrawal of wood is restricted.

2. J. Burton, "Externalities, Property Rights and Public Policy: Private Property Rights to Prevent the Spoliation of Nature," mimeographed (Kingston Polytechnic, Kingston upon Thames, England, n.d.).

3. Compare R. Windisch, "Das Motivationsproblem bei marktlicher Koordinierung knapper Umweltressourcen," mimeographed (Göttingen, 1980), p. 12.

4. Note that the curve YT'' in figure 6-1 displays the net benefit for the pollutee. If we were to draw the marginal cost curve for the firm (compare figure 7-1), transaction costs will shift the marginal cost schedule upward.

5. J.E. Meade, "External Economies and Diseconomies in a Competitive Situation," *Economic Journal* 62 (1952): 54–67.

6. This principle was used at the end of the Thirty Years' War in 1648 when the sovereign determined the religion of subjects.

Part III
Environmental-Policy Instruments

7

Incidence of an Emission Tax

In part II we analyze optimal environmental allocation and suggest different approaches in order to determine the optimal environmental solution. Environmental allocation is placed into the context of static optimization models, the economics of public goods and the theory of property rights. In chapters 7, 8 and 9, our interest shifts to environmental policy instruments. In chapter 7, we analyze how firms react to an emission tax, and what the overall incidence of an emission tax will be on environmental quality, emissions, the allocation of resources in production and abatement and sectorial structure. We thus analyze the incidence problem in detail for a specific instrument. In chapter 8, we survey the environmental policy instruments available looking at their relative advantages and disadvantages. In chapter 9 we study some institutional conditions in which policy instruments are chosen and the influence of the institutional setting on environmental policy.

The allocation models studied in chapters 3 and 4 suggest that a price tag should be attached to environmental use when the environment is treated as a receptacle for wastes. How can this price be determined? In this chapter, we discuss what information is required to establish this price for environmental policy. From a practical point of view, prevented marginal damage can hardly be determined. Rather, a quality standard has to be set, and a standard-price approach has to be used. If a standard-price approach is followed, an important question is analyzed in some detail in chapter 7. One argument is that a monopolistic producer will shift the emission tax to the consumer. We show that, even in monopoly, an emission tax will have an incentive to abate pollutants. Partial oly, an emission tax will have an incentive function to abate pollutants. Partial equilibrium analysis is not sufficient to provide a definitive answer with respect to the incidence of an emission tax. Therefore we construct a general equilibrium model in which the relative commodity price is determined endogenously. The assumptions of this general equilibrium model are specified, and the implications of the model are studied.

Standard-Price Approach

If we interpret the implications of the optimization model of chapter 4 as a guideline for economic policy, then our model indicates that in order to establish an emission tax, the following information is required: The policymaker needs information on the existing quantity of emissions, the level of abatement costs for alternative states of the environment, prevented damages and their evaluation, and diffusion between emissions and pollutants. In chapter 5 we discuss some of these information requirements in greater detail, such as specifying and evaluating prevented-damage and abatement costs. The evaluation of marginal damage is a condition that may not be given. Then the policymaker has to make an ad hoc decision on the level of environmental quality to be attained, and the target variable has to be determined in the political process. The economic dimension of the allocation problem is then reduced to the question of how the desired environmental quality can be achieved in an efficient way, that is, with minimal resource use for abatement.

This approach is illustrated in figure 7-1, where OS^0 represents the total quantity of emissions and S^0C denotes marginal abatement costs. Assume that a quality target OS' is fixed so that $S'S^0$ pollutants should be abated. Then an emission tax OT has to be set. This approach is the standard-price approach discussed by Baumol and Oates (1971). Note that figure 7-1 should be compared with other graphical illustrations in this book, such as figures 4-1, 5-2, and 6-1, all relating to the problem of how environmental quality is to be determined.

The standard-price approach dispenses with the determination of environmental-policy benefits and presents instead a procedure that achieves an environmental standard with minimal abatement costs. Since the environmental standard is politically determined and not the result of an optimizing process, the desired environmental quality can be suboptimal. Only by chance will the standard be equivalent to the optimal environmental quality.

One way to implement a fixed quality target is for the government to levy an emission tax. Assume that the government does not have information on marginal abatement costs. Then the government could use a trial-and-error process and observe how the private sector would react to a given emission tax. If the firms would abate as many pollutants as were desired by the policymaker, the emission tax would not be changed. If the resulting environmental quality were

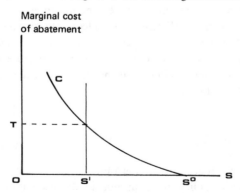

Figure 7-1. Standard-Price Approach

too low, the emission tax would have to be raised. If environmental quality were higher than expected, then the emission tax would have to be reduced.

In the case of a standard-price approach, a decisive question is: How will the private sector react to the emission tax? Will environmental quality be improved? Will the pollution-intensive sector be impeded? Will resources be transferred from production to abatement?

Reaction of Producers

In order to prepare the general-equilibrium analysis of the incidence of an emission tax, we first study how an economy adjusts to an emission tax if the product price is assumed as given. The decision of the individual producer can be explained with the help of figure 4-1a, where O_1S_1 denotes emissions and where S_1A represents marginal abatement costs. If the producer does not abate pollutants, he has to pay taxes. Tax payments are represented by the quadrangle with sides O_1T_1 and O_1S_1. If he abates pollutants, the producer's tax payment is reduced. The producer will abate pollutants as long as the marginal costs of abatement are lower than the emission tax. In figure 4-1a the producer will abate the quantity XS_1 of pollutants. If a lower emission tax than O_1T_1 is set, fewer pollutants will be abated. A higher emission tax implies that more pollutants will be abated.

Thus, the introduction of an emission tax represents an incentive to abate pollutants. The more important incentive function of an emission tax is to stimulate the search for a less pollution-intensive production technology and a more favorable abatement technology. Such technical progress would shift the cost curve of abatement to the left and reduce the total quantity of emissions. Unfortunately, this incentive for technical progress cannot be further considered in our static model.

The adaptation of the individual firm to an emission tax can be analyzed as follows. Assume that the firm maximizes profits and takes the price vector $(\tilde{p}_i, \tilde{r}, \tilde{z})$ as given. Then the problem is given by equation 4.8. Equation 4.9 indicates the profit-maximizing factor demand of the firm and implicitly defines demand functions for inputs in production R_i and abatement R_i^r. These demand equations can explicitly be written as

$$R_i = \Psi_i\,(\tilde{p}_i, \tilde{r}, \tilde{z})$$
$$R_i^r = \Psi_i^\tau\,(\tilde{p}_i, \tilde{r}, \tilde{z})$$

Divide equation 4.9 by $\tilde{p}_2$; that is, choose commodity 2 as numéraire (with $p = \tilde{p}_1/\tilde{p}_2$, $r = \tilde{r}/\tilde{p}_2$, $z = \tilde{z}/\tilde{p}_2$). Then the system of equation 4.9 and the resource restriction 3.6 consist of five equations and contain the six variables r, p, R_i, R_i^r.

The emission tax z is exogenously determined (by economic-policy decisions). For simplicity, assume that p is a constant; then we can find out how the economy reacts to the introduction of an emission tax. Total differentiation of equations 3.6 and 4.9 yields

$$
\begin{bmatrix}
a_1 & 0 & 0 & 1 \\
0 & a_2 & 0 & 1 \\
0 & 0 & -zF_1^{r''} & 1 \\
zF_2^{r''} & zF_2^{r''} & zF_2^{r''} & 1
\end{bmatrix}
\begin{bmatrix}
dR_1 \\
dR_2 \\
dR_1^r \\
dr
\end{bmatrix}
=
\begin{bmatrix}
-H_1'F_1' \, dz \\
-H_2'F_2' \, dz \\
F_1^{r'} \, dz \\
F_2^{r'} \, dz
\end{bmatrix}
\tag{7.1}
$$

with $a_i = zH_i''F_i'^2 - (\tilde{p}_i/\tilde{p}_2 - zH_i')F_i'' > 0$.

Equation 7.1 indicates the effects of a change in the emission tax on resource demand by the firm. Resources used determine output and abatement. From Appendix 7A we have

$$
H_1'F_1' > H_2'F_2' \quad \left\{ \frac{dR_1^r}{dz} > 0 \quad \text{and} \quad \frac{dR_1}{dz} < 0 \right. \tag{7.2}
$$

Resource input in the pollution-intensive sector decreases, and resource use in the abatement activity of the pollution-intensive sector increases. Total resources used in sector 1, namely in production and abatement, will decrease. A definitive statement cannot be made with regard to resource use for production in the environmentally favorable sector 2. There, resource for production use can increase or decrease. More resources can be used in the abatement activity of sector 2, so that a decrease of resource use for production in sector 2 cannot be excluded. Furthermore, we obtain the result

$$
H_1'F_1' \gtrless H_2'F_2' \quad \left\{ \frac{\Sigma \, dR_i}{dz} < 0 \quad \text{and} \quad \frac{\Sigma \, dR_i^r}{dz} > 0 \right. \tag{7.3}
$$

Resources are withdrawn from production and used in abatement. This indicates that the net emissions S decrease and that environmental quality improves. Furthermore, we know that the resource input decreases in the pollution-intensive sector.

In figure 3-3 this result can be shown graphically. Define an isoprice line for a given p and a varying z. Then the economy will move along that isoprice line from a point on the traditional transformation curve BC upward on the transformation space. The properties of this isoprice line are implicitly given by equation 4.9.

Emission Taxes in Monopoly

It is often argued that a monopolist will shift an emission tax to consumers and that consequently the incentive function of an emission tax will not apply in the case of a monopolistic producer. We want to analyze whether this argument is valid. The monopolistic producer has to take into account the same constraint as a competitive producer; however, the commodity price $\tilde{p}_i$ is not given. Instead the monopolistic producer is confronted with a demand function $\tilde{p}_i = \psi_i(Q_i)$. For simplicity, assume that the producer cannot influence the resource price and the emission tax. Then the profit-maximization problem of the monopolistic producer is given by

$$G_i = \psi_i(Q_i)\, Q_i - \tilde{r}(R_i + R_i^r) - \tilde{z}S_i$$

subject to

$$Q_i - F_i(R_i) \leqslant 0$$
$$H_i(Q_i) - S_i^P \leqslant 0$$
$$S_i^r - F_i^r(R_i^r) \leqslant 0$$
$$-S_i + S_i^P - S_i^r \leqslant 0 \qquad\qquad (7.4)$$

The reader should compare equations 7.4 with equation 4.8. The implications of the maximization problem for the monopolist are

$$Q_i \frac{\partial \psi_i}{\partial Q_i} + \psi_i(Q_i) = \frac{r}{F_i'} + \tilde{z}H_i' \qquad\qquad (7.5a)$$

$$\tilde{z} = \frac{\tilde{r}}{F_i^{r'}} \qquad\qquad (7.5b)$$

Equation 7.5a specifies that the monopolist will equate marginal revenue with marginal costs of production (including environmental costs). Because of the declining marginal revenue, the monopolist will produce a lower output compared to a firm in perfect competition. Consequently, he will produce fewer pollutants. In this sense, the monopolist is the environmentalist's friend.

Equation 7.5b specifies that the monopolist will abate pollutants as long as marginal abatement costs are lower than the emission tax. Assume O_1S_1 in figure 4-1a is total emissions of the monopolist, and let S_1A denote his curve of marginal abatement costs. Then the monopolist will abate S_1X pollutants. Equation 7.5b is identical to the case of perfect competition. Therefore, the emission tax acts as an environmental incentive even under monopolistic conditions.

General Equilibrium Approach

In the analysis of the incidence of an emission tax in perfect competition, we have assumed a constant relative commodity price p. In reality, we can expect that the relative price will change and that the change in relative price will affect sector structure and the allocation of resources. Consequently, we have to give up the assumption of a constant relative price. The relative price has to be determined endogenously in the model. Our frame of reference is the two-sector model specified in chapter 3. We introduce the following additional assumptions.[1]

Commodity demand is given by

$$C_i = D_i(p, Y) \tag{7.6}$$

where $p = \tilde{p}_1/\tilde{p}_2$ is the relative price.

Income Y is defined from the production side. There are no savings. In order to close the model, we assume that the government spends the tax receipts by redistributing them to the households. Consequently, disposable income of the households is identical to net national income at market prices and is defined as

$$Y = pQ_1 + Q_2 \tag{7.7}$$

Observe that Y includes transfers not explicitly shown and that p is the consumers' price, not the producers' price. If Y were defined with respect to the producers' price p^*, emission taxes (and transfers) would appear explicitly on the right side of equation 7.7.

Commodity markets must be in equilibrium, so that

$$Q_i = C_i \tag{7.8}$$

Additionally, we require equations 3.1 through 3.6 and equation 4.9. This system of equations contains the seventeen variables $S_i^p, S_i, S_i^r, Q_i, R_i, R_i^r, Q_i^p$, p, Y, and r and eighteen equations. The definition of Y in equation 7.7 states that the total demand is equal to income, so that in a two-sector model the equilibrium condition for one of the product markets is redundant (Walras' law) and should be omitted. By substitution the system can be simplified to

$$F_1(R_1) = D_1(p, pF_1(R_1) + F_2(R_2)) \tag{7.9a}$$
$$r = zF_i^{r\,'}(R_i^r) \tag{7.9b}$$
$$r = (p - zH_1')F_1'(R_1) \tag{7.9c}$$
$$r = (1 - zH_2')F_2'(R_2) \tag{7.9d}$$

$$\bar{R} = R_1 + R_2 + R_1' + R_2' \tag{7.9e}$$

The structure of the model is shown in figure 7-2. The model contains three subsystems: the political system, the resource market, and the commodity market. In the political system, the existing and the desired environmental qualities are compared, and an emission tax is established. The emission tax influences the resource demand for abatement and for production. Resource demand and resource supply determine the resource price; in turn, resource price affects resource demand. Resource use in production is determined by the emission tax, by the resource price, and by the commodity price p. The commodity price p is a result of demand and supply in the commodity market. Resource use in production determines gross emissions; resource use in abatement accounts for abated pollutants. Gross emissions minus abated emissions define net emissions, which, in turn, influence environmental quality.

Allocation in a General Equilibrium Model

We want to analyze how an emission tax will affect environmental quality, sectoral output, and the allocation of resources. Total differentiation and substitution of 7.9e into 7.9a to 7.9d yields

$$
\begin{bmatrix}
a_1 & 0 & 0 & 1 & -F_1' \\
0 & a_2 & 0 & 1 & 0 \\
0 & 0 & -zF_1^{r''} & 1 & 0 \\
zF_2^{r''} & zF_2^{r''} & zF_2^{r''} & 1 & 0 \\
b_1 F_1' & -D_{1Y}' F_2' & 0 & 0 & -b_2
\end{bmatrix}
\begin{bmatrix}
dR_1 \\
dR_2 \\
dR_1^r \\
dr \\
dp
\end{bmatrix}
=
\begin{bmatrix}
-H_1' F_1' \, dz \\
-H_2' F_2' \, dz \\
F_1^{r'} \, dz \\
F_2^{r'} \, dz \\
0
\end{bmatrix}
\tag{7.10}
$$

The coefficients are defined as follows:

$$b_1 = 1 - D_{1Y}' p = D_{2Y}' \tag{7.11a}$$

$$b_2 = D_{1p}' + D_{1Y}' F_1 < 0 \tag{7.11b}$$

Note that $b_2 < 0$ follows from Slutsky's rule. Let $D_{1Y\text{comp}}'$ denote the pure substitution effect. We have

$$D_{1p}' = D_{1p\text{comp}}' - D_{1Y}' D_1$$

or

$$D_{1p\text{comp}}' = D_{1p}' + D_{1Y}' F_1(R_1) = b_2 < 0$$

since the pure substitution effect is always negative. Note that equation 7.10

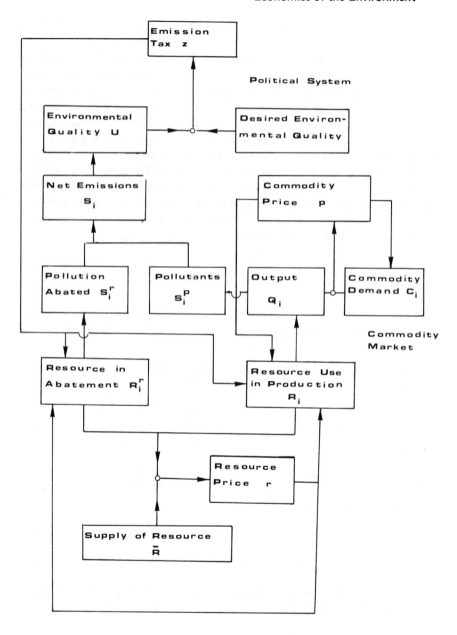

Figure 7-2. Structure of General Equilibrium Model

contains equation 7.1 as a subsystem in the first four rows and first four columns. From Appendix 7B we have the following results:

$$\Delta > 0 \quad \begin{cases} D'_{2Y} \geq 0 \\ D'_{1Y}F'_2 + D'_{2Y}F'_1 \geq 0 \end{cases} \tag{7.12a}$$

$$\frac{dR^r_1}{dz} > 0 \quad D'_{1Y}F'_2 + D'_{2Y}F'_1 \geq 0 \tag{7.12b}$$

Assuming 7.12a is given, we have

$$\frac{\Sigma dR_i}{dz} < 0 \tag{7.13a}$$

$$\frac{dR_1}{dz} < 0 \quad \begin{cases} D'_{1Y} \geq 0 \\ H'_1F'_1 > H'_2F'_2 \end{cases} \tag{7.13b}$$

$$\frac{dp}{dz} > 0 \quad \begin{cases} H'_1F'_1 > H'_2F'_2 \\ a_2 D'_{2Y}F'^2_1 p \geq a_1 D'_{1Y}F'^2_2 \end{cases} \tag{7.13c}$$

$$\frac{dY}{dz} < 0 \quad \begin{cases} H'_1F'_1 > H'_2F'_2 \\ -\eta_{1p} > \alpha > 1 \text{ with } \alpha = \dfrac{1}{1 - F'_2/pF'_1} \end{cases} \tag{7.13d}$$

where $-\eta_{1p}$ is the price elasticity of demand for the pollution-intensively produced commodity.

Allocation

Assume that both commodities are not inferior, so that their marginal propensities to consume ($D'_{iY} \geq 0$) are nonnegative. Then the determinant Δ is positive, that is, $\Delta > 0$. Assume that sector 1 is the pollution-intensive sector, that is, $H'_1F'_1 > H'_2F'_2$. Then we can conclude that resource use in the pollution-intensive sector will decline. Resource use in each abatement activity will increase; resource use in production (ΣR_i) will be reduced.

Environmental policy will shift the sector structure of the economy in favor of the abatement activities while production will be negatively affected. We can establish that production in the pollution-intensive sector will decline. In the less pollution-intensive sector 2, resource use may increase or decrease. The model allows for both cases. Thus, in one case, sector 1 and sector 2 lose resources to the abatement activity, whereas in the other case sector 1 loses resources to sector 2 and the abatement activity.

Environmental Quality

Given our assumptions, emissions will decline and environmental quality will improve. This follows from $\Sigma\, dR_i/dz < 0$ and $\Sigma\, dR_i^r/dz > 0$.

Relative Price

Equation 7.13c specifies the conditions under which the relative price of the pollution-intensive commodity will rise. We have two sufficient conditions.

1. $D_{2Y}' \geqslant pD_{1Y}'$. Under the conditions specified below, national income will decline as a consequence of environmental policy. Then $D_{2Y}' \geqslant pD_{1Y}'$ guarantees that demand for the pollution-intensive commodity 1 is reduced less than demand for commodity 2. This difference in the income effect of the two commodities ensures that the relative price of the pollution-intensive commodity must rise.

2. For $a_2 \geqslant a_1$, $|dR_1/dr| > |dR_2/dr|$ specifies[2] that (for given p and z) sector 1 is more sensitive to changes in resource price than sector 2; we may also say that sector 1 is more dependent on resource R. This condition can be interpreted as a rudimentary form of a factor-intensity condition in a one-factor model. We can expect that this condition unfolds into a set of factor-intensity conditions in a multifactor model. As a result, we know that the relative price of the pollution-intensive commodity will rise if the marginal propensity to consume this commodity is lower than the less pollution-intensive commodity and if the pollution-intensive sector depends heavily on resource R.

Sufficient conditions for a rise in the relative price can partly substitute each other. Assume that sector 1 is very pollution-intensive. Then the relative price of commodity 1 may rise even if it has a high income elasticity of demand (and if it loses demand quantities with a decline in income). Or, for identical pollution intensities of both sectors, the relative price will rise if sector 1 is characterized by a sufficiently smaller income elasticity of demand. If this is so, then sector 1 loses a smaller quantity of demand. This requires a higher adjustment in relative price. Finally, assume that sector 2 is very dependent on resource R. Then p can rise anyway, when sector 1 is sufficiently more pollution-intensive or when sector 1 has a sufficiently lower income elasticity.

National Income

Environmental policy affects net national product at market prices Y in two ways. First, resource use in production will decrease, so that for a given price p national income will fall (withdrawal effect). Second, the pollution-intensive commodity has to be revalued since the market price must include the social costs of production. The revaluation effect runs counter to the withdrawal effect.

National income will fall if the withdrawal effect outweighs the revaluation effect. This is the case if the price elasticity of demand for the pollution-intensive commodity η_{1p} is sufficiently large, that is, $-\eta_{1p} > \alpha > 1$. A high price elasticity of demand for commodity 1 ensures that the pollution-intensive sector will lose large quantities of demand so that the revaluation effect will not be too high.

From the definition of α, we have an interesting interrelation between demand conditions and the condition of emission intensity.

First, assume that sector 1 is strongly pollution-intensive so that α is close to unity.[3] Then the price elasticity does not have to be too high if the withdrawal effect is to be strong. A high pollution intensity in sector 1 means that production costs will rise sharply in sector 1, relative prices will rise, and sector 1 will lose quantities of demand even if the price elasticity of demand is not too high.

Second, if sector 1 is relatively non-pollution-intensive compared to sector 2, then α is higher than unity, and the demand for the pollution-intensive commodity must be very price-elastic in order for demand quantities to decline. In other words, in condition 7.13c a high price elasticity of demand for the pollution-intensive commodity may be substituted by a strong pollution intensity of production in sector 1.

Summary

Under the specified conditions, the introduction of an emission tax will reduce emissions and will improve environmental quality. Resource use and output of the pollution-intensive sector will decline, and resource use in abatement will increase. The relative price of the pollution-intensive commodity will rise, so that demand for it will decline. The emission tax drives a wedge between the market price and the producers' price. Finally, under the specified conditions, national income will fall. This means that there is a tradeoff between environmental quality and the maximization of national income. The effects of environmental policy are depicted in figure 7-3. The effects can also be analyzed through use of the transformation space in figure 3-3. Given an initial situation on the transformation curve *BC*, the economy moves upward on the transformation space. Whereas environmental quality is improved, national income decreases. Also, the relative price changes, sector structure, and the allocation of resources are affected.

Pollution Intensities, Factor Intensities, and Allocation Effects

The model presented can be made more realistic if additional adaptations of the economic system are considered.

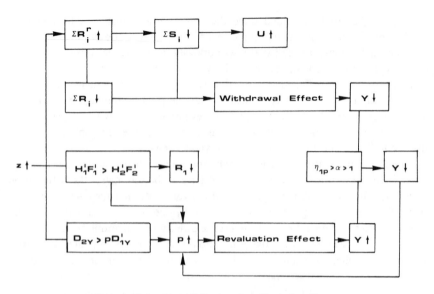

Figure 7-3. Main Effects of an Emission Tax

Two Factors of Production

In the analysis so far, we have assumed only one factor of production. If we
assume that different types of inputs are used in production and in abatement,
we can expect additional conditions for the allocation incidence of an emission
tax. Besides the pollution intensity of the two sectors, we also have to distinguish
between the capital intensity and the labor intensity of production and pollution
abatement.[4] Assume, for instance, that the pollution-intensive sector 1 is also
characterized by a labor-intensive production and by a capital-intensive abatement. Let the non-pollution-intensive sector 2 be characterized by capital-
intensive production. Then environmental policy will increase the production
costs in sector 1 and, *ceteris paribus,* reduce output there. The reduction of output means a decrease in factor demand. Since sector 1 is labor-intensive, its
demand for labor will fall relatively more than for capital. Because of the capital
intensity of abatement in sector 1, the demand for capital will rise. Under such
conditions, the relative demand of sector 1 for capital increases. If, at the same
time, sector 2 is capital-intensive and if the non-pollution-intensive sector 2 increases output, then the demand for capital rises. Since the relative demand for
capital in the economy rises, the wage-interest ratio falls. This implies that in all
activities capital will be substituted by labor; and the capital intensity will rise.
This case is illustrated in figure 7-4.

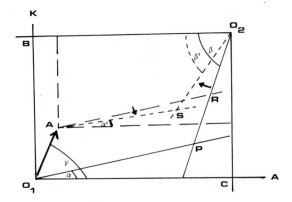

Figure 7-4. Allocation Effects in a Two-Factor Model

Assume a given factor endowment with capital endowment O_1B and labor endowment O_1C. Let K denote capital and A labor. The capital intensity of sector 1, $k_1 = K_1/A_1$, is given by $tg\alpha$. The capital intensity of sector 2 is given by $tg\beta$. In the initial situation, no environmental policy is undertaken. Point P denotes the initial allocation of resources in the Edgeworth box with O_1P denoting output of sector 1 and O_2P indicating output of sector 2.

Assume, now, that environmental policy is undertaken. Assume that a given level of abatement is specified and that O_1A indicates the withdrawal effect of resources through abatement. Note that the capital intensity of abatement is given by $tg\gamma$. It is assumed in figure 7-4 that abatement is capital-intensive, relative to production in sector 1. The withdrawal effect of resources from production means that the Edgeworth box becomes smaller. With given relative factor prices, the allocation shifts from P to R. For a given relative factor price, output in both sectors is reduced. In our example, however, we have an additional effect, the reduction of the wage-interest ratio. This means that the capital intensity will fall from $tg\alpha$ to $tg\alpha'$ in sector 1 and from $tg\beta$ to $tg\beta'$ in sector 2. This implies a substitution of capital by labor. Substitution of capital by labor affects a movement from point R to point S. Sector 2 adjusts to the new relative price and makes itself less dependent on capital.

In figure 7-4, sector 1 is assumed to be relatively pollution-intensive and labor-intensive in production and capital-intensive in abatement. It is apparent that the allocation effects depend on the factor intensities in production and abatement. There may be cases in which the result is not clear in one direction, for instance, if sector 1 is capital-intensive in production and abatement. Also, demand conditions have an impact on the output level, on the relative commodity price, and on the relative factor price. For a more thorough analysis of the allocation incidence in a two-factor world, compare Siebert et al. (1980).

Other Extensions

The allocation model discussed in this chapter could be extended in several ways in order to make it more realistic. Thus, we have assumed a given production, emission, and abatement technology. It seems to be realistic to expect that an emission tax will represent an incentive to find less pollution-intensive production technologies and to improve abatement. Furthermore, we should take into consideration that an industry consists of different types of firms. Firms differ in size, age, and technological capabilities. Consequently, an emission tax will also have an impact on industrial structure. The allocation incidence may also be different if we compare a one-product with a multiproduct firm. Moreover, the allocation incidence will vary with the type of policy instruments used. Assume for instance, that instead of an emission tax, a permit system with emission norms is used as a policy instrument. Then the emissions of an individual polluter (or a specific source of emissions) are limited by a restraint

$$S_i \leqslant \bar{S}_i,$$

so that the maximization problem of the firm stated in equation 4.8 has an additional restraint, but there are no tax payments for emissions. We can specify the profit-maximizing supply and factor demand of the individual firm; we can also determine how the individual firm and the economy as a whole reacts to a change in emission standards.

Overshooting of the Emission Tax

Our incidence analysis is undertaken in a static framework. It was mentioned earlier that in setting the emission tax the government may follow a trial-and-error-procedure. Once an emission tax is introduced, the government observes the resulting environmental quality; if it diverges from the target, the emission tax will be adjusted.

This trial-and-error-procedure may give rise to oscillations in the emission tax if the adjustments in pollution abatement take time. For instance, capital formation in the abatement activity may be a reason for a lagged response. It may take time to build pollution capital. Then a given emission tax may only yield the desired result with a time lag. If environmental policy reacts too quickly, the emission tax will "overshoot", and a misallocation of resources will result.

Notes

1. On this approach compare Siebert (1978a).

2. Differentiate the factor-demand conditions 7.9 for given p and z with respect to r:

$$\frac{dR_i}{dr} = \frac{1}{(p_i/p_2 - zH_i')\,F_i'' - zH_i''F_i'^2} = -\frac{1}{a_1}$$

and

$$\left|\frac{dR_1}{dz}\right| > \left|\frac{dR_2}{dz}\right| \Leftrightarrow a_2 > a_1$$

3. Note that $pF_1' = r + zH_1'F_1'$ and $F_2' = r + zH_2'F_2'$, so that $H_1'F_1' > H_2'F_2'$ implies that $F_2'/(pF_1') < 1$.

4. Gronych in chapter 8 of Siebert et al. (1980) treats assimilative capacity as an input to production. Environmental policy then determines environmental endowment and can be interpreted similarly as an exogenous change in factor endowment.

Appendix 7A: Reaction of the Individual Firm

The determinant of equation 7.1 is given by

$$A = -a_1 a_2 z \, (F_1^{r''} + F_2^{r''}) + z^2 F_1^{r''} F_2^{r''} \, (a_1 + a_2) > 0 \tag{7A.1}$$

Define

$$A_1 = a_2 pF_1' \, (F_1^{r''} + F_2^{r''}) - z^2 F_1^{r''} F_2^{r''} \, (H_1' F_1' - H_2' F_2') \tag{7A.2}$$

$$A_2 = a_1 F_2' \, (F_1^{r''} + F_2^{r''}) + z^2 F_1^{r''} F_2^{r''} \, (H_1' F_1' - H_2' F_2') \tag{7A.3}$$

The solutions are

$$\frac{dR_1}{dz} = \frac{A_1}{A} \tag{7A.4}$$

$$\frac{dR_2}{dz} = \frac{A_2}{A} \tag{7A.5}$$

$$\frac{dR_1^r}{dz} = \frac{A_3}{A} = -\frac{F_2^{r''}}{A} \, (a_1 F_2' + a_2 pF_1') \tag{7A.6}$$

Appendix 7B:
General Equilibrium Model

We have

$$\Delta = -b_2 D - a_2 D'_{2Y} F_1'^2 z (F_1^{r''} + F_2^{r''}) + z^2 F_1' F_1^{r''} F_2^{r''}$$
$$(D'_{1Y} F_2' + D'_{2Y} F_1') \tag{7B.1}$$

Define

$$\Delta_1 = -b_2 Z_1 + F_1' F_2'^2 D'_{1Y} (F_1^{r''} + F_2^{r''}) \tag{7B.2}$$

$$\frac{dR_1}{dz} = \frac{\Delta_1}{\Delta} \tag{7B.3}$$

$$\frac{dR_2}{dz} = \frac{\Delta_2}{\Delta} \tag{7B.4}$$

$$\Delta_2 = b_2 Z_2 + F_1'^2 F_2' D'_{2Y} (F_1^{r''} + F_2^{r''}) \tag{7B.5}$$

$$\frac{dR_1^r}{dz} = \frac{\Delta_3}{\Delta} \tag{7B.6}$$

$$\Delta_3 = -b_2 Z_3 - F_1' F_2' F_2^{r''} (D'_{1Y} F_2' + D'_{2Y} F_1') \tag{7B.7}$$

$$\frac{dp}{dz} = \frac{\Delta_5}{\Delta} \tag{7B.8}$$

$$\Delta_5 = -D'_{1Y} F_2' Z_2 - D'_{2Y} F_1' Z_1 \tag{7B.9}$$

$$\frac{dY}{dz} = \frac{1}{D} [(F_1^{r''} + F_2^{r''}) F_1'^2 F_2'^2 + (b_2 - Q_1 D'_{1Y})$$
$$(-pF_1' Z_1 + F_2' Z_2) - F_1' Z_1 Q_1] \tag{7B.10}$$

8

Policy Instruments

In this chapter, we study how the basic ideas of allocation theory can be implemented and which policy instruments can be used to reach a desired environmental quality. The set of available policy instruments is reviewed. The basic message of allocation theory for practical policy is that environmental scarcity must be taken into consideration in individual decisionmaking. We study in some detail the regulatory approach, emission taxes, and pollution licenses. Furthermore, water associations are considered. They represent an interesting institutional arrangement by which the costs of environmental-quality targets can be attributed via cost sharing to individual polluters.[1]

Transforming Quality Targets into Individual Behavior

The problem of using environmental-policy instruments consists of finding institutional arrangements or policies such that a given target of environmental quality is reached by the individual decisions of the polluters. How can we transform a quality target for an environmental medium into the emission (and abatement) behavior of individual agents? This problem can be studied from different angles of the doctrine of economic thought which are all more or less related to each other.

According to the principal-agent literature (Fama 1980; Grossman and Hart 1983), the policy maker as a principal has chosen the desired environmental quality and attempts to influence the decisions of the individual agents, namely the households and the firms, in such a way that the target is eventually reached. The government does not exactly know how the agents behave; more specifically, it does not have all the information which the agents have, for instance on abatement technology. The problem then is to devise an institutional arrangement and to define incentives in such a way that the behavior of the individual agents contributes to the overall target.

From the point of view of the property rights literature, finding the appropriate institutional arrangement is just a manifestation of devising new property rights that allow to express environmental scarcity. Compare our discussion in chapter 6.

A related concept can be found in the problem of *Ordnungspolitik* stressed by the German Freiburg school in the 1930's. The question here was to devise a frame of reference or a set of rules (Ordnungsrahmen) for an economy defining the operating space for private activities.

Finally, from the discipline of economic policy in the European tradition, the problem of environmental policy instruments can be interpreted as a transformation problem, namely the question of chosing the best policy instrument in order to reach the set target.

Available Policy Instruments

We may distinguish among the following instruments (Bohm and Rusell 1985).

1. The policymaker attempts to influence the targets of private subjects in such a way that the social impact of private decisions is considered more carefully; that is, the political leader tries to change the orientation of households and producers.
2. Pollution abatement is interpreted as a government activity; it is financed by general taxation.
3. The government pays subsidies in order to induce abatement activities or reduce pollution. The subsidies are financed by general taxes.
4. A regulatory approach is followed in which the government specifies the maximum amount of emissions per firm or per equipment (emission norms, permits). When a quality target is violated in an environmental medium, no new permit can be issued.
5. A price per unit of emission is charged (emission tax, effluent charge) with the intent to induce abatement or less pollution-intensive technologies.
6. By fixing the quality target, the policymaker determines the tolerable total quantity of all emissions, that is, the sum of emission rights for an environmental medium. These emission rights are given to those who are willing to pay the highest price; that is, they are auctioned among competing users in an artificial market for pollution licenses.
7. Associations for specific environmental media are formed that either determine the quality target themselves or implement the quality target which is specified by the policymaker. The role of these associations is to distribute the costs of achieving a desired environmental quality to the polluters; the attribution of costs should be undertaken in such a way that incentives for abatement are created.

Criteria for Evaluating Instruments

The choice of a specific environmental policy must take into account a set of criteria.

Ecological incidence. Environmental-policy instruments are chosen in order to transform a given environmental quality into a desired condition. Therefore an important criterion is that the instrument induce abatement and improve environmental quality.

Economic efficiency. Environmental policy results in significant costs. These consist of resource costs and target losses to macroeconomic policy objectives. Since these costs mean forgone opportunities, the level of costs will determine the scope of environmental policy. Consequently, a given quality target has to be reached with minimum costs.

Information. For the practical application of environmental-policy instruments, it is crucial to know what kind of information is presupposed by the various instruments, to what extent this information can be technically provided, and how much the required information will cost.

Management costs. Information costs represent only one aspect of the performance costs of an environmental-policy instrument. Management expenses also include the costs of implementation and control of the instruments as well as the possible costs in the form of forgone flexibility (bureaucratization).

Practicability. Environmental policy instruments cannot be regarded in an organizational, institutional, or political vacuum. The choice of instruments can also be influenced by how much opposition is generated among various parties such as policy administrators or special-interest groups.

Time lag of incidence. This criterion refers to the question of how long it will take until an environmental-policy measure improves environmental quality.

Transition problem. The introduction of environmental-policy instruments represents an abrupt change in the frame of reference of individual behavior. Consequently, we must ask how an environmental-policy instrument will resolve the resulting transition problem.

Seriousness of the problem. The estimation of the environmental problem is a further determinant of the instruments to be chosen. If the environmental problem is regarded as being very serious for a certain environmental medium, then the status of ecological efficiency possibly acquires a higher rank in comparison to economic efficiency. If the environmental situation is estimated such that after consideration of the transition costs, a short-term solution is not imperative, then the criterion of economic efficiency becomes more important.

Type of problem. Since instruments have the function of transforming a given situation into a desired one, the choice of the instruments is unavoidably dependent on the type of problem. Therefore special importance should be placed on whether the same instruments can be used for different environmental media and whether—even if only one environmental medium is considered— different environmental problems can be distinguished for an environmental medium. These differences require that various instruments be employed.

In theory (compare chapter 4), the choice of a policy instrument is determined by maximizing welfare. In practice, the choice of a policy instrument is a multidimensional problem. There are many criteria to be considered. One can expect that a specific environmental-policy measure can be favorable with regard to some criteria and unfavorable concerning others.

Moral Suasion

Moral suasion is an attempt to influence the preferences and the targets of private economic subjects including managers in such a way that the social consequences of private decisions are considered. It includes a change of ethical norms with respect to nature and ecological problems. This approach may bring about results, but since the economic success of an enterprise is the central element of a free-market system, we cannot rely on firms to consider the social effects of their economic decisions. Rather, it should be the task of the economist to change the frame of reference (the data corona) of private economic decisions in such a way that social costs are internalized.

Government Financing and Subsidies

One approach to the environmental problem would be that the government has to undertake pollution abatement and that abatement activities have to be financed by general taxation. If we take into account environmental conditions, this approach is not very feasible for air pollution. Also, it seems to be a good principle to prevent emissions from entering environmental media instead of abating them after they have entered the media. An increase in government activity along these lines would reduce the role of the private sector and increase that of the public sector. This would negatively affect the decentralization of the economy. Therefore, we have to look for other policy instruments. The role of the government in this respect is to redefine the conditions of individual activity in such a way that private costs do not differ substantially from the social costs of individual activities. The provision of a public good does not mandate that the good is actually produced or even financed by the government. Adequate institutional arrangements may be all what is called for in order to ensure the provision of public goods.

Subsidies are proposed in a number of forms in environmental policy. Quite a few objections can be raised against subsidies. They have to be financial by general taxes, and in most industrialized countries subsidies already account for a large part of the budget. Also, whereas most subsidies are motivated by social policies such as health care or agriculture, the environmental problem is an allocation question. The main objection to subsidies, however, is that subsidies stimulate the pollution-intensive commodity. They take over a part of the environmental damage. Because of this subsidization, the enterprise does not need to introduce these costs into its price. Therefore, the price of the pollution-intensive commodity is too low in comparison to commodities being produced favorably to the environment. The price structure as an allocation guideline does not change as is desired. In comparison to a desired optimal situation, excessive quantities of pollution-intensive commodities should be limited. The subsidy systematically distorts the economic price mechanism and causes a false allocation of resources, as discussed in chapter 2. In the following considerations, we focus on the regulatory approach, emission taxes, and pollution licenses.

Regulatory Approach

The regulatory approach seeks to reach a given quality target for an environmental system by regulating individual behavior. The typical instruments are pollution permits, that is, allowances to emit a specific quantity of a pollutant into an environmental system. Permits are issued until the quality target has been reached; then no further permits are issued[2] (Siebert 1982*i*; 1985*b*).

Regulations can take different forms according to what they specify. The usual permit is a property right to emit a maximum quantity of pollutants. Other types of regulations are obligations to reduce a given amount of pollutants, in absolute or in relative quantities. Still other examples of this approach include regulations which stipulate the state of technology to be applied in abatement or production or which monitor the type of input to be used. Product norms may define the quantity of pollutants which are contained in goods (for example, DDT in agricultural products) or which emerge through the use of commodities (noise emitted through the use of commodities such as a car). Production quantities may be limited, or production of a specific product may be prohibited. Finally, the location of firms may be forbidden in a specific area.

The regulatory approach has been widely used in environmental policy. Thus, water- and air-quality management in the United States is based on a permit system (Mills 1978). Air-quality policy is also based on a permit system in Europe and Japan.

The advantage of the regulatory approach is seen in its ecological incidence. If the quality target is properly set and if private emitters do not violate the relevant laws, then the quality target will be reached. This argument makes the regulatory approach very attractive to environmentalists. It is claimed that the regulatory approach may have advantages in the case of environmental risks (see chapter 14). Unfortunately, the regulatory approach has severe shortcomings.

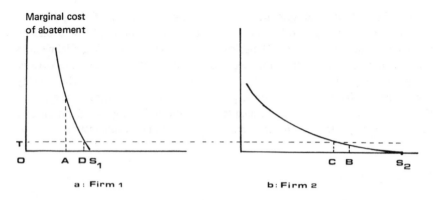

Figure 8-1. Effect of an Instruction to Reduce Emissions

Inefficiency

The regulatory approach requires a set of emission rules that apply to all emitters of a specific pollutant. The policymaker planes the economic subsystems by using a general approach, and thus he is not able to take into account particular differences. Therefore, the regulatory approach is inefficient. As an example, consider an obligation to reduce a given amount of pollutants by x percent. We neglect the announcement effect which would clearly indicate that the level of pollutants should not be reduced before the instrument is applied (in fact, more pollution should be produced now so that one will be faced with only a relatively small reduction later). In figure 8-1, the marginal abatement costs of two firms are shown. Firm 1 has relatively unfavorable abatement costs, whereas firm 2 can abate at lower costs. If both firms have to reduce their emissions by one-third, firm 1 will abate S_1A with relatively high abatement costs, and firm 2 will abate S_2B with relatively low abatement costs. Abatement is inefficient in the sense that firm 2 can abate BC of the pollutants at a lower cost than firm 1 can abate AD. An emission tax OT shows the efficient solution.

The inefficiency argument implies that resources are wasted. Thus, the opportunity costs are too high. Since the costs of environmental policy will have an effect on the target level, inefficient abatement implies less environmental quality. Therefore, the regulatory approach reduces the chances for an effective environmental policy.

Bureaucracy

Government agencies have to issue permits specifying the allowable quantity of emissions for specific equipment within the firm. For instance, in the North

Rhine Westfalia region of West Germany, air-quality policy attempts to regulate each stationary source of emission (Dreyhaupt 1979). We may call this approach the "individual stack policy" where the government regulates each individual facility. In North Rhine Westfalia, about 10,000 permits are said to exist relating to air quality, not counting the de-facto permits of older facilities. According to Mills (1978, p. 186), 46,000 permits were issued in the United States for water pollution as a result of new legislation in the period from 1972 to 1976. We may doubt whether a government agency has all the necessary information to make a proper assessment in such matters. We may also note that such decisions may create an atmosphere in which government interference with individual decisions, even in other fields, becomes a widely-accepted practice. Incidentally, in West Germany the time required to obtain pollution permits for traditional facilities averages about three years.

No Scarcity Price

The regulatory approach allocates pollution permits on a first come, first served basis. This is not a very feasible allocation mechanism. Some companies receive permits at a zero price; others are charged at a price of infinity (that is, this factor of production is not available). The approach does not solve the common-property problem of environmental use.

Grandfather Clause

As a practical problem, the permit approach can only be used for new facilities; old installations have a de-facto permit either through an explicit grandfather clause or through the impossibility of reworking existing permits.

Newcomers and Dynamic Firms

The regulatory approach views the economy as being a static entity. When no more permits can be issued, newcomers cannot begin to produce or to locate in a region and dynamic firms cannot expand. Permits represent a protection for existing firms; permits tend to perpetuate the given structure of existing firms. Spatial structure is likely to become encrusted. This consequence of the regulatory approach is not only to the disadvantage of business; it also negatively affects labor. New firms may not be able to locate in a region although they may provide interesting and improved employment opportunities.

State of Technology

Permits very often require that the producers use the existing state of technology. For instance, the air-quality law in West Germany stipulates such a condition. This condition has a very interesting implication: The government will try to prove that new technologies are possible whereas the entrepreneur will use his energy to show that these new technologies are not feasible or not economical. We have feedback on the economic system. Whereas in a market economy it is the role of firms to find new technologies, given our scenario, firms will relinquish this function to the government.

Productivity Slowdown

The grandfather clause is an incentive to use old technology. The state of the art requirement encrusts the given technology and does not introduce a decentralized incentive to improve abatement and production technology. And the closing off of a region to a newcomer reduces mobility and implies efficiency losses. All these phenomena reduce productivity or result in a slowdown of productivity increase.

The Role of Courts

In most countries, government decisions can be made subject to checks by the courts. For instance, in West Germany the residents or the firms affected by a permit may go to the administrative courts on at least two levels. There are examples where a court has withdrawn a permit already granted by local administration only to have a higher court reverse this decision after a year or two. Regulations give a greater role to the courts in the allocation process. But, excluding exceptional cases, allocation of resources cannot be undertaken by the courts.

These disadvantages of the regulatory approach to the environmental problem suggest that the economist has to search for other solutions by which scarcity is correctly expressed. Therefore we consider the possibility of introducing prices accounting for environmental scarcity.

Emission Taxes

The intent of an emission tax is to introduce a scarcity price for emissions. In chapters 4 and 5 we discuss the level at which the emission tax has to be set. In the following analysis, we examine some problems connected with emission taxes.[3]

Reaction of Firms

In chapter 7 we analyze the reaction of firms to an emission tax. In this inquiry, we undertook a static analysis. Now, for policy considerations, we have to take into account all possible reactions to an emission tax. One of the most crucial reactions is the inducement of improved abatement technologies. Each individual firm has a definite incentive to improve its abatement technology and to reduce tax payments. Figure 8-2 summarizes possible reactions. It shows that the decisive adaptations have to take place within the firms. After these adjustments have been implemented, relative prices will change and demand will be adjusted accordingly.

Tax Base

The correct tax base for an emission tax or an effluent charge is the quantity of emissions, measured in pounds or tons. In practical policy, we can expect that information problems will arise and that alternative tax bases need to be used. Figure 8-3 shows some tax bases.

Assume that the quantities of emissions are not known and that we have to use proxies for emissions. Then we can show that we will not obtain the desired reactions. Let an emissions indicator such as SO_2 be considered representative of all air pollutants such as CO, NO_2, and particulates. Then, by taxing the indicator, we stimulate abatement of SO_2 but not of the other pollutants. It is quite possible that in the process of abating SO_2, other emissions will be increased. A similar indicator problem arises in water-quality management if emissions are calculated in units equivalent to the wastes per inhabitant. In all these cases, the indicator should be constantly revised.

If pollution-intensive inputs are taxed, we introduce an incentive to economize on these inputs; however, this target may be reached with more emissions. In this context, the problem of the second-best solution arises. Assume that we want to differentiate the tax according to a reasonable criterion such as levying a higher tax rate in winter than in summer.[4] If the tax base is the SO_2 content of heating oil, firms will not pollute less in winter but will buy more oil in summer and store it. Or assume that you want to use a higher tax on heating oil in a metropolitan center than in the countryside because of more severe pollution in the metropolitan center. Then we will have interregional trade, and in order to prevent it, we will have to create an artificial monopoly for the oil supplier in town.[5]

If the tax is based on pollution-intensive outputs rather than emissions, we only obtain a change in relative price and in demand. There is no response originating in the abatement and production activities. Tax bases such as capital input or sales will distort reactions even further. Finally, if a rather general tax is

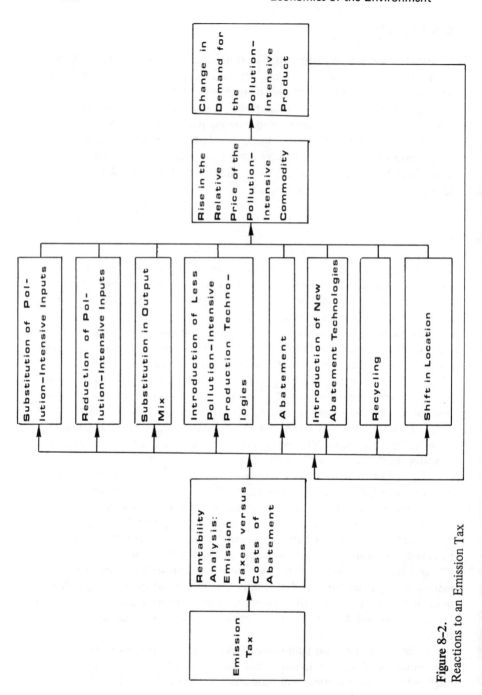

Figure 8-2.
Reactions to an Emission Tax

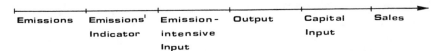

Figure 8-3. Tax Bases of an Emission Tax

levied, such as a Waldpfennig on transactions in general, the emission tax looses all its incentive functions.

Measuring Emissions

It is an important question of environmental policy whether emissions can be measured within reasonable cost parameters. Note that this question also arises for the regulatory approach because, with permits, quantities of emissions are specified. Examples of measuring experience for water management can be found in Kühner (1979). Another survey of measuring technologies is given by Anderson (1977). In West Germany, the cost of measuring CO, SO_2, NO, HC, and particulates amounts to 40.000 German marks ($23,000) per stack and per year.[6] Self-reporting is the usual practice in monitoring emissions in the case of permits. Self-reporting, backed up by occasional checks and by measurement of the ambient environmental quality, seems to be a practical approach to the measurement problem.

Interaction of Pollutants

When pollutants are diffused or when interactions such as synergisms occur, the link between emissions and quality variables seems to be destroyed. This problem, however, relates not only to emission taxes but also to regulation and pollution licenses. We must require that the political process which establishes the quality target also determine the total quantity of tolerable emissions. This would imply that diffusion processes would be taken into consideration. The point is that quality targets are given and appropriate emission taxes must be found so that these targets will be reached.

In setting these taxes, one must consider that an emission tax for pollutant A may lead to more pollutants of another type B. For instance, the tax for emission A may induce a new production technology with more emissions of type B. Or an emission tax may reduce emissions into the environmental medium α, but increase emissions into medium β. Therefore, a correct vector for emission taxes has to be found so that the appropriate relative prices for different types of emissions are set. It is a tricky problem to find the correct relative price among pollutants.

Emission Tax as a Political Price

Who will set the emission tax? One procedure is for the legislature to specify a
nationally uniform tax rate. This approach has been followed in West Germany's
effluent charge for water wastes. This law defines a unit of emission based on an
emission indicator. Prior to 1986, 25 German marks will be charged per unit of
emission; in 1986 the rate will increase to 40 marks per unit. The law was passed
in 1978 with the established tax rates being valid until 1986. Allowing for the
time required to prepare and enact such laws, prices have to be fixed which will
apply for a period of ten years or more.

Another procedure would be for the legislature to define the quality targets
for different environmental media with respect to the most important pollutants and to transfer the right to determine emission taxes to an independent
government agency. The agency would be limited by the quality targets; its role
would be to set prices and adjust them in such a way that the targets would be
reached.

Such an institutional setting would be consistent with nationally uniform
environmental-policy instruments; it could also be applied to a regionalization of
environmental policy. For instance, the national legislature may define national
quality targets while the regional authorities may set additional regional emission
taxes (compare chapter 10).

Pollution Licenses

Pollution licenses limit the total quantity of tolerable emissions for an environmental medium in a political process. Then these emission rights are sold to
those wanting to use the environment as a waste receptor. The limited quantity
of emission rights is allocated through an artificial market where polluters represent demand and the government determines supply.

Pollution rights must be transferable. If a firm learns that it can abate emissions at lower costs, it must be able to sell its pollution rights to another polluter.
Or if a firm wants to locate in a different area, it must be able to acquire pollution rights by inducing abatement in an existing firm. The transferability of
pollution rights brings about flexibility in the allocation of the limited quantity
of tolerable emissions.

This approach is beneficial because it combines the advantages of the regulatory approach with the advantages of emission taxes. By specifying the total
quantity of tolerable emissions, environmental quality is clearly determined;
there is no uncertainty with respect to the total quantity of emissions. In addition, a price is charged for using the environment as a waste receptor. Another
advantage compared to emission taxes is that the government does not have to
worry about the correct price relationship among different types of pollutants.

The government only has to set the quality targets for different environmental systems. Once these quality targets are specified, the market will find the correct relative prices. Substitution will take place until a set of "equilibrium prices" for pollution rights is found such that demand equals supply of pollution rights.

Pollution rights may be easily used in the case of regionalized environmental policy (compare chapter 11). Assume that environmental policy sets different quality targets for regional media, for instance, in order to protect a specific area of natural beauty. Then fewer pollution rights would be supplied for this area. The price for a pollution right would be higher; consequently, either more abatement would take place, or fewer pollution-intensive sectors would locate in that region.

The following problems are connected with pollution rights (Bonus 1984; Noll 1982; Tietenberg 1980).

Delineation of Regions

Whereas emission taxes may be used nationwide, pollution rights presuppose regional delineation of environmental media since the total quantity of rights must be defined for a specific area. Pollution rights are easier to implement for a river system than for an air system. As we show in chapter 10, interregional diffusion is an important issue in this context. If we have two regions, each with different environmental scarcity, it may be profitable to locate firms in those places of the less polluted area that are very close to the polluted region (economies of agglomeration). Thus, pollution rights may induce a spatial structure that is not desired. It may be necessary to introduce zoning in this case. Zoning may also be required if we have concentrations of pollution within an environmental region. However, zoning implies that pollution rights may have to be differentiated according to zones within an environmental region. This could restrict transferability and thus would take away some of the advantages of this proposal.

Complementarity in Demand

A given facility requires a set of pollution rights where pollutants normally are in a constant relation to one another. If such technical conditions are given, the transferability of pollution rights may be reduced. It is interesting to note, however, that some substitution already takes place within a firm if a firm has more than one facility.

Auctioneering the Pollution Rights

One procedure for allocating pollution rights is to auction them. For instance, all pollution rights would be sold each year on a specific date in public bidding. An argument against this procedure is that firms are confronted with the risk of not receiving a pollution right, an event which could endanger their existence. From an allocation point of view, the auction merely serves to sell and buy a factor of production. Although firms may get used to this procedure, we have to recognize that a firm usually has some certainty on the availability of factors of production such as capital, land, and labor. If the market process withdraws factors of production from a firm, it normally does so over a period of time. However, in the case of an auction for pollution rights for each year, we may have abrupt changes. This discontinuity in the availability of a factor of production may be prevented if bidding is done at more than one date, or if pollution rights last longer than the intervall between bidding dates.

Pollution Rights According to Initial Pollution

The problem of uncertainty may be prevented by giving pollution rights to the existing polluters. In this case, one could ask them to reduce pollution by a given percentage over a number of years and grant them the right to emit the residual amount. Newcomers to the region could buy a pollution right from existing firms. Although the incentive to reduce pollution would exist once this policy were implemented, there would be undesired announcement effects between the time that the measure were proposed and made effective. That is, firms would have an incentive to produce many pollutants upon learning of this policy consideration in order to receive a larger quantity of pollution rights later. Since it would take a long time to enact and possibly clarify (through the courts) such as institutional arrangement, the announcement effect may be important.

Transferability

The announcement effect can be avoided if the idea of pollution rights is combined with the regulatory approach. In the first phase, emission norms for facilities may be specified which implicitly grant a right to pollute up to a specified volume. Then these implicitly defined rights may be made transferable. In the long run, a price for pollution rights would be established, and emission rights would be allocated via the price mechanism.

Duration of Rights

Pollution rights may be defined on a temporary basis or without a time limit. If they are defined temporarily, it may be for a year or according to the life span of the facility. The allocation effects and the practicability of pollution rights may vary with these temporal definitions.

Integration into Existing Laws

All environmental-policy instruments have to be integrated into the existing legal framework. Very often economists make proposals that are ideal from their point of view but which do not take into consideration existing legal restrictions. In many countries, permits are used as an instrument of environmental policy. These permits specify the maximum amount of emissions allowed by a specific facility or firm per year. Very often they are granted on a temporary basis which is related to the life span of a facility. Furthermore, the permits are frequently granted at virtually a zero price. If these permits were combined with a price tag, a feasible allocation mechanism could be introduced.

Restricting Access to the Regional Labor Market

Pollution rights are a factor of production in fixed supply. If a large firm in a region can get hold of a factor in limited supply, for instance land, it may control access to the region by other firms or the expansion of existing firms. Similarly, the benefit of buying a pollution right to a large firm may consist in controlling the regional labor market. The large firm is induced to buy pollution rights since this may reduce the output of other firms and, concomitantly, reduce the competing demand for labor in a region (Siebert 1982d; Bonus 1982). Thus, the large firm can increase its labor supply in a region by buying pollution rights.[7]

The Bubble Concept

Some properties of transferable discharge permits have been implemented in the bubble concept, introduced by air quality policy in the U.S., first in the form of offsets in 1977 and then the in form of the bubble in 1979. As in European air quality laws, U.S. policy regulates the individual stack by permits and by specifying maximally permissible level of emissions. The innovation of the bubble concept consists in allowing several sources of emissions to define themselves as a bubble. The emission sources of a bubble have to satisfy the tolerable quantity of emissions of all sources added up so that environmental quality cannot decrease. A single source, however, may emit more than its specific permit allows if another source in the bubble pollutes less. Environmental policy is not interested in the pollution through an individual stack, but in the impact on environmental quality of a bundle of sources. As an example, in one of the first bubbles, a Dupont plant in Chambers, New Jersey, was allowed to neglect 119 smaller process oriented emission sources of volatile organic components by reducing up to 99 percent (instead of the prescribed 85 percent) at seven major stacks.

The advantage of the bubble consists in cost reduction. By allowing abatement where it is cheapest, less resources have to be used for pollution abatement. Also, the bubble concept introduces an incentive to reduce the costs of abatement and to search for new technologies at the decentralised units of the economy. It thus prevents the most important disadvantage of the regulatory approach, namely treating technology as a constant.

Delineation of the Bubble

The creation of a bubble underlies a set of conditions. First, membership in a bubble is voluntary (in contrast to the water association on the Ruhr, see below). Second, the bubble has to respect the given regulation; it cannot pollute more as a whole than allowed by permits of the individual sources. Third, emission sources must be near to each other. Fourth, as a rule, the bubble relates to a homogeneous pollutant and not to different pollutants. Bubbles for different pollutants would presuppose that environmental policy can determine the equivalence of different quantities of different pollutants which does not seem practical yet. So far, bubbles refer to three pollutants, namely SO_2, particulates and volatile organic components. Thus, there are restraints in defining a bubble. Whereas efficiency would like to see the bubble relatively large, environmental considerations imply limits on transferability (controlled trading). Finally, hazardous material is subject to binding national emission norms, and trading here is not possible.

It is relatively easy to create a bubble when the emission sources are part of one plant or one firm. The bubble can also be introduced when emission sources of different firms are involved. Then it is a matter of contractual arrangement and compensation payments between the partners involved. Consider a firm with unfavorable abatement costs and a binding environmental restraint. It would be profitable for the firm to induce another firm with a better cost situation to undertake abatement.

Other Forms of the Bubble

Besides the bubble as described above, three other institutional arrangements should be mentioned.

Offsets. In those areas where the desired environmental quality is not yet established (non-attainment areas), new emission sources wanting to locate must make an arrangement with existing sources by which the increase in pollution is more than offset by abatement at an existing source. By surpassing the emission norms, an existing emission source can establish an "offset"; and it can transfer the offset to a newcomer. Offsets are thus instrumental in improving environmental quality in non-attainment areas; moreover, they allow newcomers to locate in a region.

Banking. Emission reductions which surpass the regional reduction (or overfulfill a standard) can be banked. They then can be transferred at a future point of time, and they can be used in a bubble in the future. The condition is that the reductions are of a permanent nature, that they can be quantified and that they can be controlled.

Netting. The expansion or modernization of a plant has to satisfy the new source review requirement. Insofar as the additional emissions of an expansion are not too important and if a firm remains within the limits of the bubble, the administrative review of the new source is not necessary. This rule relates both to attainment and non-attainment areas.

This is an example how the time needed for the permit procedure can be cut down. The development of these so-called *NSPS* bubbles (new source performance standards) is still in a state of flux (Council on Environmental Quality 1984, p. 63). For instance, a broad definition of a facility may be one aspect of a *NSPS* bubble).[8]

Some Problems

In transplanting the U.S. bubble concept into another institutional setting such as German air quality management, some problems of the bubble concept emerge. One problem is that the base line from which emission reductions may be defined, is blurred. Permits very often do not define precisely tolerable emission per year; they may relate to volume flows, and hours of operation per year may not be specified. Consequently, all existing permits would have to be redefined which represents a sizable task. Moreover, no formal permits may exist for old facilities. Another question is that the bubble concept is difficult to apply in a setting where permits heavily rely on the state of art with tolerable emissions being not clearly specified. Also, it is difficult for legal thinking to waiver the application of the state of the art if an offset can be provided elsewhere.

Institutional Arrangements for Cost Sharing

Besides regulation, emission taxes, or pollution rights, a quality target can be transformed into individual behavior through a mechanism which shares the costs of reaching the targets and simultaneously develops an incentive system that guarantees efficiency. The water associations of the Ruhr area in Germany represent such an approach (Kneese and Bower 1968; Klevorick and Kramer 1973).

The water associations of the Ruhr area (Ruhr, Emscher, Lippe, Wupper, Niers, Erft, Left Lower Rhine, and Ruhr Water Dam Association) represent organizations in which membership is mandatory for every polluter. The general assembly of the association determines the water quality to be attained. When the required environmental-quality level is known, the association can determine the amount of capital equipment, investment, and operating costs that it must spend to attain these standards. Thus, the total costs of abatement are specified. The problem then consists of allocating these costs to the individual polluter. Costs are attributed in such a way that the costs to the individual polluter are related to his quantity (and quality) of pollution. This creates an incentive to abate pollutants.

For instance, the "Emschergenossenschaft" has developed an index that defines the quantity of unpolluted water necessary to dilute polluted water to the level where damage to a test fish is prevented. By this method, a quality target can be fixed; at the same time, different types of pollutants can be expressed in a homogeneous dimension. The formula is (Kneese and Bower 1968, p. 250; Johnson and Brown 1976, p. 123)

$$V = \frac{S}{S^Z} + \frac{1}{2}\frac{B}{B^Z} + \frac{K-30}{2K^Z} - F$$

where V is the dilution factor, S the materials subject to sedimention in centimeters per liter, S^Z the permitted S, B the biochemical oxygen demand BOD_5 in milligrams per liter after sedimentation, B^Z the permitted BOD_5, K the potassium permanganate oxygen ($KMNO_4$) used, K^Z the permitted K in milligrams per liter, and F a coefficient of fish toxicity. Let V_i be the dilution factor for polluter i, and let E_i be the quantity of wastewater. Then the cost share α_i is given by

$$\alpha_i = \frac{V_i E_i}{\displaystyle\sum_1^n V_i E_i} \quad \text{with} \sum_1^n \alpha_i = 1$$

If total costs are denoted by C, then the cost share for the individual producer is given by $C_i = \alpha_i C$. The polluter can influence C_i by reducing α_i, that is, by reducing V_i and E_i. Thus, there is an incentive to reduce pollution.

The Ruhr Association uses population equivalents (PEs) as a measure of pollution (Kneese and Bower 1972, p. 60). Dividing the total costs of abatement by the sum of all population equivalents PE, the price p per population equivalent is obtained: $p = C/\Sigma$ PE. The cost share for the individual polluter is given by $C_i = p\text{PE}_i$.

For industrial polluters, the quantity of population equivalents is determined as follows. First, a coefficient of 0.5 PE is used per employee. Second, wastewater is evaluated with 0.01 PE/m^3. Third, special coefficients are used for specific sectors. For instance, 0.85 PE/ton of paper is the coefficient used in paper sulfide production; other examples of coefficients include 31 PE/ton of sulfuric acid used in metal finishing or 0.35 PE/ton of raw cabbage used in the production of sauerkraut. The coefficients vary for the firms within an industry, depending on the production and abatement technology used. For instance, for metal finishing, the coefficient varies between 31 and 6 PE/ton of sulfuric acid used (Kühner 1979). Thus, an incentive is introduced to abate pollutants.

There are some interesting institutional features of the water associations. Voting rights vary with the volume of effluent charges paid and consequently with the volume of pollution produced; thus, the largest polluter has the greatest number of votes. In spite of this rule, analysis shows that the decisions of the associations seem to have been reasonable. Klevorick and Kramer (1973) have researched this problem and have shown that most environmental concerns have been taken care of by the associations. One reason for this success is that institutional safeguards have been introduced. For instance, in the Niers Association, the downstream polluters receive 75 votes before the remaining 225 votes are distributed according to the paid effluent charges. In the Lippe Association, coal mines cannot have more than 40 percent of the votes.

Combining Standards and an Emission Tax

In practical environmental policy, one may want to have the certainty of emission standards and the incentives of an emission tax at the same time. Then a standard and an emission tax may be combined as shown in figure 8-3 (Bohm and Russell 1985). A standard $\bar{S}$ limits emissions; for the remaining emissions

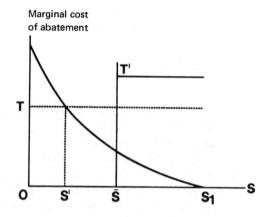

Figure 8–4. Combining Standards and an Emission Tax

$O\bar{S}$, an emission tax OT is levied. Such an emission tax introduces an incentive to reduce emissions to OS' and to shift the marginal cost curve of abatement downward. Apparently, such a combination only works if the tax rate OT is higher than the marginal abatement costs to meet the standard. In addition or alternatively, a non-compliance fee $\bar{S}T'$ can be used if the standard is surpassed.

Taxonomy of the Environmental Problem and Policy Instruments

In this chapter we have discussed the most important approaches which transmit environmental-quality targets into the pollution behavior of industrial polluters: regulation, emission taxes, pollution licenses, the bubble concept and cost sharing. We should point out that the policy instruments used vary with the problem at hand. In chapter 2 we develop a taxonomy of the environmental problem. Our discussion mainly applies to the problem where pollutants arise as a joint output of production. If other problems prevail, different policy instruments from the ones discussed in this chapter may be necessary. For instance, if pollutants are contained in products, such as DDT in agricultural goods, we may have to use product norms. A similar problem arises with respect to pharmacological products. If pollutants are introduced into the environment via new products, such as occurs in the chemical industry, emission taxes may not be effective or practical. Also, if monitoring costs are prohibitive, emission taxes cannot be used. Assume, for instance, that measuring pollution of cars is impractical. Then a product norm for cars (or a tax for pollution-intensive cars) may be the appropriate policy instrument. Finally, wastes already in the environment such as toxic materials in land-fills call yet for another approach (for instance the Superfund).

Notes

1. On environmental-policy instruments, compare Kneese and Bower (1968), Kneese and Schultze (1975), Mills (1978), and Siebert (1976c, 1982b).

2. This procedure is for instance followed in the German Bundesimmissions-schutzgesetz.

3. A more detailed analysis can be found in Siebert (1976c). Also compare Siebert (1982b).

4. Organization of Economic Cooperation and Development, *Instruments for Controlling Sulfur Dioxide Emissions from Fuel Combustion in Stationary Sources: A Case Study of Norwegian Measures,* prepared by F. F. Førsund and S. Strom (Paris, 1973), p. 23.

5. Ibid. p. 24.

6. Information from industry.

7. The question arises whether a similar argument holds for the product market. Assume that a sector of the economy happens to be located in an environmental region. Then the large firm may use pollution rights to restrict the output of its competitors. The large firm has an incentive to buy more pollution rights than it needs for production since pollution rights will not be available to its competitors. Consequently, in this case, pollution rights may strengthen the position of a dominant firm.

8. Compare for instance the "Tunnelofen" case in German environmental law.

The Political Economy
of Environmental Scarcity

In this chapter, we review some of the principles which should govern environmental policy, we study some of the implications of these principles and we indicate why the political process often deviates from them. The center of the stage is dominated by the opportunity costs principle which requires that the opportunity costs of using the environment as a receptacle of wastes as well as a public consumption good have to be taken into account. In a decentralized economy, these costs have to be attributed to the subsystems of the economy, for instance through the polluter pays principle. Additional requirements for environmental policy are the principle of long-run orientation and the principle of interdependence. The chapter also briefly looks at environmental legislation in the last twenty years.

The Opportunity Cost Principle

Scarcity means that there are competing uses. And competing uses imply that opportunity costs arise. These are defined as costs of an opportunity foregone, that is the loss of utility by excluding an alternative use. Economics is the story about opportunity costs. The opportunity cost principle requires that if a scarce resource or good is put to a specific use, the opportunity costs have to be considered. The benefits of a specific use have to outweigh its opportunity costs. The opportunity cost principle guarantees that goods and resources are put to their best use; it is a manifestation of the principle of rationality.

As a guideline for environmental policy, the opportunity cost principle mandates that a specific use of the environment has to bring in its opportunity costs in form of benefits. If the environment is used as a receptacle of waste, the opportunity costs consist in the loss of environmental quality. The use of the environment for assimilative purposes cannot be continued if the opportunity costs, that is the loss of environmental quality, is greater than the benefits of this use, i.e. facilitating the production of private goods. If, on the other hand, the environment is used as a public good for consumption, the opportunity costs are given by the implied restraint on the assimilative capacity and, consequently, on the production of private goods. Thus, the opportunity cost principle works both ways, it calls for comparing the opportunity costs of using the environment as a receptacle of wastes as well as a public good for consumption.

The opportunity costs of using the environment as a public good can be easily determined through the evaluation by the market. Resources needed for abatement, output of private goods foregone, and the loss in national income are all evaluated by market processes. The opportunity costs of using the assimilative services, however, run into the problem of determining the value of a public good, that is of environmental quality lost. As discussed, here the free rider problem arises. Since the environment is a public good and can be used in equal amounts by all, individuals or groups can take the position of a free rider not contributing to the cost of environmental quality. Institutional mechanisms have to be developed which ensure that free rider behavior in evaluating environmental quality is reduced. We are far away from ideal solutions in this context (compare chapter 5). The existence of the free rider phenomenon and lacking institutional mechanisms to prevent free rider behavior are one reason why the political economy of the opportunity cost principle looks more blurred in reality than in the textbook.

Consider a global environmental good such as the ozone layer (see chapter 10). If a country takes the free rider position not indicating its willingness to pay, for instance its willingness to reduce the application of freon, the value of the ozone layer cannot be adequately determined. Similarly, a group in a society with a strong preference for environmental protection can easily take the position of a free rider in demanding an especially intense environmental protection if the group does not contribute to the costs of that policy, i.e. if they do not carry the burden. Or, a group not interested in environmental protection may push for a generous use of the environment's assimilative services.

The political importance of free rider positions will depend on quite a few factors: In the case of a pure public good, the free rider exists. If some of the publicness can be taken away by an appropriate institutional arrangement, for instance by regionalizing the good, part of the free rider issue disappears. The institutional mechanism of aggregating individual preferences is of importance: A proportional voting system may make it easier for specific groups to influence the environmental quality target than a majority voting system. And the institutional legal framework such as constitutional protection may, admittedly in an extreme case, determine societal preferences by the preference of a specific individual who receives legal or constitutional protection.

The Polluter Pays Principle

To require that for society as a whole the opportunity costs of a specific resource use should be outweighed by its benefits does not yet specify how the opportunity costs are allocated to the subsystems of a society. For a decentralized economy with autonomous decision making by the subsystems, it is a wise principle to have private benefits of an economic action outweigh its overall opportunity costs to society. The subsystem then carries all the costs arising, both to itself and to the society as a whole. The opportunity costs are allocated to those units that cause them. This is the polluter pays principle of environmental policy.

The polluter pays principle is an institutional manifestation of the opportunity cost principle. It can be applied once environmental quality targets are established, and in that sense it circumvents the free rider problem. The principle has a number of advantages: It allocates the opportunity costs of environmental protection in a reasonable way. The individual polluter has an incentive to reduce pollutants; the divergence between private and social costs is abolished, and commodity prices do include environmental costs as well as traditional factor costs.

A priory, the polluter pays principle can take many forms such as emission taxes, compensation procedures as in Japan's environmental policy or liability rules. The polluter pays approach is the documentation of the more general question of an appropriate institutional setting for allocating the opportunity costs of environmental protection to the subsystems. It may also be interpreted as a solution to an incentive problem.

The polluter pays principle only looks at an institutional mechanism to allocate the opportunity costs of environmental protection. The analogon would be an incentive mechanism for allocating the opportunity costs of environmental degradition to the consumers of the environment as a public good.[1] Apparently, this would be an incentive-compatible arrangement in which the free rider no longer exists and in which the consumer of the environment, by determining the target, would also take into account society's cost to reach the target.

The political economy of the polluter pays principle shows a whole array of deviations.

As a first condition, the polluter has to be identified. Of course, it is helpful for the application of the polluter pays principle if that problem can be solved by measuring emissions and removing possible controversial issues into acceptable and practical institutional rules and away from the courts such as in the Japanese compensation schemes. Liability litigation may not be practical. A case in point for a deviation from the polluter pays principle are hazardous wastes already in the environment (old land-fills, "Altlasten").

Second, the specific constraints of the policy maker and his vote maximizing behavior will induce him not to apply the polluter pays principle if it will hurt his constituency. Subsidies and financing through general taxation are less troublesome. Why bother to signal the opportunity costs to the polluter if votes get lost? Similar arguments apply when the polluter pays principle negatively affects specific sectors of the economy relevant to the policy maker or if it creates regional unemployment.

Third, the policy maker is unwilling to abide by the polluter pays principle if he is in the upwind or upstream position. In the case of an interregional spillover, there is an incentive to ask for a compensation and to apply the victim pays principle. Very often, in a lose interpretation, the polluter will display behavior analogous to the free rider, for instance by claiming that environmental damages are negligible.

Finally, we meet the free rider again in the case of global environmental goods.

The Principle of Long-Run Perspective

The opportunity costs of environmental degradation or environmental protection cannot be defined in a static setting; they must be defined for a longer time horizon.

With respect to the environment, pollutants accumulate over time (see chapter 12), and damage often will only become apparent with the passage of time. Examples are the accumulation of DDT in food chains, the transport of freon over two to three decased into the ozone layer and the eventual penetration of nitrites into ground water systems. Often, these long-run diffusion functions are not known, and the eventual impact on the environment will only come to light at a later stage. There is uncertainty involved (see chapter 14). Consequently, environmental policy is well advised to also include the long-run opportunity costs of environmental degradation. This requirement implies that environmental policy should not merely consist in responses to pollution, but should be preventive or anticipatory (O'Riordan 1985; Simonis 1983).

Not only must the opportunity costs of environmental degradation be specified in the long run but also the opportunity costs of environmental protection. Abatement activities are capital-intensive, and it takes five or ten years to build up the pollution-control capital (for instance water purification facilities including a sewage transportation system). The adjustment of production processes, changes in the sectorial structure, relocation of firms are phenomena that occur over a decade or more. Continuity of environmental policy is therefore a prerequisite.

A long-run orientation of environmental policy is also relevant because the application of specific instruments takes a long time. For instance, eight years passed between the legislation on Germany's effluent fees in water management (1978) and the application of the full rate in 1986, with a least five additional years of deliberation. As an another example, the state of the art, as defined by German air quality policy in 1973, was only changed in 1986 after thirteen years.

The demand for a long-run thrust of environmental policy contrasts markedly with the actual environmental policy observed. Of course, the old landfills are an example of a rather short-run orientated environmental policy not anticipating future damage. The policy maker very often has an extremely high discount rate, and critics say, four months before an election it is well above thirty percent. Perceptions on environment problems including public opinion and preferences as established by the political process shift quickly over time, and it seems that the policy maker is tempted to follow such shifts quickly.

The Principle of Interdependence

Environmental systems are interdependent and represent a complex network of interaction. It is commonplace by now that environmental subsystems are related to each other in a multitude of ways. Distinguishing different environmental media such as air, water, or land is only an auxiliary analytical device to grasp the complex problem.

The interdependence of environmental media implies an interdependence among pollutants from the point of view of environmental policy. This interdependence is due to the following reasons:

Pollutants are linked through environmental systems and diffusion between them. Pollutants ambient in the air can be deposited into water systems, and pollutants ambient in rivers, lakes and the ocean can get into the atmosphere by evaporation. Similar relationships exist between air and land as well as water and land. Besides diffusion in a physical sense, for instance through gorund water systems, diffusion may occur through ecological systems such as food chains (bio-diffusion).

Pollutants may be linked to each other by the emission technology. A pollutant may either be discharged to the atmosphere, to water system or placed into landfills. The assimilative roles of different media of the environment may be substituted against each other. This also means that abatement technologies are substitutive. If one medium is regulated, emissions may switch over to another medium.

Finally, pollutants may be interrelated through the production technology. If a specific pollutant is reduced, another may increase. For instance, cutting down carbon monoxide in engines is likely to increase nitrogen oxides.

Environmental policy must take these interdependences between environmental media, between abatement, emission and production technologies and between pollutants into account. If environmental policy addresses itself to only a particular media, a particular pollutant, or a particular abatement or production technology, it is likely to fail in the long run. Very quickly, new problems will popp up. Consequently, environmental policy has to be integrative and encompass all environmental media and pollutants.

As an example in which interdependence was neglected, environmental policy in the U.S. and in some European countries during the early seventies can be quoted from hindsight. Environmental policy centered on air and water quality management, neglecting land and landfills where quite a few hazardous pollutants ended up. As another example, we have lowered the level of larger suspended air-borne particulates in Europe in the late sixties and in the early seventies considerably, only at the expense of increasing thinner particulates and exchanging local pollution by a long-range transfer of pollutants.

The political economy suggests that it is rather difficult to follow a systematic and holistic approach. Policy often is peacemeal and the policy maker adheres to a police power approach, waiting for a problem to develop, to be recognised as an important question by the public including the media, and then stepping in. This behavior leads to *ad hocery,* and the dominating environmental issues shift around.

Major Environmental Legislation

The environmental issue came to the foreground in the sixties, for instance through such diseases as Itai-Itai in Japan, through the eutrophication of lakes and the decline in air quality. In the late sixties and in the early seventies, legislation for air quality and water management was passed in most of the industrialized countries. Legislation seems to have followed an interesting time pattern. Air quality management was the object of the first major environmental legislation such as U.S. Clean Air Act (1970) and the Bundesimmissionsschutzgesetz (1982) and the Technische Anleitung zur Reinhaltung der Luft (1983) in Germany. As a second step, legislation for water quality management was introduced such as the U.S. Clean Water Act (1972) and Germany's water management (Wasserhaushaltsgesetz) and effluent fee law (Abwasserabgabengesetz) in 1976. In a later stage, when some problems of landfills became apparent, the environmental medium land was regulated, for instance through the Superfund in the U.S. (1980) and the Abfallbeseitigungsgesetz in Germany in 1980. Moreover, toxic and hazardous materials including product qualities were regulated, for instance in the Chemikaliengesetz (1980) and the Atomgesetz (1980) in Germany.

The initial major laws were revised for instance the amendment of the U.S. Air and Water Acts in 1977, the introduction of the bubble concept in the U.S., the new Technische Anleitung zur Reinhaltung der Luft 1986. In these revisions, shortcomings in the protection of the environment were corrected; moreover, it was attempted to introduce more economic incentives; at the same time, environmental regulation came under the attack under the heading of deregulation.

Besides the shift in emphasis on different environmental issues and the issue of deregulation, other aspects have changed the importance of environmental policy. Whereas in the late sixties and early seventies the environmental issue was pressing, in the middle and late seventies and the early eighties, the oil crisis was dominating the political arean. The unusual increase in the oil price represented a supply shock for the world economy, requiring economic adjustments in an institutional setting that had reduced flexibility. Energy conservation was the pressing problem, and alternative energy sources became more important. Environmental constraints, for instance for coal, were not judged so important. Whereas this evaluation still is characteristic for the United States in 1986, the development in Europe went somewhat different with Germany's "Waldsterben" giving new fire to the environmental debate. New legislation was passed on large electricity generating facilities (exceeding a capacity of 50 Megawatts) (Groß-feuerungsanlagenverordnung 1982) and new rules for catalytic devices in cars were introduced.

A review of the different political signals for the German energy industry and their environmental impact is quite telling. "Move away from oil" was the political message at the second energy crisis in 1979/80; energy supply was encouraged to diversify into coal and atomic energy. Electricity was hailed a "pure" energy. Then came the Waldsterben, and coal came under severe pressure. SO_2-reduction was the big issue. Once the firms had adjusted to this orientation in their planning, NO_x was receiving the attention. Then in 1986, Tschernobyl puts into question atomic energy including electricity. One may wonder which impact on environmental policy the next energy price rise will have. It seems to be rather difficult to have continuity in such a context.

Besides these short remarks, it is beyond the scope of this book to study the political process by which environmental policy is formed, to analyze the role of voting and of the voting system, of parties, of party behavior, of pressure groups, of public opinion, of the legal system including constitutional aspects and of the courts as well as of bargaining behavior in international environmental issues. It seems rather realistic that all these phenomena will imply that actual policy will deviate from the principles such as the opportunity costs principle. There are many reasons in the political arena to forget opportunity costs. It seems the economist's role to keep stressing the importance of the opportunity costs and of environmental use as an allocation problem.

Notes

1. One pragmatic approach in this context is the Benefitor's Principle (Nutznießer-Prinzip) stressed by Meissner (1985). Note, however, that this principle merely is a way of financing; it does not solve the free rider issue.

Part IV
Environmental Allocation in Space

10 International Dimension

In the previous chapters we consider a point economy without any spatial dimensions. In the next two chapters we introduce the spatial dimension into our analysis. When we take into account the spatial extent of the environmental system, we introduce a set of interesting allocation problems. In the following discussion we study the environmental allocation of spatial systems from a global, national, and regional perspective.[1]

Environmental Systems in Space

Environmental systems are defined over space. Depending on the spatial extent of the environmental media, we can distinguish among the following types of environmental goods (Siebert 1985a).

Global environmental goods, such as the earth's atmosphere or the ozone layer. In this case, the environmental system is used as a public consumer good and as a receptacle of wastes for the earth as a whole.

International environmental goods limited to spatial subsystems of the world, such as the Mediterranean and the Baltic Sea. These goods extend over at least two nations.

Transfrontier environmental systems[2] which transport pollutants from one nation to another (for example, the potassium salt carried by the Rhine River and the acid rains originating in Western Europe and falling on Sweden). Transfrontier pollution can be subdivided into two types: one-way and two-way. One-way transfrontier pollution occurs when the wastes from one country are transported to another and environmental quality in the country of origin remains unaffected. Classic examples are the pollutants carried from a source upstream to a location further down the river and pollutants transported by the westerly winds to the east. In two-way transfrontier pollution, wastes are also transported back to the country of origin, that is, through atmospheric conditions and changing winds. The situation becomes more complex when different pollutants are transmitted through different environmental media.

National environmental goods where environmental boundaries coincide with political frontiers.

Regional environmental goods within one country such as metropolitan air regions or river systems.

Microlevel environmental systems such as small ponds or even smaller units.

The existence of different spatial environmental systems implies that we have different types of environmental problems and also that alternative solutions may be necessary for different cases. In this chapter we analyze the international aspects. In the next chapter, regional environmental allocation is discussed.

Global and Transfrontier Pollution

One basic problem confronting those trying to treat international and transfrontier pollution is that there exists no international authority empowered to implement environmental protection measures. Consequently, problems must be solved by international bargaining processes which involve the divergent interests of two or more states.

The tolerable level of pollution, the willingness to pay for improved environmental quality, and the bargaining position of the nations may differ considerably among countries. This is due to the fact that the intensity of environmental use among countries differs, that national preferences vary, and that national incomes have different levels.

Because environmental services are a public good, it is not possible to exclude from use those nations which are not willing to pay for the conservation of environmental quality. Countries cannot be forced to contribute to the financing of antipollution measures. Thus, the free-rider problem must be considered when one deals with global and international environmental goods.

A variety of approaches have been proposed for solving international and transfrontier environmental problems (Walter 1975; Markusen 1975; Pethig 1982; Arnold 1984, Kuhl 1986).

International Agency

In national environmental-quality management, water quality is controlled through the establishment of water-management authorities. It is conceivable that similar cooperatives might be formed to control the quality of the oceans or even of the atmosphere. Nations could surrender a part of their sovereign rights concerning the environment to an international environmental agency which could tax emissions and thereby control transfrontier environmental quality. The introduction of a tax would create an incentive (for instance, for the upstream polluter) to reduce the emission of pollutants. If countries could agree on an international tax, the national environmental agency could set a supplementary tax on emissions within its own borders. This proposal represents the international application of the "polluter pays" principle. However, it is politically unrealistic since nations are not willing to relinquish their sovereignty over this area.

Pollution Rights

Pollution rights could be granted by an international agency. Again, this procedure seems highly unrealistic. Alternatively, countries could bargain for pollution rights. In such a bargaining process, the free-rider problem arises. Bargaining positions may differ. For instance, the downstream party has a high stake in persuading the polluting upstream nation to reduce its use of the environment at a zero price. On the other hand, the upstream party attempts to continue emitting pollutants without compensating the victimized recipient. The result of the bargaining process depends on the relative strength of the parties, which is also affected by international public opinion.

Cost Sharing

The costs of pollution abatement could be shared by the countries involved. The costs of attaining and maintaining an acceptable level of quality in the transfrontier environmental medium would be added and distributed among the countries according to a set rate. Once again, many problems arise with this proposal. Since costs are determined by the desired level of environmental quality, how much environmental quality should be strived for? By what criteria can abatement costs be attributed to different countries?

Reciprocal-Compensation Procedure

In the case of transfrontier pollution, the reciprocal-compensation principle has been proposed (OECD 1973). This principle is based on the assumption that in the bargaining process, the polluter will exaggerate the costs of pollution abatement in order to reduce the demands of the other country. Similarly, it is expected that the victim will exaggerate the extent of the incurred damages, in order to maximize the assessment of corrective measures needed. In order to avoid this deliberate falsification of information about the damages and costs of the respective abatement, it has been suggested that an international fund be established to which the polluting country would pay according to its assessment of the damages and the victimized land would pay according to its assessment of the costs of abatement. This approach is designed to guarantee that the factors determining the emission tax are set as realistically as possible. The funds collected from the two parties would then be redistributed to them for the implementation of the environmental-protection measures. It is essential that the countries not know the rate by which the tax receipts will be redistributed because this information would distort their estimates of the costs and damages.

Nationalization

It is possible to "nationalize" parts of international goods, as has been done by some countries in the declaration of 200-mile zones along coastlines. However, in most cases, this does not provide an answer to environmental problems because international spillover effects cannot be excluded.

National Environmental Policy and International Repercussions

National environmental goods are characterized by the fact that their spatial dimension corresponds to the political boundaries of a country; that is, the quality of these environmental goods can be controlled by national environmental policy. At first glance, one would not expect such environmental goods to have international dimensions. However, this cursory view is incorrect.

The environment as a public-consumption good can influence the trade position of a country in the service sector (tourism) if the public good is limited to national space, for example, a beautiful landscape. The role of the environment as a receptacle of wastes is even more important. In this function, the environment is a production factor and therefore a determining factor of comparative price advantage. If a country is richly endowed with assimilative services by nature, it will have a trade advantage over a country only scarcely equipped with assimilative services. The abundance or the scarcity of environmental endowment is influenced by the following conditions:

1. The *natural assimilative capacity,* that is, the capacity of the environmental systems to reduce pollutants by natural processes.
2. The *demand for assimilative services* of the environment, measured by the quantity of emissions released into the environment. As we know, emissions depend on consumption, production, and emission technology as well as on abatement technology and abatement incentives.
3. The *value accorded to the public-consumption good* "environment." Evaluation of the environment will depend on preferences, income level, population density, and institutional arrangements for revealing true individual preferences. Instead of assessing environmental quality, a tolerable level of emissions can be established as a target by using the standard-price approach.

If one takes into account differences in environmental endowment among countries, the following questions arise:

Does environmental endowment (or environmental policy) affect the comparative price advantage of a country?

To what extent will a change in comparative advantage influence trade flows, location decisions, the balance of payments, the terms of trade, and the exchange rate?

Does environmental policy in one country have an impact on environmental quality in another country? Does a strict environmental policy in one country imply such a change in international specialization that environmental quality in the other country will decline?

Are gains from trade affected by environmental disruption?

How does the environmental problem relate to trade policy? Do environmental-policy instruments create trade barriers? Can trade-policy tools such as import duties serve to reach environmental targets?

Environmental Policy and Comparative Advantage

A basic hypothesis explaining trade is that a nation will export a commodity if it has a comparative price advantage in producing that good. Let $p = p_1/p_2$ denote the price relation of the home country in the autarky situation, and let p^* be the price relation of the foreign country. Then the condition for establishing trade is $p \gtreqless p^*$. If $p < p^*$, then the home country has a comparative price advantage for commodity 1, and thus it will export commodity 1. If $p > p^*$, then the home country has a comparative advantage for commodity 2, and it will export commodity 2.

Comparative price advantages of the home country for commodity 1 can be explained by the following factors: a more favorable endowment in the home country of the factor that is intensively used in the production of commodity 1, such as capital, labor, or raw-material endowment; a more favorable productivity in the home country in the production of commodity 1 (that is, advantages in technical knowledge which are based on technological, organizational, and management systems as well as on the capabilities of the workforce), and a relatively lower demand for commodity 1 in the home country.

Environmental abundance or scarcity is also a factor which influences the comparative price advantage of a country. Assume that the home country pursues an environmental policy because the given environmental quality is not acceptable. Assume further that an emission tax is levied. Then we know from equation 7.13 that, under some conditions, especially when $H_1'F_1' > H_2'F_2'$, we have $dp/dz > 0$. In a closed economy, the relative price of the pollution-intensive commodity increases if an environmental policy is undertaken. This means that the comparative price advantage of the home country is reduced. The competitive position of the country is negatively affected, and exports will be reduced.

The Heckscher-Ohlin theorem can be extended to trade with pollution-intensive commodities.[3] The Heckscher-Ohlin theorem states that given identical demand and identical technologies among countries, a country richly endowed with a factor of production will export that commodity which heavily uses the abundant factor. Let the home country be richly endowed with environmental services. Let z represent the correct indicator of environmental scarcity; that is, assume that environmental policy finds the ideal or correct shadow price. If we assume that the home country is richly endowed with environmental services, we can express this situation as $z < z^*$, where z is the emission tax of the home country and z^* is that of the foreign country. Because $dp/dz > 0$, we have $p(z) < p^*(z^*)$ if $z < z^*$, so that the environmentally rich country will export the pollution-intensive commodity. The country with limited environmental attributes will export the commodity which is not pollution-intensive.[4]

Figure 10-1 explains this argument. Now, $AGBCH$ represents the transformation space of the home country as it was derived in figure 3-3. In order to keep the diagram simple, we do not show the transformation space of the foreign

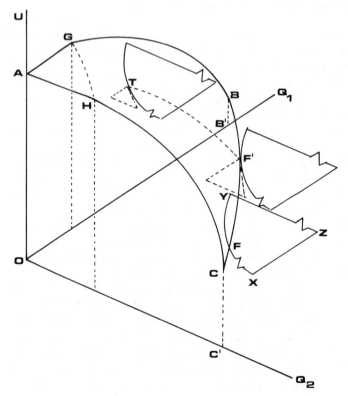

Figure 10-1. Trade Effects of Environmental Policy

country. Rather, we indicate its production block XYZ where environmental quality is not explicitly considered for the foreign country. Furthermore, the production block is drawn scaled down for simplicity. Note that the production block of the foreign country XYZ lies horizontally in the UQ_1Q_2 space.

We want to analyze different cases. First, assume that no environmental policy is undertaken and that the home country commences trade. Point F denotes the autarky situation in which relative prices diverge so that $p < p^*$. In order to interpret the diagram, we assume that the home country is a small country so that the foreign country dictates the relative price p^*. Assume that the trade equilibrium is given at point F', where the production block of the foreign country is tangential to the transformation space of the home country. The home country specializes in the production of commodity 1. This happens to be the pollution-intensive commodity. As a consequence of international trade, the home country will produce more of the pollution-intensive commodity, and environmental quality will decline. Remember, we are assuming that no environmental policy has been instituted yet.

Second, assume that the home country is in autarky (point F), that is, that there is no trade. Then if environmental policy is undertaken, p must rise since the environmental costs of production are attributed to the pollution-intensive commodity 1. The home country will move up the transformation space (starting from point F) and have a lower comparative advantage. In figure 10-2, curve $B'C'$ represents the projection of the transformation curve onto the Q_1Q_2 plane in the case of no environmental policy. Curve $B'C'$ can be taken from figure

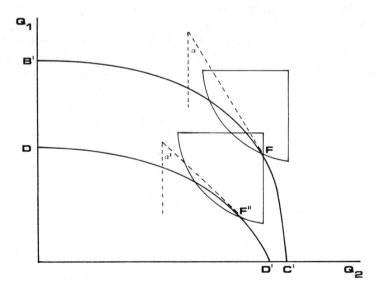

Figure 10-2. Comparative Advantage and Environmental Policy

10-1. Point F represents the autarky situation. Curve DD' is a transformation curve for a higher environmental quality. Point F'' is the new autarky point. When $tg\alpha' > tg\alpha$, it signals that p has risen and that the home country's comparative advantage has declined.

Environmental Policy and Trade Flows

A reduction in the home country's comparative price advantage indicates that potential exports of the pollution-intensive commodity will fall. If we want to analyze the change in actual exports arising from environmental policy, we must start from an initial trade equilibrium and ask how the trade volume will be affected by environmental policy.

In figure 10-1, this problem can be expressed as follows. Consider point F', which denotes a trade equilibrium without environmental policy. How does environmental policy of the home country affect this trade equilibrium?

In the initial situation F', the trade flows are shown by the trade triangle at point F'. If the home country pursues an environmental policy, its export advantage will fall. One can expect that the export quantity of the home country will decrease.

If we assume that the home country is small, the relative price p of situation F' will be dictated by the foreign country. In this case, we can define an isoprice line for constant $\bar{p}$ and alternative emission tax rates for the home country. This isoprice line $F'T$ indicates the adjustment process which will occur in the home country. The export quantity is reduced for a given relative price. The imports also have to decrease. The trade triangle depicted by the triangle drawn at point T becomes smaller. If we assume that the home country is not small, then p becomes a variable. Under these conditions, we should expect that the environmental policy of the home country will lead to an increase of p in the world market. Thus, the new trade position, which takes into account the home country's environmental policy, lies to the left of the isoprice line $F'T$. Because of this influence by the home country on relative price p, its comparative advantage is reduced even more. A formal analysis of this problem for a two-country model is given by Siebert (1979a) and Siebert et al. (1980).

The basic idea of these models is to introduce equilibrium conditions of the world market and the budget constraints. The equilibrium conditions of the two-country case require that the world markets be cleared, that is, that the excess demand of both countries add to zero,

$$E_i(p_i, z) + E_i^*(p_i^*) = 0 \tag{10.1}$$

where E_i^* denotes the excess demand of the foreign country. For the commodity prices of the home country p_i and the foreign country p_i^*, we have

$$p_i = p_i^* w \tag{10.2}$$

where w specifies the exchange rate (for example, with the dimension of dollars per German mark). The balance of payments B is defined as

$$B = -(p_1 E_1 + p_2 E_2) \tag{10.3}$$

Total differentiation of equations 10.1 through 10.3 with respect to z answers the question of under which conditions environmental policy affects the variables in the system.

1. If constant exchange rates are assumed, the system of equations tells us how the balance of payments changes with environmental policy.
2. If flexible exchange rates are assumed, we obtain information about the changes in the exchange rates (revaluation or devaluation).
3. In both cases one obtains statements about the change of commodity flows and variations in the terms of trade.

Location Advantage

The change in comparative price advantage indicates variations not only in potential trade flows but also in location advantage. If environmental policy is pursued in countries poorly endowed with assimilative services, then the production conditions of the pollution-intensive sector will be negatively affected. Its production costs will rise. At the same time, the relative location advantage of an environmentally rich country improves. If capital is internationally mobile, one can expect that, *ceteris paribus*, capital of the environmentally poor country will be transferred to the environmentally rich country. The effects of environmental policy on the location advantage will also depend on the type of policy instrument used. An emission tax will serve to correct relative prices and will change comparative advantage; a permit system will be likely to make location space temporarily unavailable, and thus it may have much stronger effects on location.

International Specialization and Environmental Quality

In the case of transfrontier pollution, environmental quality of the foreign country is influenced by the pollutants which are transferred from the home country to the foreign country by environmental media. The environmental policy of the home country can affect environmental quality in the foreign country even if the home country's pollution is confined to national environmental media. This comes about by specialization and trade. For example, assume that the home country introduces an emission tax and thereby impairs its comparative price advantage for the pollution-intensive commodity. Its exports will fall, and the production of the pollution-intensive commodity will be reduced. A reallocation of resources takes place. However, resource use is increased in the abatement process while resources are withdrawn from the pollution-intensive sector. Production in the environmentally favorable sector is expanded. In sum, the environmental quality of the home country has to increase.

What kinds of adjustment processes take place in the foreign country which does not pursue an environmental policy? Since the comparative price advantage of the home country deteriorates for the pollution-intensive commodity, the comparative price advantage of the foreign country rises. It is profitable for the foreign country to increase the production of this commodity. In the foreign country, a reallocation of its resources occurs in favor of the pollution-intensive commodity so that emissions increase and environmental quality abroad worsens. In short, the environmental policy of the home country negatively affects the environmental quality in the foreign country through specialization and by trade.

Does this "pollute thy neighbor via trade" thesis mean that the home country can impose detrimental environmental conditions on the foreign country? For instance, can the industrialized nations export their pollutants to the developing countries via trade? Is this a new type of imperialism a "pollution imperialism"? The answer to these questions is no, for the following reasons.

First, environmental policy involves costs for the concerned nations, namely, in terms of the resources used as well as the target losses in other policy areas (unemployment, the loss of the comparative price advantage). A country is only willing to tolerate these costs of a better environmental quality to a certain extent.

Second, the costs of a better environment (costs of pollution abatement) increase progressively, thereby placing severe limitations on environmental policy. Third, the environmentally rich country can protect itself by introducing environmental-policy measures. By imposing such measures as emission charges on polluting products, the environmentally rich country will reduce the attractiveness of these goods for internationl trade and thereby avoid specialization in the production of environment-intensive products. In this way, the environmentally rich country can maintain or improve the quality of its environment.

The Equalization of Prices for Emissions

Under certain conditions, the emission tax will adjust itself at home and abroad in the long run. Assume that environmental policy reacts to a change of environmental scarcity in both countries and that it correctly reflects environmental scarcity. The home country is assumed to be scarcely endowed with environmental services and the foreign country richly endowed in this respect. Then, in the initial situation, the emission tax is high at home and low abroad. For a high price of environmental use the home country will specialize in a more environmentally favorable production; conversely, the foreign country, having a smaller emission tax rate, will endeavor to specialize more in the production of pollution-intensive goods. The environmental quality increases in the home country and decreases abroad. In the long run, *ceteris paribus*, the emission taxes have to approach one another through international trade and through specialization. A key assumption in this prognosis is that these countries have the same production technology. If this condition is not valid, then the emission taxes are not likely to converge. Note that identical shadow prices do not imply identical environmental qualities.

Factor mobility between two areas (nations, regions) also works towards the equalization of environmental shadow prices. Assume that commodities are immobile and that traditional resources (labor, capital) are totally mobile between two areas and infinitely divisible while the environment is an immobile factor of production. Then the emission tax will adjust itself in the long run between the areas. The mobility of labor and capital will be sufficient to equalize the price of the immobile factor "environmental abundance" assuming identical and linear-homogeneous production functions for each sector in the two regions.

This tendency of equalization of the factor price of the immobile factor of production through the mobility of other factors of production or the exchange of commodities, however, does not work, when the mobility of labor also depends on regional environmental quality and when the evaluation of environmental quality is determined by individual preferences (majority voting). Individuals will migrate to the area with a better environmental quality and increase the demand for environmental goods there, raising the emission tax. In the vacated area, however, the demand for environmental quality will decrease and the emission tax has to fall there. Due to the fact that labor mobility depends on the wage rate and on regional environmental quality, the labor market may be segmented. The polluted area may have a higher wage rate and a lower emission tax; the emission tax may not be identical between regions. Apparently, this argument is more relevant in an interregional context, for instance in a Tiebout scenario (1956).

Environmental Policy and Gains from Trade

The "pollute thy neighbor" thesis points to an important, previously neglected aspect. The primary motivation for engaging in foreign trade is the prospect of gains, that is, that countries expand their consumption opportunities through trade. If a country exports the pollution-intensive commodity, it reduces its environmental quality. So, in this case, the traditionally defined gains from trade with regard to commodities 1 and 2 have to be compared with the deterioration of environmental quality. Trade pays for an economy only when net welfare increases, that is, when the traditional gains from trade overcompensate the deterioration of environmental quality. From this consideration it also follows that in an open economy, the reduction of the gains from trade can be considered as target losses of environmental policy.

This argument can be clarified through figure 9-1 where F is the autarky situation and F' is the initial trade equilibrium without environmental policy. Engaging in trade, that is, moving from F to F', creates gains from trade as indicated by the trade triangle at F'. The home country can reach a consumption point outside its transformation space. Pursuing environmental policy, that is, moving from F' to T, implies a higher environmental quality and a smaller trade triangle. The shrinking of the trade triangle can be considered to be an indicator of smaller gains from trade in the traditional sense. It can be shown that the emission tax has to be set in such a way that the net welfare gains of introducing an emission tax are zero (Siebert 1977c).

If the home country exports the less pollution-intensive commodity, it will improve its comparative advantage by implementing an environmental policy. Its gains from trade will be increased for given terms of trade.

In the discussion so far, we have not considered the case where the home country may influence its terms of trade. Assume that the home country exports the pollution-intensive commodity. Then its terms of trade will improve if environmental policy reduces excess supply of the commodity at home and if excess supply of the import commodity is increased. We know from the traditional gains-from-trade discussion that a high price elasticity of demand for the pollution-intensive commodity and a low price elasticity of supply at home represent such conditions. Similarly, we must require low import demand and high export supply elasticities abroad.

Up to now, trade theory has not taken into account environmental degradation in defining the gains from trade. Gains from trade should, however, be specified as the net improvements in well-being, rather than in terms of consumption availabilities. It then becomes necessary to weigh traditional gains from trade against environmental degradation. An open economy must be prepared to accept lower traditional gains from trade for the sake of an improved environmental quality.

Environmental Regulation and Protection Against Trade

Trade distortions arise if product norms are used as a policy instrument. An example is the intended introduction of catalytic devises car as a product name by Germany and the trade barriers deriving therefrom in the European Common Market. Other examples are tolerable amounts of pesticides in consumption goods or emission norms for (capital goods) machinery. These barriers to trade through product standards are aggravated if one discriminates between product standards for domestic and foreign goods. GATT regulations do not permit a discrimination and product standards should be applied on import goods as well as on import substitutes. In reality, however, product standards can be formulated in such a way as to permit national industries to meet the standards more easily than foreign competitors.

Product norms as trade barriers are only one aspect of a wider problem, namely whether environmental protection necessarily also implies protection against trade.

We have seen that environmental policy will reduce the comparative advantage of the pollution-intensive sector. Consequently, the sector loses outout and employment. It is realistic that specific groups of society will be negatively affected by environmental policy, such as the export- and import-substitute sector and workers (or trade unions) in these sectors. These political forces will ask for compensations or countervailing measures to make up for the loss of their relative autarky position. If these political groups are successful, environmental policy may give rise to new trade distortions.

Environmental abundance or scarcity is a factor in foreign trade which should be included in determining comparative advantage like other traditionally recognized factors, such as resources, technical knowhow, and so on. It would not make sense that pressure groups with strong interests (export and import industries, unions) attempt to compensate for the environmental advantages of other countries through trade-policy measures. By levying tariffs on imports or subsidizing their own exports, environmentally poor countries might attempt to protect their domestic industries that produce pollution-intensive goods. For economic reasons they might try to counteract their own environmental-policy measures. The costs of such a policy are bound to be high in the long run since such a policy means that each country will try to compensate its comparative disadvantage by policy measures. A country poorly endowed with labor will protect itself against labor-intensive imports; a country poorly endowed with capital will protect itself against capital-intensive imports; a country poorly endowed with technical knowledge will protect itself against technology-intensive inputs. And a country poorly endowed with environmental services will protect itself against pollution-intensive goods. In such a scenario, the idea of the advantages of international specialization is dead.

Notes

1. For a more detailed discussion of the international aspect, compare Siebert (1977c, 1978a, 1985), Siebert and Antal (1979e, chap. 10), Siebert et al. (1980). Also compare Pethig (1976, 1982) and Walter (1975).

2. Note that tranfrontier pollution is characterized by a diffusion function T with environmental quality in one region j being determined by emissions not only of region j, but – via the diffusion function T – also by emissions of region i.

$$U^j = (E^j, T(E^i))$$

For instance, T may be uni-directional. In contrast, for an interregional public good, the diffusion function cannot be explicitly defined and we have

$$U^k = (E^j, E^i)$$

Compare Siebert 1985, p. 132.

3. Compare any textbook of international trade.

4. It is conceivable that the comparative price advantage is "turned around" by environmental policy. In such a case the home country would export the environmentally favorable product.

11 Regional Aspects of Environmental Allocation

In contrast to global or international environmental systems, regional media relate to the spatial subsystems of a nation such as river systems, groundwater systems, or air regions. Regional media may also cut across national political boundaries, as occurs in the upper Rhine Valley where France, Germany, and Switzerland are linked. In this chapter we present a spatial-allocation model for a two-region system where pollutants are transmitted via environmental media from one region to another. The implications of the allocation model are derived and explained. The basic result is that emission taxes have to be differentiated according to regional conditions. The institutional problem of whether environmental allocation should be undertaken by national or regional authorities is discussed. Finally, we look into some practical problems such as interregional equity requirements and the relationship between regional environmental policy and regional planning.

The Problem

What is so special about environmental allocation in a regional setting? We focus on three components of the problem: delineation of environmental regions, interaction among regions, and policy approaches to environmental allocation. These issues introduce factors concerning the problem of environmental allocation that were not considered previously.[1]

Delineation of Regions

The space which a country occupies can be viewed as consisting of different sets of regions; for instance, we may distinguish among economic areas, political entities, and environmental regions which vary with environmental media. A *region* can be defined as a set of spatial points that either are homogeneous with respect to some variable (criterion of homogeneity) or are more intensively interrelated to one another than to other spatial points (criterion of functional interdependence). We may construct economic regions according to sociocultural or historical criteria or by using such economic variables as industrial structure, rates of unemployment, per capita income, or intensity of economic exchange via commodity exchange and factor mobility. Correspondingly, environmental regions may be defined by environmental characteristics. For instance, interaction among spatial points through environmental media such as the groundwater system, a river system, or a meteorological system may define an environmental region.

Environmental regions for different media will not be identical. In figure 11-1, sections 1 through 6 may denote air regions, and x may indicate a river system. Regions for different environmental media may overlap. Moreover, environmental regions and economic areas are not identical. An economic area may be delineated according to industrial structure (that is, a coal district) or the state of development (depressed area), while an environmental region is defined according to the spatial extent of an environmental system. For instance, in figure 11-1, areas 1 through 6 may be interpreted as economic or planning regions, and x may be considered to be an environmental system.

Interactions among Regions

Environmental regions are interrelated. Environmental disruption in one area will cause repercussions in other areas. Similarly, environmental policy for one region will have an impact on other areas. We may distinguish among the following mechanisms of interaction.

1. Environmental regions are interrelated in that pollution in one area will affect the environmental quality of another region by the interregional diffusion of pollutants to the other areas (interregional spillovers). This problem is similar to the case of international diffusion.

2. Economic regions are interrelated through the mobility of commodities. For instance, a strict environmental policy in one economic region may lead to an increased specialization of less pollution-intensive commodities while

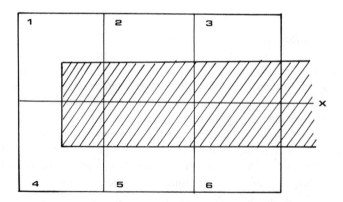

Figure 11-1. Delineation of Regions

another area could specialize in more pollution-intensive commodities. The exchange of goods will affect regional environmental quality.

3. Similarly, factors of production may migrate among regions, leaving those areas where factor prices have been reduced as a result of environmental policy.

4. Residents may migrate among regions owing to differences in environmental quality. Note that residents are not necessarily identical to workers and that environmental quality and wages both determine the mobility of labor. If residents have an influence in the political process, their mobility will affect the target values established for environmental quality.

5. Administrative or planning regions may be interrelated in the sense that the environmental quality in one area is an argument variable in the welfare function (of the inhabitants) of the other region (that is, amenities in one area are esteemed by the inhabitants of another area), either because the other region assigns a value per se to these public goods or because the region uses them during holidays for recreational purposes (temporal mobility of residents). Also, demonstration effects may occur among regions, with environmental quality in one area influencing the achievement levels in other regions.

6. Administrative regions may be interrelated by institutional arrangements such as a grants-in-aid system among regions. Also, the assignment of different types of taxes and expenditures to regions may create an interdependency among regions. This occurs if regions interact in the political process of assessing taxes and allocating expenditures to administrative levels. More unlikely, regions may have to interact in order to determine the volume of expenditures (that is, for interregional public goods) or taxation (financing interregional public goods). In this context, the country's constitution plays an important role. Federal states such as Switzerland or the United States may have institutional arrangements different from those of a central state such as France (Frey 1979).

Problems of Regional Allocation

With respect to the interdependency among regions, the following questions of spatial environmental allocation arise:

Should nationally uniform or regionally differentiated environmental policy instruments be used?

Should environmental policy be pursued by national or regional agencies?

Should the desired level of environmental quality be regionally differentiated or nationally uniform?

Can the different types of regions (economic areas, environmental systems) be delineated consistently?

What are the spatial effects of the various environmental instruments, and what relationship exists between regional planning and environmental policy?

Spatial-Allocation Model

For simplifying purposes, a two-region case is considered.[2] We use the same functions as in chapters 3 and 4. Every region has two production functions, two pollution functions, two abatement functions, and a damage function. Subscripts denote sectors; however, superscripts now indicate regions, not individuals as in chapter 4. Furthermore, we assume that the welfare functions are separately formulated for each region; that is, the regional welfare W^j is affected by only the regionally produced commodity Q_i^j and the regional environmental quality U^j:

$$W^j = W^j(Q_1^j, Q_2^j, U^j) \qquad j = 1, 2 \tag{11.1}$$

This function neglects the interregional interdependence of welfare functions. Residents of region 1 are indifferent to the environmental quality of region 2. For instance, we do not take into account the possibility that region 2 may be the recreation area of region 1 or that residents of one region may care about scenic landscapes in the other area. For simplicity, note that we also assume that output determines regional welfare. This means that there is no interregional exchange of commodities.

In order to explicitly consider the interregional diffusion of pollutants, it is assumed that pollutants are transported from region 2 to region 1 through environmental systems. Let S^{21} denote the quantities of pollutants being transported from region 2 to region 1. Here S^j represents the ambient pollutants in the environment of region j, S_e^j the gross emissions of region j, S_r^j the abated emissions, and $\overline{S^{aj}}$ the regional assimilative capacity, which is given exogeneously. Then pollutants in region 1 are defined as[3].

$$S^1 = S_e^1 + S^{21} - S_r^1 - \overline{S^{a1}} \tag{11.2}$$

Pollutants in region 2 are given by

$$S^2 = S_e^2 - S^{21} - S_r^2 - \overline{S^{a2}} \tag{11.3}$$

It is assumed that the quantity of "exported" pollutants represents a given part of net emissions and is non-negative[4]

$$S^{21} = \alpha^{21}(S_e^2 - S_r^2 - \overline{S^{a2}})$$ (11.4)

The resource is intersectorally and interregionally mobile, so that we have

$$\overline{R} = \sum_j \sum_i R_i^j + \sum_j \sum_i R_i^{rj}$$ (11.5)

Furthermore, the definitions

$$S_e^j = \sum_i S_i^{pj}$$ (11.6)

and $$S_r^j = \sum_i S_i^{rj}$$ (11.7)

and equations 3.1, 3.2, and 3.3 apply.

Regional Implications of a National Environmental Policy

In the following we assume that the definition of property rights for environmental use is vested with a national authority and that the national government maximizes social welfare for a system of regions ("politique pour la nation", Boudeville 1966). Environmental policy maximizes the welfare of the two-region system under restrictions 3.1 through 3.3 and 11.2 through 11.7. The applicable approach and its implications are illustrated in Appendix 11A.

We can expect that optimal allocation dictates that interregional spillovers are accounted for in the shadow prices of the economy. The polluter pays principle requires that a region bears the environmental costs that it causes in another area. Shadow prices should also reflect differences in environmental scarcity between regions. In the short-run, we can expect that environmental scarcity prices will be differentiated regionally. In the long run, when all adjustments have taken place, there is, under certain conditions, a tendency towards the equalization of environmental shadow prices. Finally, we can also expect that the target values of environmental quality may differ among regions.

Regional Differentiation of the Emission Tax

Prices for Pollutants

From equation 11A.2j one obtains the shadow price of pollutants ambient in the environment:

$$\lambda_S^1 = \lambda_S^2 + \lambda^{21} \tag{11.8}$$

Because of 11A.2b and i we have

$$\lambda^{21} = \lambda_S^1 - \lambda_S^2 = -W_U^{1'} G^{1'} + W_U^{2'} G^{2'} \tag{11.9}$$

for the shadow price of the pollutants exported by region 2. The following three cases can be distinguished:

1. If there is no difference between the marginal damages $W_U^{i'} G^{i'}$ in both regions, then $\lambda^{21} = 0$ holds in the optimum, and the marginal evaluation of pollutants is identical for both regions.
2. If $\lambda^{21} > 0$, that is, if region 1 has a higher marginal damage than region 2, then one unit of pollutants is evaluated as being more important in region 1.
3. If $\lambda^{21} < 0$, one unit of pollutants causes a smaller marginal damage in region 1 than in region 2. The shadow price λ^{21} thus can be interpreted as representing "differential damage."

Price for Emissions

The different evaluation of pollutants appears in the shadow prices for emissions (emission tax rates). For the shadow price of emissions in region 1 we have

$$\lambda_{S_i^P}^1 = \lambda_S^1 = \lambda_{S_i^r}^1 = -W_U^{1'} G^{1'} = \frac{\lambda_R}{F_i^{r1'}} \tag{11.10}$$

In region 1 the shadow price of emissions corresponds to the shadow price of pollutants and the shadow price of abated emissions. Similarly, as in the model for a closed economy (compare equations 4.6b and c), we have as a condition for the optimum that the emission tax rate must be equivalent to the prevented marginal damage and the marginal costs of abatement.

For the shadow price of emissions in region 2 we have

$$\lambda_{S_i^P}^2 = \lambda_S^2 + \alpha^{21} \lambda^{21} = \lambda_{S_i^r}^2 = -W_U^{2'} G^{2'} + \alpha^{21} \lambda^{21} = \frac{\lambda_R}{F_i^{r2'}} \tag{11.11}$$

The shadow price of emissions in region 2 is no longer identical with the evaluation of the pollutants in region 2. The following cases have to be delineated:

1. If no interregional diffusion of pollutants takes place, that is, $\alpha^{21} = 0$, the shadow price of emissions in region 2 is, in the optimum, equivalent to the marginal costs of abatement and the prevented marginal damage of region 2.

2. If a unit of pollution causes the same marginal damage in regions 1 and 2, that is, $\lambda^{21} = 0$, then it does not matter in terms of the evaluation of pollutants in which region a unit of pollution is released into the environment. A differential damage does not arise. The emission taxes in the two regions are identical.

3. If a unit of pollution causes a higher damage in region 1 than in region 2 ($\lambda^{21} > 0$), then the shadow price of emissions in the optimum is determined not only by the marginal damage caused in region 2 but also by the differential damage caused in region 1. The argument goes as follows: Region 2 is "relieved" by the diffusion of pollutants, and therefore its marginal damage decreases. On the other hand, the quantity of pollutants increases in region 1, and the marginal damage rises there. The polluters of region 2 have to bear the social costs of pollution which arise from region 2 as well as from region 1.

4. If a unit of pollution causes a smaller damage in region 1 than in region 2 ($\lambda^{21} < 0$), then the shadow price for emissions can be set lower compared to the situation described in item 3. In this case, region 1 is still sufficiently endowed with assimilative capacity. Since this assimilative capacity is not used by region 1, it can be utilized by region 2 through interregional diffusion.

Location Advantage

The regional differentiation of emission taxes affects the shadow prices of commodities and therefore the absolute price advantage or location advantage of a region. As implications we have

$$\lambda_{Q_i}^1 = W_{Q_i}^{1'} + H_i^{1'} G^{1'} W_U^{1'} = W_{Q_i}^{1'} - H_i^{1'} \frac{\lambda_R}{F_i^{r1'}} \tag{11.12}$$

$$\lambda_{Q_i}^2 = W_{Q_i}^{2'} + H_i^{2'} (G^{2'} W_U^{2'} - \alpha_{21} \lambda^{21}) = W_{Q_i}^{2'} - H_i^{2'} \frac{\lambda_R}{F_i^{r2'}} \tag{11.13}$$

The shadow price of a commodity is determined by its regional evaluation and by the environmental costs which arise in its production. The environmental costs have to be subtracted from the social evaluation; $\lambda_{Q_i}^j$ thus denotes the producers' price of commodity i, not the consumers' price. For region 2 the environmental costs contain not only the environmental damages of region 2 but also the differential damage which arises because of the interregional diffusion of pollutants.

Consider the case in which environmental policy is changed in such a way that interregional diffusion is explicitly considered. Then by assuming $\lambda^{21} > 0$, additional costs arise for region 2. The production incentive in region 2 for commodity i is reduced. In the case where $\lambda^{21} < 0$, on the other hand, region 2 can continue to transmit pollutants to region 1. Region 2 receives a production advantage because of the unused assimilative capacity in region 1.

The location advantage of region 2 also is influenced by the assimilative capacity of region 1. Assume that the assimilative capacity of region 1 is reduced. Then λ^{21} must rise, and the production incentive in region 2 will be smaller. On the other hand, if the assimilative capacity in region 1 is increased, λ^{21} will be smaller and the production incentive in region 2 will rise.

Diagrammatic Explanations

The implications of the regional allocation model may be explained diagrammatically. Figure 11-2 shows the marginal damage and the marginal abatement costs for region 1 (figure 11-2a) and region 2 (figure 11-2b). Because of equation 11.10 the emission tax rate in region 1 must equate prevented marginal damage with the marginal costs of pollution abatement. For region 2 the differential damage has to be taken into account because of equation 11.11.

In order to be able to interpret our results, we assume an initial situation in which both regions have the same characteristics and in which no interregional

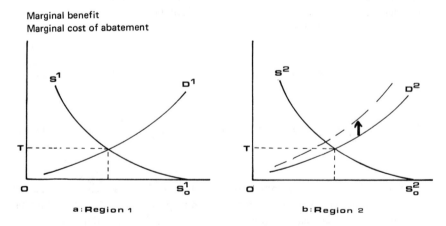

Figure 11-2. Emission Taxes with Differences in Evaluation

diffusion takes place. Then the optimal solution is identical for both regions. The shadow price for emissions is OT in both regions. This situation is depicted by figure 11-2.

The reader should note that figure 11-2 represents partial equilibrium analysis and does not contain all the interdependencies treated in the model. Thus, the marginal-cost curve of emission abatement presupposes an optimal value for λ_R. Furthermore, the marginal-damage curve will shift if the quantity of emissions OS^j varies with the output vector in both regions.

Beginning with a frame of reference providing identical conditions and an identical emission tax in both regions (figure 11-2), we analyze what causes a higher emission tax in region 2.

Greater Damage

A unit of pollution may cause a higher level of marginal damage (in value terms) for region 2 when $S^1 = S^2$. The marginal-damage curve in region 2 shifts upward. This may occur if region 2 has a higher population density because then a unit of pollution will cause greater damage. It is also conceivable that the type of industrial activity in region 2 could account for the higher damage. Region 2 may have a different ecological system which is more vulnerable to pollution. The higher marginal damage implies a higher emission tax for region 2 in the optimum.

Higher Evaluation

The physical damage caused by one unit of pollution is valued higher in region 2 than in region 1. This may be due to differences in the respective preference functions; that is, residents of area 2 may be more environmentally minded. Also, citizens in region 2 may have a higher per capita income and may evaluate nature more highly. Finally, an area's value may be enhanced when it incorporates a specific function (recreation) or represents a value per se (amenity of the landscape). In these cases, the curve of the prevented marginal damage has to be drawn higher for region 2, and a higher emission tax has to be set (compare figure 11-2b).

Smaller Assimilative Capacity

Region 2 may have a smaller assimilative capacity than region 1. Let us assume that given an initial situation, the assimilative capacity of region 2 decreases. This means that the quantity of ambient pollutants increases (figure 11-3b).

Marginal benefit
Marginal cost of abatement

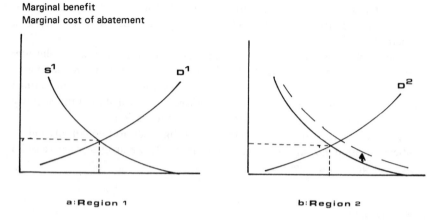

a:Region 1   b:Region 2

Figure 11-3. Regional Allocation with Differences in Assimilative Capacity

The emission tax in region 2 will have to be set higher, and the quantity of pollutants to be abated will increase. Note that in this case we have a complex chain of reactions which is not shown in figure 11-3*b*. The higher emission tax may lead to a smaller output, less pollution, and a shift in the cost curve of abatement. Also, the shadow price for the resource may change and thereby prompt the marginal-cost curve to shift again.

Higher Demand for Assimilative Services

Region 2 may have a higher demand for assimilative services than region 1. The demand for assimilative services depends on such factors as the level of regional development, the industrial mix, and the population density. The higher demand for assimilative services of region 2 can also be attributed to the fact that region 2 uses a more pollution-intensive production technology and emits a greater quantity of pollutants for identical output vectors. This case should be treated analogously to the case where region 2 has a lower assimilative capacity.

Higher Costs of Abatement

Region 2 has higher marginal costs of abatement. This presupposes that the abatement technology varies regionally and that technical knowledge of abatement processes cannot be transferred interregionally, either because information concerning inventions in abatement technology meets with spatial obstacles or because innovations in both regions are not proportionately possible. This latter

Marginal benefit
Marginal cost of abatement

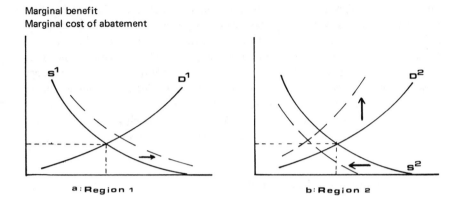

Figure 11-4. Regional Allocation and Interregional Diffusion

situation could arise if in one area older, less efficient abatement technologies exist. The disadvantageous marginal costs of abatement can also be based on a higher factor price in the case where partial immobility of factors exists. In figure 11-3 the case of disadvantageous marginal costs is illustrated by a higher curve of the marginal abatement costs.

The results can be treated comparably with the analysis of problems arising from international specialization. Those factors requiring regional differentiation of emission taxes also exhibit comparative advantages. The reader is reminded, however, that the institutional conditions for both problems are different. The basic difference is that internationally no effective environmental agency exists, whereas nationally an agency monitoring a two-region system is feasible.

Interregional Diffusion

The emission tax is influenced by interregional diffusion of pollutants. In figure 11-4 we analyze the effects of this diffusion. Let $\lambda^{21} > 0$. If interregional diffusion takes place and if region 2 exports pollutants, then, *ceteris paribus,* the marginal-cost curve of pollution abatement in region 2 shifts to the left because the quantity of ambient pollutants in the environment diminishes. In region 2 the tax rate and the quantity of abated pollution fall (arrow to the left in figure 11-4b). In region 1, on the other hand, the tax rate rises and the quantity of abated pollution increases (arrow in figure 11-4a). If the interregional diffusion is not accounted for, region 2 will have a location advantage through this interregional-diffusion factor. This has the same effect as an extension of the assimilative capacity; region 1 bears social costs which it has not caused. If an environmental policy is initiated, the polluters of region 2 will have to bear the environmental costs which they have caused in region 1 (differential damage). If the differential damage is introduced by environmental policy, the marginal-damage curve in region 2 will shift upward (figure 11-4b). This implies that a higher emission tax will be set in region 2. Furthermore, the marginal-cost curve in region 2 will shift upward (figure 11-4b). This again implies that a higher emission tax will be set in region 2. Furthermore, the marginal-cost curve of abatement in region 2 will shift, since λ_R varies. Although we do not consider this effect further, it is important to recognize its potential impact.

Resource Mobility and Adjustment of Emission Taxes

If resources are totally mobile between the two regions and infinitely divisible, then the emission tax will adjust itself in the long run between the regions. This results from the following consideration:

Assume that in a given situation the assimilative capacity in region 2 is smaller than in region 1. Then, *ceteris paribus,* the emission tax in region 2 is initially higher. With a higher shadow price of emissions in region 2, the producers' price for commodities in this region is lower. Region 2 has a lower location advantage. With resources being mobile, firms leave region 2. Pollution in region 2 decreases, and it increases in region 1. The price of pollutants will fall in region 2 because of the lower level of pollution. In region 1, the price of pollutants will rise. Abatement will be stimulated in region 1, but marginal productivity of abatement will be reduced (that is, marginal abatement costs will rise in region 1). Thus, the emission tax in region 1 has to rise because of a higher level of pollution and because of increasing abatement costs. In region 2, however, the emission tax will be reduced. In the long run, the emission taxes in the two regions have to be identical if factors of production are completely mobile.

This model does not consider interregional trade because we did not distinguish between output and consumption goods. Interregional commodity exchange can also adjust the emission tax in the long run. Let us assume that we have identical production, pollution, and abatement functions for commodity *i* in both regions. Then the region which is richly endowed with assimilative capacity will specialize in the production of the pollution-intensive commodity. This implies that the demand for assimilative services increases in the region with environmental abundance. If we also assume a progressive increase of abatement costs, the emission tax will be adjusted accordingly between the regions. It can be shown that emission taxes will equalize under specific conditions, for instance identical and linear production and emission functions, identical and linear abatement functions, and identical and linear-homogeous overall production technology (Siebert 1985, p. 140).

If the evaluation of environmental quality is determined by individual preferences, the mobility of residents also works toward an adjustment of the emission tax between the regions. Individuals will migrate to the region with a better environmental quality and increase the demand for environmental goods there. The emission tax has to rise. In the vacated region, however, the demand for environmental quality will decrease.[5]

One can expect that this long-run tendency toward an equalization of emission taxes will not be relevant given the limited planning horizon of practical policy. The structure of space is "congealed" at a given time in the sense of burned clay. This means that factors are partially immobile and that the environmental policy should not set the long-run optimal tax rates which are applicable for total mobility, but rather only those prices which consider the partial immobility of resources. The theoretically interesting phenomenon of emission-tax equalization does not relieve environmental policy of a regional differentiation of the emission tax.[6]

Differences in Environmental Quality

Identical shadow prices for pollutants do not imply identical environmental qualities in both regions. Assuming $\lambda_S^1 = \lambda_S^2$, we have from equations 11A.2b and 11.A2i in the appendix:

$$\frac{W_U^{1'}[G^1(S^1)]}{W_U^{2'}[G^2(S^2)]} = \frac{G^{2'}(S^2)}{G^{1'}(S^1)}. \qquad (11.14)$$

Only if both the (concave) utility function and the (concave) damage function are identical in both regions, will $\lambda_S^1 = \lambda_S^2$ imply that environmental qualities are identical in both areas. If, however, the utility and damage functions differ, $\lambda_S^1 = \lambda_S^2$ does not necessarily imply identical environmental quality in the optimum.

Siting Issues and the National Interest

The location of private and public large-scale ventures (airports, power plants) has become a major political issue, especially in densely populated economies. No allocation problem arises when all layers of society experience a net benefit, i.e. the region (local community) and the nation both have a net advantage. A problem arises when the benefits of a large-scale project and its costs relate to different regions and when at least one layer of society (a region) experiences a net loss that cannot be compensated. Then, from a national perspective, a region has to experience a net loss if the system as a whole can gain. From the regional perspective some protection is warranted. We have a problem of a constitutional dimension. The basic question is whether the constitution of a country should protect a minority of citizens experiencing the opportunity costs (for instance in a region) or whether a group of society can be expected to tolerate the opportunity costs in order to allow overall net benefits.

Regional versus National Authorities

If environmental policy is to be regionalized, the question arises as to whether environmental policy should be undertaken by autonomous regional authorities or by the national government. This assignment problem may differ according to the prevailing organizational scheme, namely, whether the question applies to central states or to federal states. One basic problem concerns interregional spillovers. Either the administered area must be large enough to internalize all externalities, so that there will be no interregional spillovers, or a mechanism must be found which will monitor interregional diffusion, implement an interregional-diffusion norm, or place an appropriate shadow price on the pollutants crossing regional borders. The assignment problem must be solved in such a way that a high-stack policy (that is, increasing the height of the stacks in order to get rid of pollution) is not undertaken by a region. If interregional spillover is a relevant problem, then handling the spillover is a precondition to the regionalization of environmental authorities.

Regional authorities have the advantage of being able to identify regional preferences through such mechanisms as referenda or party voting. Regionalization implies that to some extent people can determine their way of living without being controlled by decisions of the central government or even international agencies (such as the European Economic Community). In the classical federal state such a Switzerland and the United States (Frey 1979), regional preferences are assumed to differ among regions; goal conflicts are solved by regional authorities according to the preferences of the regional population. A pure federalism presupposes that no serious interregional spillovers exist. The role of the federal government is limited to a "skeleton law" (Frey) on environmental protection to guarantee that spillovers are internalized.

Another, but related approach is Olson's concept of fiscal equivalence (1979). This approach describes an institutional arrangement in which the group of people benefiting from environmental policy (experiencing environmental damage) are more or less identical with those financing environmental improvement. The task of an institutional arrangement then consists in finding such a delineation of environmental regions that guarantees the spatial overlapping of benefits and costs. However, creating fiscal equivalence for different types of public goods (that is, schools, theaters, dumps, transportation systems, river systems, air regions) may create a net of multiple organizational units. Organizations for different types of public goods will be characterized by overlapping spatial areas and may present a system of differing spatial grids (Olson 1979). The organizational structure will be even more complex if the organizations not only provide public goods but also have taxing rights. Consequently, the question arises as to whether a set of different regions is a practical solution.

Applying the Tiebout theorem (1956) to environmental allocation, an optimal solution can be found for local environmental qualities under a set of given conditions. The most important prerequisite (Stiglitz 1977) is that interregional spillovers are not serious and that consumers are mobile and vote with their feet. Each voter will migrate to the region in which he can maximize his utility. An equilibrium is reached when no consumer is induced to change his location. The willingness-to-pay for the regional environmental qualities is expressed correctly. Thus, voting with one's feet will guarantee a Pareto-optimal environmental allocation.

Independent regional authorities will have a number of difficulties to overcome.

First, the consistent delineation of environmental regions creates severe problems. Since environmental media differ in spatial extent, regions related to different environmental media will overlap spatially. Also the interdependency existing among environmental regions because of technology and the economic system has to be considered because emissions released into one medium A can also be transmitted (at least partly) to medium B. Although these coordination problems will also arise for a national environmental policy, we can expect that independent regional authorities will have greater difficulties in trying to solve them.

Second, regional authorities are not likely to take into consideration the interdependency of regional welfare functions, that is, that the environmental quality of region 2 can also be an argument variable in the welfare function of region 1. Consequently, the institutionalization of independent regional authorities implies suboptimization.

Third, it is doubtful whether regional authorities will take into account the interregional diffusion of pollutants. The pollution-exporting region regards the export of pollutants as a welcome extension of its assimilative capacity. The price of environmental use is set too low in the pollution-exporting region; this region has a location advantage at the expense of other regions. In the importing regions, the shadow prices are set too high; they reduce the production of pollution and goods more than is economically desirable.

Some Restraints on Regional Authorities

The conflict between regional autonomy and the necessity to solve the spillover problem may require some restraints on regional authorities.

In the case of interregional bargaining among independent regional authorities, we can expect the same problems as occurred in the case of transfrontier pollution. "The victim pays" solutions are very likely and experience suggests that even these solutions may not be easily implemented. Consequently, one may think about introducing some restraints, for instance on grants by the national government, in order to induce solutions.[7] On an international scale, this approach is rather impractical.

Alternatively, national environmental policy could formulate "interregional-diffusion norms" for pollutants. These would define the quantity of pollutants that a region would be permitted to "export" via environmental systems to another area per period (for example, in the case of water management, the water quality of a tributary as it joins the main river). Thus, it would be conceivable to combine a system of independent water-management agencies (such as the *Agence de Bassins* in France) with a system of interregional-diffusion norms. But diffusion norms cannot be fixed once and for all (in contrast to quality norms). Diffusion norms have to be adaptive to changes in population density, industry mix, environmental conditions, and scientific discoveries. It will be extremely difficult to change such diffusion norms in a world of independent regional agencies. A national agency could more easily adapt pollution shadow prices to new economic, ecological, and social developments.

Note that in the previous analysis we assumed that independent environmental agencies can determine the quality targets for regional systems. Alternatively, one can consider an institutional arrangement with a smaller regional autonomy. For instance, regional authorities could be empowered to impose a regional supplementary tax. Those regions with a strong environmental preference or with a special need for environmental protection could levy an additional tax besides those rates already established by the national agency.

Regional water associations (see chapter 8) represent an institutional setting which allows a regionalization of environmental policy. The delineation of the environmentel system (river system) can be easily achieved. Moreover, the spillover problem can be solved if water quality at the mouth of a river or of a tributary is specified by interregional bargaining or by national laws. Interregional diffusion norms then are identical to ambient standards at a given spot of a river and they can be considered as the target variable of environmental quality.

Cooperative and Non-cooperative Solutions of Bargaining

In the bargaining process between autonomous regions, we meet all the problems of environmental policy "in nuce". Environmental quality is a public good; and the environmental media are common property resources, consequently the downwind region has no property title to force abatement in the polluting area; it is not possible to exclude the polluting area from using the environment as a receptable of waste. The polluting area can behave as a free rider. Without clearly defined rights, both regions have to determine the tolerable level of pollution in a bargaining process. Three cases have to be distinguished.

One-directional spillover. In a scenario in which the upwind region used the environment as a free good bargaining implies that both regions can only benefit if the pollute compensates the polluter to reduce pollution in the upwind region (victim-pays-principle). Unilateral action of the downwind region cannot improve efficiency. When bargaining costs are neglected, a solution of the game is found in which marginal damage prevented (in the downwind country) equals marginal costs of abatement (in the upwind country). This bargaining result represents a Coase solution (1960) and a Nash solution (1950) in a cooperative game. A non-cooperative solution does not exist.

Multi-directional spillover. When spillovers are multi-directional, each region has a threat potential irrespective of compensation. A cooperative and non-cooperative solution may exist. In the case of non-cooperative behavior, reaction functions $S^i = \Psi^i(E^j)$ are determined and an equilibrium point or a Nash equilibrium of the game is sought. A Nash equilibrium requires that the solution cannot be improved to the advantage of both regions. This implies individual rationality, i.e. the solution must be at least as favorable as the initial situation for each participant.[8]

Common environmental systems. The bargaining solutions differ when environmental quality relates to an environmental system common to more than one region (country) such as the ozone layer. The reaction function has to take into account that each polluter hurts himself. Consequently, unilateral action may now improve the welfare of one player (Pethig 1982).

Regional Autonomy and Environmental Media

Solutions to the assignment problem vary according to the environmental media and according to the instruments used (compare taxanomy problem).

Noise is a regional problem, and so it may be partly controlled by regional authorities. However, since product norms should not be differentiated regionally, an antinoise policy must be nationalized.

Water-quality management can be handed over to regional authorities if interregional-diffusion norms can be controlled and if they can be easily altered to respond to changing needs. In the case of water, observe that interregional-diffusion norms are identical to ambient standards in a river, and these norms can be considered to be the target variables of environmental quality. If water management relies exclusively on emission taxes as set by regional authorities and does not incorporate interregional-diffusion norms, then the taxes should be determined so as to take into account downstream damages.

Bargaining may be necessary to set this tax. Such a procedure seems very impractical. Alternatively, one could conceive of a surcharge levied by some national or interregional agency that would encompass downstream damages. Again, this seems impractical. In the case of water management, the use of regional authorities operating within the constraints determined by interregional-diffusion norms seems to offer a practical solution. Only if the problem of interregional diffusion is negligible can a national emission tax be used.

In the case of air-quality management, the solution varies, again depending on the preferred policy instruments and the magnitude of interregional pollution. If such pollution is negligible, regional management can be utilized. Otherwise, air-quality management must be undertaken nationally, since bargaining among regions seems unrealistic. A national emission charge can be combined with a regional surcharge wich is levied by regional authorities. Note that a regional surcharge can account for regional differences in tastes and environmental endowments. If interregional diffusion is of a significant magnitude, however, the surcharge must also account for damages in the polluted area. Consequently, the surcharge cannot be established by the polluting region. Once again, interregional diffusion complicates the picture and requires the imposition of a surcharge by a national or an interregional agency.

Toxic wastes and toxic materials contained in products should be controlled nationally according to liability rules or through product norms.

Environmental Equity and Specialization of Space

Welfare maximization for the nation as a whole can imply that regions will reach different welfare levels. Interregional specialization can also mean that regions will achieve differing amounts of environmental quality. This result can be in conflict with a spatially interpreted equity goal. Therefore, one possible strategy is to introduce restrictions on the interregional differences in welfare (Siebert 1975b). In practical economic policy, one can expect that the restrictions are not defined with respect to the regional welfare level, but rather in relation to the determining factors of regional welfare. Thus, articles 72 and 106 in the Constitution of the Federal Republic of Germany require that living conditions be similar for all regions. This requirement may be interpreted to mean a similarity in environmental quality. Therefore, we could introduce additional constraints into our allocation model, such as $U^1 = U^2$, which would require identical environmental quality among regions. Alternatively, we could require that a minimum quality $U^j \geqslant \overline{U^j}$ be reached in each region.

If the equity constraint is not formulated in terms of regional welfare, but rather is broken down into different constraints on welfare determinants, then the constraint becomes more restrictive through partitioning. Typical welfare determinants are social overhead capital, environmental quality, and income per capita. Identical welfare could be achieved in these regions by a judicious combination of these determinants. Interregional constraints on each welfare determinant, however, reduce the solution set considerably. In practice, constraints are not implemented rigorously and thus are used more as guidelines. Since these equity considerations may be thought of as a spatial implication of a welfare approach, a state of this type can be classified as a welfare state with a federal structure (Frey 1979).

An alternative approach to equity restrictions on environmental quality is a specialization among regions, such as a "black-spot policy" where pollution-intensive activities are concentrated in certain areas (for example, Sweden).[9] This spatial-separation approach attempts to bring about a specialization of national territory and relies heavily on land-use planning as an instrument of environmental-quality management. This approach allows for better protection of less polluted areas; at the same time, it concentrates the "public bad" in designated areas. Also, there is a strong incentive to locate the black spots near the border so that the burden is shifted to the neighbor (such as in the case of Sweden where black spots are located near Norway).

Environmental Policy and Regional Planning

Environmental policy will have an impact on spatial structure. Regional planning will influence environmental allocation in space. Will these policy areas work harmoniously and consistently?

Consistency relates to the following problems: (1) If there is only one policy target, do the policy instruments all work in the same direction? (2) Are the policy instruments consistent over time? (3) Do the policymakers at different levels all work toward attaining the target? (4) If there are different policy targets, to what extent is there a goal conflict, and are these goal conflicts resolved rationally?

Since environmental policy relates to different environmental media, environmental policy areas will overlap. A high emission tax for residuals in the atmosphere may introduce an incentive to emit these pollutants into the region's river system instead. We cannot fault individual firms or households for substituting processes at politically set prices. The problem is whether the policymaker can react adequately to changing conditions and whether the policymaker can anticipate the reactions of individuals. If the decision-making process of environmental policy is rather slow and emission taxes are rigid, inconsistencies in environmental policies can arise. It is necessary that policy instruments used for different media be coordinated: emission taxes should set the correct relative prices among pollutants for different media or, if one favors direct controls, the correct structure of emission norms.

Regional planning (or land-use planning) can be regarded as instrumental for environmental policy, especially by preventing pollution-intensive firms from locating in agglomerated areas. On the other hand, environmental policy may be an instrument of regional policy. Environmental policy can be considered an attempt to attribute social costs to economic activities. In this interpretation, environmental policy helps to correctly express regional comparative advantage. For instance, a region with a large endowment of assimilative capacity may experience an increase in its comparative advantage owing to environmental policy. A heavily industrialized area may have experienced an artificial comparative advantage before environmental policy was implemented. Its agglomeration economies may have been overestimated. If both regional planning and environmental policy are efficiency-oriented, one should not expect goal conflicts. However, if other targets such as environmental equity are introduced, then goal conflicts are likely to arise.

Finally, as is discussed in the following chapters, the time profile of an emission tax will influence the spatial structure at each moment in time, and the structure of space will influence the future allocation of space. If environmental policy has to correct its price signals very often, spatial structure will have a ratchet effect on future location decisions. Costs of adaptation are involved in adjusting spatial structure to the revised price signals.

Notes

1. For a survey of the problem, compare Siebert (1979b, 1979d, 1985).

2. For a more detailed discussion, compare Siebert (1975b). Also compare Tietenberg (1979).

3. We here analyze a static allocation problem and neglect that pollutants accumulate over time. Compare chapter 12 and for the regional context Gebauer (1982).

4. We are only interrested in inner solutions with S^i, $S^{21} \geqslant 0$. Formally, nonegativity constraints could be additionally introduced into the maximization problem of Appendix 11A. We then would explicitly introduce an inner solution.

5. Compare the Tiebout theorem (1956).

6. Compare Potier (1979).

7. Introducing an additional restraint for instance by a reduction of grants from the federal government could transform the non-cooperative game into a cooperative game.

8. On the postulates of a Nash-equilibrium in the environmental context compare Pethig (1982, p. 80). Also compare Kuhl (1986).

9. Interregional spillovers may be of an intertemporal nature. Pollutants transported into a region may accumulate there over time. The problem then has to be analyzed as a cooperative or non-cooperative differential game which shows the properties of a steady-state in a two-region system and the time paths of pollution in both regions towards the steady state (Gebauer 1982).

Appendix 11A:
A Regional Allocation
Model

Environmental policy maximizes the welfare of the two-region system. The Lagrangean expression is

$$L = \sum W^j(Q_1^j, Q_2^j, U^j) - \sum_j \sum_i \lambda_{S_i^p}^i [H_i^j(Q_i^j) - S_i^{pj}]$$

$$- \sum_j \sum_i \lambda_{Q_i}^j [Q_i^j - F_i^j(R_i^j)]$$

$$- \sum_j \sum_i \lambda_{S_i^r}^j [S_i^{rj} - F_i^{rj}(R_i^{rj})]$$

$$- \lambda_S^1 \left(\sum_i S_i^{p1} - \sum_i S_i^{r1} + S^{21} - S^1 - \overline{S^{a1}} \right)$$

$$- \lambda_S^2 \left(\sum_i S_i^{p2} - \sum_i S_i^{r2} - S^{21} - S^2 - \overline{S^{a2}} \right)$$

$$- \sum_j \lambda_U^j [U^j - G^j(S^j)]$$

$$- \lambda_R \left(\sum_j \sum_i R_i^j + \sum_j \sum_i R_i^{rj} - \overline{R} \right)$$

$$- \lambda^{21} \left[\alpha^{21} \left(\sum_i S_i^{p2} - \sum_i S_i^{r2} - \overline{S^{a2}} \right) - S^{21} \right] \qquad (11A.1)$$

The approach in 11A.1 should be analyzed analogously to equation 4.5. The equations are the welfare function, pollution function, production function, pollution-abatement function, definition of ambient pollutants in the environment, damage function, and resource constraint.

The Kuhn-Tucker conditions are

$$\frac{\partial L}{\partial Q_i^j} = W_{Q_i}^{j\,'} - \lambda_{S^p}^j H_i^{j\,'} - \lambda_{Q_i}^j \leqslant 0 \qquad Q_i^j \frac{\partial L}{\partial Q_i^j} = 0 \qquad (11A.2a)$$

$$\frac{\partial L}{\partial U^j} = W_U^{j\,'} - \lambda_U^j \leqslant 0 \qquad U^j \frac{\partial L}{\partial U^j} = 0 \qquad (11A.2b)$$

$$\frac{\partial L}{\partial R_i^j} = \lambda_{Q_i}^j F_i^{j\,'} - \lambda_R \leqslant 0 \qquad R_i^j \frac{\partial L}{\partial R_i^j} = 0 \qquad (11A.2c)$$

$$\frac{\partial L}{\partial R_i^{rj}} = \lambda_{S_i^r}^j F_i^{rj\,'} - \lambda_R \leqslant 0 \qquad R_i^{rj} \frac{\partial L}{\partial R_i^{rj}} = 0 \qquad (11A.2d)$$

$$\frac{\partial L}{\partial S_i^{p1}} = \lambda_{S_i^p}^1 - \lambda_S^1 \leqslant 0 \qquad S_i^{p1} \frac{\partial L}{\partial S_i^{p1}} = 0 \qquad (11A.2e)$$

$$\frac{\partial L}{\partial S_i^{p2}} = \lambda_{S_i^p}^2 - \lambda_S^2 - \alpha^{21}\lambda^{21} \leqslant 0 \qquad S_i^{p2} \frac{\partial L}{\partial S_i^{p2}} = 0 \qquad (11A.2f)$$

$$\frac{\partial L}{\partial S_i^{r1}} = -\lambda_{S_i^r}^1 + \lambda_S^1 \leqslant 0 \qquad S_i^{r1} \frac{\partial L}{\partial S_i^{r1}} = 0 \qquad (11A.2g)$$

$$\frac{\partial L}{\partial S_i^{r2}} = -\lambda_{S_i^r}^2 + \lambda_S^2 + \alpha^{21}\lambda^{21} \leqslant 0 \qquad S_i^{r2} \frac{\partial L}{\partial S_i^{r2}} = 0 \qquad (11A.2h)$$

$$\frac{\partial L}{\partial S^j} = \lambda_S^j + \lambda_U^j G^{j1} \leqslant 0 \qquad S^j \frac{\partial L}{\partial S^j} = 0 \qquad (11A.2i)$$

$$\frac{\partial L}{\partial S^{21}} = -\lambda_S^1 + \lambda_S^2 + \lambda^{21} \leqslant 0 \qquad S^{21} \frac{\partial L}{\partial S^{21}} = 0 \qquad (11A.2j)$$

$$\frac{\partial L}{\partial \lambda} \geqslant 0 \qquad \lambda \frac{\partial L}{\partial \lambda} = 0 \qquad (11A.2k)$$

These conditions should be compared to Appendix 4B.

Part V
Environmental Allocation in Time
and Under Uncertainty

12 Long-Term Aspects of Environmental Quality

The Problem

In our analysis thus far, we have studied environmental allocation in a static context. However, environmental systems are used not only by one generation, but by a number of generations. Today's use of the environment may affect the role of the environment in the future. Consequently, the environmental-allocation problem also has to be interpreted over time.

Pollutants accumulate over time. Today's emissions influence environmental quality in the future. This problem of intergenerational allocation is studied in chapter 12.

Environmental constraints have repercussions on economic growth by limiting the availability of the environment as a receptacle of wastes, consequently, resources have to be used for environmental protection and cannot be allocated to production. This relationship of environmental policy and economic growth is studied in chapter 13.

Some of the impact of pollution will occur in the distant future, and we do not have adequate information on the specific effects. In contrast to our analysis so far, uncertainties are involved relating to the damage function, the accumulation of pollutants and possibly to environmental policy instruments. These problems are taken up in chapter 14.

In this chapter, we are interested in the competing use of the environment as a good for public consumption and as a waste receptacle. If today's generation emits pollutants into the environment and if these pollutants accumulate over time, then environmental quality for future generations will be negatively affected. We want to examine, then, how the environment may be optimally allocated over time, what level of environmental quality should be envisioned for future periods, and what implications arise for the setting of a shadow price of environmental use over time. The interdependency between today's use of the environment and future environmental quality can be explained as follows:

1. A number of pollutants are accumulated by environmental systems and remain in the environment for several years, decades (as with DDT), or thousands of years (as in the case of radioactivity). Some pollutants that enter the environment today will harm future generations; that is, some pollutants will have long-term effects.

2. One cannot dismiss the possibility that pollutants will be responsible for irreversible damage to the ecological equilibrium in the future. There is the risk

that changes may occur in the environmental system which humans may not be able to reverse.

3. Some environmental systems regenerate by delicate natural processes, such as take place in the production of oxygen by phytoplankton. Emissions can disturb these processes and influence the capability of environmental systems to regenerate over time. Similarly, the pollutants emitted into the environment today can impair the future assimilative capacity of environmental systems.

4. The capital stock in production and abatement and a given sectoral structure are passed on to the next generation; it may be unable to change these structures immediately because the mobility of labor and capital is insufficient.

5. We pass on a given production and abatement technology to future generations. Since the institutional setting of today's economy defines the incentives of finding new technologies, our institutional rules may also have an impact on the future.

Environmental use today influences future environmental quality through interdependencies in the ecological system as well as in the economic system. We therefore must decide to what extent the intertemporal interactions among generations should be considered in our current decisions.

The following questions arise: What environmental quality should be maintained today, and how much environmental quality should be left for future generations? Which emission technologies and how much capital in abatement processes should we hand over to future generations? How should the price of environmental use (or a system of emission standards) be set over time? How can one avoid that the price for emissions oscillates and that these oscillations cause wrong investments? For which planning period should an environmental agency maximize welfare? To what extent should minimal values (for example, for the quality of environmental media) be stated for irreversible damages in order to protect future generations? What kinds of shifts in demand for the public good "environment" come about over time (for example, shifts in preferences or shifts due to increases in income)? What is the magnitude of the income elasticity of demand for environmental quality? What are the effects of changes in demand on the price of environmental use? What adjustment processes take place for emissions when environmental-policy measures are introduced (for example, technological adjustment processes or location shifts)? How soon should the time path of prices be known so that the desired adjustment processes can operate without causing wrong investments?

In the following analysis, we restrict ourselves to developing a simple dynamic allocation model in which merely the accumulation of pollutants is taken into account as interdependency between periods.

Dynamic Model

We assume that the economic planner intends to maximize social welfare over time. The welfare of future generations is discounted because of the time preference by a rate of $\delta > 0$. Welfare ω for the planning period $[0, \infty]$ thus will be calculated at its discounted value:

$$\omega = \int_0^\infty e^{-\delta t} W(Q_1^t, Q_2^t, U^t)\, dt \tag{12.1}$$

Equation 12.1 raises two important issues. First, we assume that a social-welfare function exists not only for one generation but for all future generations. All problems of information and institutional aspects discussed in chapter 5 are assumed away. Second, the normative problem arises as to whether we should discount the welfare of future generations and if so, by which discount rate.

The maximization of social welfare has to satisfy restrictions for every period. These constraints are known from the static allocation problem (chapter 4). Also, the quantity of pollution is given at the initial point of time 0, that is, $S(0) = \overline{S}$.

The maximization problem should at least incorporate an interdependency which connects the variables of different periods. In the following analysis we assume[1] that

$$\dot{S} = \sum S_i^p - \sum S_i^r - \overline{S}^a \tag{12.2}$$

This equation of motion represents the change in accumulated quantities of pollutants $\dot{S}$, emissions in one period $\Sigma\, S_i^p$, abated quantities of pollutants $\Sigma\, S_i^r$, and assimilated quantities of pollutants $\overline{S}^a$. The implications of this approach are depicted in Appendix 12B. Readers not familiar with control theory should first consult Appendix 12A.

Implications

Implications that are related to a point in time, namely, the conditions for optimality that must be fulfilled in every single period, are equivalent to the implications of the static optimization approach.

1. From condition 12B.4a it follows that the shadow price of commodities λ_{Q_i} has to be set in such a way that it is equivalent to the social evaluation of a commodity for consumption minus its environmental costs. Observe that in condition 12B.4a the shadow prices and marginal utilities of commodities are cal-

culated at current value. However, condition 12B.4a can also be interpreted in terms of discounted values.

2. From conditions 12B.4c and d it follows that the resource price in production, as well as in abatement, is equal to the marginal value of the resource.

3. The dynamic allocation problem consists of finding a use of the environment over time as a good for public consumption and as receptive medium such that the value of the welfare function will be maximized. This optimal allocation of environmental use over time and the resulting allocation of the resource in production and abatement (primal) correspond to an optimal time path of the shadow price (dual).

Condition 12B.4g represents the equation of motion for the auxiliary variable $\mu(t)$ at current value:

$$-\dot{\mu} = -\delta\mu + W'_U G' \tag{12.3}$$

Equation 12.3 clearly shows that the change of the shadow price in period t at current value depends on the discount rate, the level of the shadow price, and the marginal damage in the period. From equation 12.3 it follows that

$$-\dot{\mu} \gtreqqless 0 \quad -\mu(t) \gtreqqless -\frac{1}{\delta} W'_U G' \tag{12.3a}$$

$$-\dot{\mu} \gtreqqless 0 \quad -{}^0\mu(t) = -\mu(t)e^{-\delta t} \gtreqqless -W'_U \frac{G'}{\delta} e^{-\delta t} \tag{12.3b}$$

The auxiliary variable $\mu(t)$, which in this approach is defined at current value, can be interpreted as follows: Let ${}^0\mu(t)$ denote the present value of $\mu(t)$. Then we have ${}^0\mu(t) = \mu(t)e^{-\mu t}$. The auxiliary variable ${}^0\mu(t)$ measures the marginal contribution of the state variable S at point t to the optimal value of the welfare function; that is, ${}^0\mu(t)$ tells us how one unit of pollution, ambient in the environment (entered exogenously into the economy at time t), changes the present value of the welfare function. Now ${}^0\mu\dot{S}$ defines the change in welfare caused by a variation in the state variable occurring at t, and $\mu(t) = {}^0\mu(t)e^{\delta t}$ denotes the change in value of the welfare function at current value (Arrow 1968, pp. 87, 93–94). And μ can be regarded as the shadow price for pollutants; it is negative.[2] The shadow price for pollutants can also be viewed as a user cost. It represents the opportunity costs of today's environmental use to future generations since μ indicates a change in the welfare function caused by an additional unit of pollution (that is, the welfare loss of future generations).

In equation 12 3b, ${}^0\mu$ characterizes the total marginal damage for all periods, that is, the damage in period t and in the future. Thus, when a unit of pollution is increased at t, the change of the welfare function is discounted to period 0. On the right side of equation 12.3b, we have the negative "capital" value of a pollutant ambient in the environment at period t (prevented marginal damage discounted to period 0). The *capital* value of a unit of pollution at the beginning of period t is the value of the utility flow (marginal damage) in this period divided by the discount rate.[3] This capital value is calculated only from the utility flow in period t and thus does not consider, as does $-\mu$, the damage in future periods. The right hand side of equation 12.3b can be regarded as the capitalized loss of period t, from a period-egoistic point of view.[4] The shadow price of pollutants $-\mu$, on the other hand, takes into account future periods. Thus, we obtained the following result.

If the total marginal loss for all periods is greater than the capitalized loss in period t, the shadow price of pollutants has to rise (case of a high future loss). If, on the other hand, the total marginal loss is smaller than the capitalized loss of period t, the shadow price of pollutants should fall (case of a low future loss).

4. The time profile of the shadow price of pollutants ambient in the environment influences the shadow prices of the other variables and therefore the adjustment processes of the system. With a high future damage and a rising shadow price of pollutants, the producers' price falls, the production of commodities (especially the pollution-intensive) is repressed, and the incentive for abatement rises (compare conditions 12B.3a through c). The temporal variation of the shadow price favoring high actual or high future prices is relevant for the steering of the economic system. A bias, for example, in favor of relatively high actual prices, causes a strong structural change between abatement and production. A policy fostering an increase in the shadow price penalizes the pollution-intensive sector and requires adjustment processes adequately strong in the initial periods.

Three Strategies for Dynamic Environmental Use

The canonical equations 12.2 and 12.3 of the optimization problem allow a statement to be made about the optimal time path of the shadow price $\mu(t)$ for alternative initial situations S_0 (pollution level S in period 0). The optimal environmental allocation and the optimal time path of the shadow price $\mu(t)$ are depicted with the help of figures 12-1 and 12-2. First we discuss the equations $-\dot{\mu} = 0$ and $\dot{S} = 0$.

The $-\dot{\mu} = 0$ Curve

The equation of motion for the shadow price of pollutants, because of equation 12.3b, can be interpreted as follows: When the $-\dot{\mu} = 0$ curve applies,

$$-\dot{\mu} = 0 \Leftrightarrow -\delta\mu + W'_U G' = 0 \tag{12.4}$$

$$-\mu\big|_{\dot{\mu}=0} = -\frac{1}{\delta} W'_U G' \tag{12.4a}$$

The $-\dot{\mu} = 0$ curve progressively increases if $G''' < 0$ and $W''' > 0$ (figure 12-1a). This follows from

$$\frac{d(-\mu)}{dS} = -\frac{1}{\delta}(G'^2 W''_U + W'_U G'') > 0$$

$$\frac{d^2(-\mu)}{dS^2} = -\frac{1}{\delta}(2W''_U G'G'' + G'^3 W'''_U + W'_U G''' + W''_U G'G'') > 0$$

The $-\dot{\mu} = 0$ curve characterizes situations in which the total marginal loss in all periods equals the (periodic-egoistic) capital value of a unit of pollution; that is, we see that for $\dot{\mu} = 0$, $-\mu = (1/\delta) W'_U G'(S)$. The distance $\overline{SP}$ in figure 12-1a thus characterizes the periodic-egoistic capital value of an additional unit of pollution at point $\overline{S}$, as well as the total loss in all periods, that is, the shadow price of emissions.

For a given S, if the shadow price of emissions is set higher than the periodic-egoistic capital value of an additional unit of pollutant, that is, if $-\mu > \overline{SP}$ and $-(1/\delta) W'_U G'(\overline{S}) = \overline{SP}$ (point A), then the shadow price of the auxiliary variable has to rise in time because $-\mu > -(1/\delta) W'_U G'(\overline{S})$ for $-\dot{\mu} > 0$. For all cases in which $-\mu$ lies above the $-\dot{\mu} = 0$ curve, $-\mu$ has to rise (upward arrow in figure 12-1a). On the other hand, for a given S, if the shadow price of emissions is set lower than the periodic-egoistic capital value (point B), from $-\mu < -(1/\delta)$ $W'_U G'(\overline{S})$ for $-\dot{\mu} < 0$ it follows that $-\mu$ falls. Cases of $-\dot{\mu} < 0$ then lie beneath the $-\dot{\mu} = 0$ curve (downward arrow in figure 12-1a).

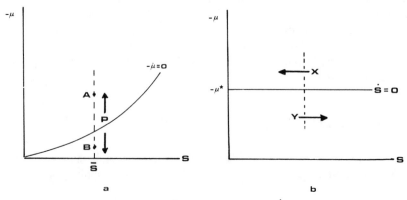

Figure 12-1. The $-\dot{\mu} = 0$ Curve and the $\dot{S} = 0$ Curve

The $\dot{S} = 0$ Curve

The equation of motion 12.2 can be interpreted as follows: The resource use in production and in abatement activity depends on the level of the shadow price $-\mu$. With an increasing $-\mu$, more resources are used in abatement and fewer are used in production. If the assimilative capacity is zero, we have

$$\dot{S} = \sum_i H_i \{F_i[R_i(-\mu)]\} - \sum_i F_i^r [R_i^r(-\mu)] \qquad (12.5)$$

A high $-\mu$ reduces the production of pollutants and makes the quantity of abated pollutants increase. A low $-\mu$ implies a greater production of pollutants and a smaller abatement. One can expect a shadow price $-\mu^*$, for which $\dot{S} = 0$, or

$$\dot{S} \gtrless 0 \Leftrightarrow \sum_i H_i\{F_i[R_i(-\mu)]\} \gtrless \sum_i F_i^r [R_i^r(-\mu)] \Leftrightarrow -\mu \lessgtr -\mu^* \qquad (12.6)$$

Thus, the curve $\dot{S} = 0$ is a horizontal line with an axial section $-\mu^*$. Above the straight line $-\mu^*$, $\dot{S} < 0$ holds true, that is, S falls (point X). Beneath the straight line $-\mu^*$, $\dot{S} > 0$ is valid, that is, S increases (point Y in figure 12-1b).[5]

Phase Diagram

Combining figure 12-1a and b results in figure 12-2. The four regions in figure 12-2 indicate how the variables $-\mu$ and S change for alternative initial situations. The changes of $-\mu$ and S are represented by Pontryagin paths. The run of these Pontryagin paths is indicated by the arrows in the four regions.

In figure 12-2, P characterizes a situation in which the values $-\mu$ and S do not change. For a given initial level of pollution, the path to a steady state $(-\mu^*, S^*)$ ensures the maximization of the welfare function. Both curves in figure 12-2 divide the first quadrant into four regions. Regions II and IV represent nonoptimal policies; regions I and III each contain a stable path.

Region IV depicts the path to an "ecological paradise." Assume that for an initial situation $S'(0)$ economic policymakers will adopt a tax which lies above the $\dot{\mu} = 0$ curve. Then the production of commodities will be repressed and abatement stimulated until production contracts to zero.

Region II describes the path to an "environmental collapse." In the initial situation $S'(0)$, if environmental policy chooses a shadow price which lies beneath the $-\dot{\mu} = 0$ curve, then abatement is repressed and production increases. The quantity of pollutants rises, and environmental quality decreases.

Regions I and II both contain a stable path. For an initial situation $S''(0)$, if a shadow price is chosen that decreases in the long run, then the quantity of pollution is reduced to S^*. However, for an initial situation $S(0)$, the time profile

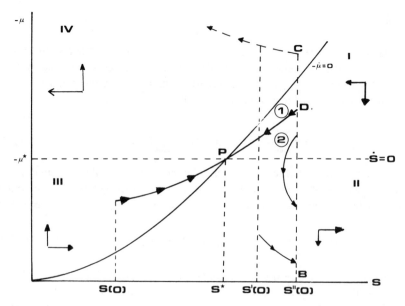

Figure 12-2. Optimal Stock of Pollutants and Time Path of the Emission Tax

of the shadow price must be chosen in such a way that the economy gradually adapts to the pollution norms (not yet exhausted in the initial situation). If an economy adopts a tax in region III (or I) and its associated time path, it is not ensured of attainment of the long-term optimal situation. A tax not lying on the stable path (for example, arrow 2) leads away from the optimal path. Figure 12-2 clearly depicts that the correct setting of the shadow price for intertemporal use represents a path over a sharp ridge. If the shadow price "loses its way," the system falls into the undesired (nonoptimal) regions II and IV. The strategy of region I and III, therefore, has to be interpreted as "moving slowly into a pollution norm."

Adjustment Costs

For practical economic policy, it cannot be excluded that the policymaker "jumps" between the regions of the phase diagram. Assume that the system has a quantity of emissions $S'(0)$ in the initial situation. If the economic policy adopts too low an emission tax, the system shifts to B. Now let the environmental issue be noticed by the voters, so that the politician is forced to react. If he now chooses a tax rate corresponding to point C (region IV), the system shifts in the wrong direction. The optimal tax on path 1 that should be applied in region II makes clear that this tax rate has to be set higher in situation S'' than in the initial situation S'. This demonstrates that the situation has deteriorated as a result of government intervention, compared to the initial situation $S'(0)$. The higher tax rate indicates policy failure. The transition of the tax rate from points B to D also shows that wrong price signals had been set and that a revision of the tax rate brings about adjustment costs.

Social Discount Rate and Environmental Allocation

The social discount rate decisively influences the intertemporal use of resources. From equation 12.3 it follows that the higher the time preference (discount rate), the lower the absolute shadow price should be. The reduction of δ shifts the $-\dot{\mu} = 0$ curve upward (compare figure 12-3a).

If a lower discount rate prevails, in contrast to path 1, environmental policy must adopt path 2 with a higher shadow price. If one considers the stable path 1 in region I of figure 12-2 for a given discount rate as a system of reference, then for a policy of a decreasing shadow price for emissions, a reduction of the discount rate implies an increase of the shadow price in every period (except for $T = \infty$).

The shadow-price increase is equivalent to a change in resource use over time. A lower discount rate produces a smaller quantity of emissions in the future (greater protection of future generations) and, at the same time, a price increase for use of the environment as a receptacle of pollution today. These higher costs of environmental use today can also be interpreted as opportunity costs, that is, forgone use of the resources employed in abatement. A lower discount rate raises the user costs and favors future generations.

For an initial situation $S'(0)$ and a policy of an increasing shadow price (path 3), a change in the discount rate can cause a reversal in policy. Now,

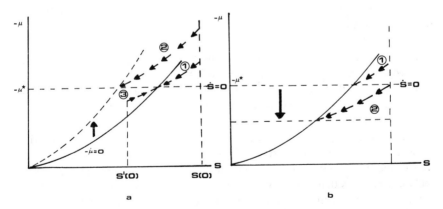

Figure 12-3. Effects of an Increase in the Discount Rate and in Assimilative Capacity

instead of an increasing shadow price, a policy of a decreasing shadow price (path 2) has to be followed.

Further Determining Factors of the Shadow Price of Emissions

The simple allocation model presented takes into account only a single intertemporal context, namely, the accumulation of pollutants. There are, however, many other interdependencies among periods which also affect the shadow price of emissions and thus the intertemporal environmental use.

Assimilative Capacity

If the quantity of pollutants $\overline{S^a}$ assimilated by the environment increases parametrically, the $\dot{S} = 0$ curve shifts downward (figure 12-3b). The time path of the shadow price that should be chosen in pursuit of a greater assimilative capacity necessitates lower taxes now and in the future, but may not change the bias in the time profile of the shadow price.

Wealth of Future Generations

Future generations may be richer than we are today. Neglecting irreversibilities of allocation decisions, the wealth of future generations may favor the adoption of a high discount rate and a low shadow price for pollutants.

Technical Progress

Wealth of future generations can also manifest itself through improved technical knowledge. If one expects that resources will be used with greater productivity in the future, or that the production of commodities and emission technologies will be less pollution-intensive, we can set a lower shadow price today, compared to path 1 in figure 12-2.

Also, technical progress in abatement activities permits today's shadow price to be set lower. Technical progress, then, ensures that in spite of a high pollution level in the initial period, a lower pollution level can be attained in the future. Technical progress that reduces pollution in production and encourages improvements in the abatement technology allows one to set a lower tax rate at present (compared to path 1 in figure 12-2).

If it is presumed that technical progress in abatement depends on the emission-tax level, then the statement must be corrected to account for the long time lag of the technological incentive effect of an emission tax. The endogenization of technical progress in abatement and emission technology (dependent on the level of the emission tax) possibly causes a change in the time profile of the shadow price in favor of higher actual prices.

The abatement technology is specific to environmental media and economic sectors. Therefore, it is possible that technical progress in abatement may differ among the sectors and environmental media. If technical progress in future abatement favors the pollution-intensive sector, the shadow price for emissions can be set lower.

Capital Formation in Abatement

If a policy of a decreasing shadow price for emissions over time is pursued and if economic agents expect $-\mu$ to be constant, then too much capital will be tied up in abatement. This implies a misallocation of resources. This distorted allocation can be changed in the long run only if the excessive capital locked in abatement is mobilized via depreciation. The longer it takes to depreciate, the stronger the misdirection of capital will be.

An analogous argument applies to labor used in the abatement branch, provided that labor is temporally immobile and labor mobility is connected with costs (retraining, migration costs, costs of frictional unemployment). Furthermore, we can apply an analogous argument to the factors used in the improvement of assimilative capacity. Capital formation and partial immobility of labor in the abatement branch require a lower shadow price in the initial periods (compared to path 1 in figure 12-2).

Here, the importance of announcement effects becomes distinct. It seems to be more effective to influence private investments with an appropriate fixing of the shadow price than to moderate the effects of a wrong fixing of prices through policy instruments.

Sectoral Structure and Immobility of Factors

If one considers a two-sector model with a pollution-intensive and an environmentally favorable sector, a policy of a decreasing emission tax means that the pollution-intensive sector is repressed in the initial situation. Capital and labor migrate to the environmentally favorable sector (and costs of friction occur). In the course of time, however, the emission tax is decreased, so that the status of the time-consuming reallocation process is changed while the reallocation itself continues. With a falling tax rate, reallocation has to be partly canceled. The temporal immobility of invested capital and labor and the adjustment processes that come about from a change in the sectoral structure require that the shadow price of emissions be set lower than in earlier periods.

Longevity of Pollutants

The pool of pollutants in any period consists of short- and long-lived pollutants. If, *ceteris paribus,* the composition of pollutants changes while long-lived pollutants increase relative short-lived pollutants, then the actual shadow price will have to be set higher.

Other Factors

Intertemporal environmental allocation is influenced by other determinants, such as the risk of unknown future damages, the risk of irreversibilities (see chapter 14), and location decisions.

The previous considerations, which are not contained in the simple model, represent a number of significant factors relevant to setting shadow prices for emissions. These factors indicate that regions and stable paths which differ from those shown in figure 12-2 can be obtained.

Notes

1. In equation 12.2 the case can obviously arise that, because of the exogenously given assimilative capacity $\overline{S^a}$, more pollutants are assimilated than the stock of pollutants plus net emissions. This case must be excluded. This can be done by assuming that a constant part of the stock of pollutants is reduced. For simplicity, we assume equation 12.2. It should be noted that equation 12.2 in this chapter replaces equation 3.4. New pollutants do not disappear automatically at the end of a period; rather, they expire at the rate $\overline{S^a}$.

2. The economic argument suggests that $dW/dS(t) = {}^0\mu(t) < 0$ and therefore $\mu(t) \leqslant 0$, for ${}^0\mu(t_0)$ states how a unit of pollution, put into the system at time t_0, affects the present value of the welfare function. From 12B.4e it follows that $-\mu = \lambda_{S_i^p}$. Since $\lambda_{S_i^p} \geqslant 0$, $\mu \leqslant 0$ (that is, μ is not positive).

3. Note that the capital value can be determined by the interest rate and interest revenue. For an interest rate of 6 percent and an interest revenue of $12 per period, the capital value amounts of $200 at the beginning of the period.

4. Note that the minus sign on the right side of equation 12.3 ensures that we measure the marginal prevented damage.

5. If the assimilative capacity is sufficiently large, the $\dot{S} = 0$ curve would coincide with the horizontal axis and a penalty on pollution would not be necessary.

Appendix 12A:
Control Theory

If x denotes the state variable of a system and m the control variable, the control problem is

$$\max_{\{m(t)\}} J = \int_{t_0}^{\infty} e^{-\delta t} I(x, m, t)\, dt \qquad (12A.1)$$

subject to the restrictions

$$\dot{x} = f(x, m, t) \qquad x(t_0) = x_0 \qquad \{m(t)\} \in U$$

where $I\,(\ldots)$ and $f\,(\ldots)$ are continuously differentiable functions; t_0 and x_0 are parameters (namely, t_0 characterizes the initial point in time and x_0 the initial value of the state variable); $\{m(t)\}$ is the control trajectory, which has to be an element of the control set U. The integral of the values of the I function from time t_0 to infinity must be maximized. The $\dot{x}$ function is the equation of motion of the system.

The maximum principle is applied while the Hamiltonian function is defined as $\tilde{H}(x, m, t) = I(x, m, t) + \mu f(x, m, t)$, and its value is maximized at every point in time by a convenient choice of time paths $\{m(t)\}$, $\{\mu(t)\}$, and $\{x(t)\}$. The maximization of the value for the $\tilde{H}$ function at every point in time in the planning period $t \in [0, \infty]$ requires the fulfillment of the following necessary conditions:

$$\frac{\partial \tilde{H}}{\partial m} = 0 \qquad (12A.2a)$$

$$\dot{x} = \frac{\partial \tilde{H}}{\partial \mu} \qquad (12A.2b)$$

$$\dot{\mu} = \mu\delta - \frac{\partial \tilde{H}}{\partial x} \qquad (12A.2c)$$

The maximization of the Hamiltonian function for every period (that is, a convenient choice of the control variables at every point of the optimal trajectory) is ensured by $\partial H / \partial m = 0$ (if no further restrictions occur). The equation $\dot{x} = \partial H / \partial \mu$ represents the equation of motion of the system. Note that equation 12A.2b is obtained by differentiating the Hamilton function with respect to

Table 12A-1
Optimality Conditions

Present Values	Current Values
$H = I(x, m, t)e^{-\delta t} + \lambda f(x, m, t) + \lambda_j(\ldots)$	$\widetilde{H} = I(x, m, t) + \mu f(x, m, t) + \lambda_j(\ldots)$
$\dfrac{\partial H}{\partial m} = 0$	$\dfrac{\partial \widetilde{H}}{\partial m} = 0$
$\lambda = -\dfrac{\partial H}{\partial x}$	$\dot{\mu} = \delta\mu - \dfrac{\partial \widetilde{H}}{\partial x}$

Here $\widetilde{H} = He^{\delta t}$, $\mu = \lambda e^{\delta t}$, $\widetilde{\lambda}_j = \lambda_j e^{\delta t}$, and $\dot{\lambda}e^{\delta t} = \dot{\mu} - \delta\mu$.

the multiplier and that it yields the constraint of the system, similar to static optimization problems.

The Hamiltonian function can be formulated at present (discounted) value or at current value. Shadow prices must be interpreted in the same way. The last paragraph used the formulation at current value. The value of the H function, as well as the shadow price, should be interpreted at current value in this case.

In order to determine the transversality conditions, define a K-function according to Long and Vousden (1977) with

$$K(T, \xi) = \xi x(T) \tag{12A.3}$$

where T is terminal time and ξ is a multiplier relating to the state variable in terminal time. Then we have as terminal conditions

$$\xi x(T) = 0 \quad \xi \geqslant 0 \tag{12A.3a}$$

$$\frac{\partial K}{\partial x(T)} = \xi = e^{-\delta T}\mu(T) \tag{12A.3b}$$

$$\frac{\partial J}{\partial T} = e^{-\delta T}H(T) = 0 \tag{12A.3c}$$

12A.3c determines terminal time T. If the Hamiltonian, that is the performance indicator of a period T, does not contribute any more to present value of the target function, it is not worthwhile to continue the program. Note that this condition can only be interpreted for finite solutions because

$$1 \quad \lim_{t \to \infty} e^{-\delta T} \to 0.$$

Equations 12A.3a and b imply

$$e^{-\delta T}\mu(T)x(T) = 0 \text{ for finite time.}$$

If additional restrictions $g(x)$ occur, the Lagrangean function is

$$\tilde{L} = \tilde{H} + \tilde{\lambda}_j g(x)$$

$$\tilde{H} = I(x, m, t) + \mu f(x, m, t) \qquad (12A.4)$$

where the Lagrangean function and multipliers are noted at current value. Then the necessary conditions are

$$\frac{\partial \tilde{L}}{\partial m} \leqslant 0 \qquad m \frac{\partial \tilde{L}}{\partial m} = 0 \qquad (12A.4a)$$

$$\dot{\mu} = \mu\delta - \frac{\partial \tilde{L}}{\partial x} \qquad (12A.4b)$$

$$\dot{x} = \frac{\partial \tilde{L}}{\partial x} \qquad (12A.4c)$$

The transversality conditions 12A.3a–b hold; condition 12A.3c changes into

$$e^{-\delta T} L(T) = 0. \qquad (12A.4d)$$

Table 12A-1 compares the formulation at present value and at current value. For $\dot{\lambda} = -\partial H/\partial x$ it follows by definition that $\mu = \delta\mu - \partial H/\partial x$. If $\partial H/\partial m = 0$, we have also $\partial \tilde{H}/\partial m = 0$ because $\partial H/\partial m = (\partial \tilde{H}/\partial m)e^{-\delta t}$.

Appendix 12B:
A Dynamic Allocation Model

The allocation problem for environmental use is presented in its dynamic aspect by the maximization of a welfare function as

$$\omega = \int_0^\infty e^{-\delta t} W(Q_1, Q_2, U) \, dt \qquad (12B.1)$$

under the following restrictions:

$$\dot{S} = \sum_i S_i^p - \sum_i S_i^r - \overline{S^a} \qquad (12B.2)$$

where $\overline{S^a}$ denotes the quantity of pollutants that is assimilated per period. Equation 12B.2 is the equation of motion for the system which indicates to what extent the pool of pollutants varies per period.

The initial condition of the system is given by

$$S(0) = \overline{S} \qquad (12B.3)$$

Furthermore, the restrictions of the static allocation approach of equations 3.1 through 3.6 apply for every period. If the problem is formulated in periodical values, the maximization problem is

$$L = W(Q_1, Q_2, U) + \mu \left(\sum_i S_i^p - \sum_i S_i^r - \overline{S^a} \right) - \sum_i \lambda_{S_i^p} [H_i(Q_i) - S_i^p]$$

$$- \sum_i \lambda_{Q_i} [Q_i - F_i(R_i)]$$

$$- \sum_i \lambda_{S_i^r} [S_i^r - F_i^r(R_i^r)]$$

$$- \lambda_U [U - G(S)]$$

$$- \lambda_R \left(\sum_i R_i + \sum_i R_i^r - \overline{R} \right) \qquad \text{max}$$

Necessary conditions for an optimum are

$$\frac{\partial L}{\partial Q_i} = W'_{Q_i} - \lambda_{S_i^p} H'_i - \lambda_{Q_i} \leqslant 0 \qquad Q_i \geqslant 0 \qquad Q_i \frac{\partial L}{\partial Q_i} = 0 \qquad (12\text{B}.4a)$$

$$\frac{\partial L}{\partial U} = W'_U - \lambda_U \leqslant 0 \qquad\qquad U \geqslant 0 \qquad U \frac{\partial L}{\partial U} = 0 \qquad (12\text{B}.4b)$$

$$\frac{\partial L}{\partial R_i} = \lambda_{Q_i} F'_i - \lambda_R \leqslant 0 \qquad\qquad R_i \geqslant 0 \qquad R_i \frac{\partial L}{\partial R} = 0 \qquad (12\text{B}.4c)$$

$$\frac{\partial L}{\partial R_i^r} = \lambda_{S_i^r} F_i^{r\prime} - \lambda_R \leqslant 0 \qquad\qquad R_i^r \geqslant 0 \qquad R_i^r \frac{\partial L}{\partial R_i^r} = 0 \qquad (12\text{B}.4d)$$

$$\frac{\partial L}{\partial S_i^p} = \lambda_{S_i^p} + \mu \leqslant 0 \qquad\qquad S_i^p \geqslant 0 \qquad S_i^p \frac{\partial L}{\partial S_i^p} = 0 \qquad (12\text{B}.4e)$$

$$\frac{\partial L}{\partial S_i^r} = -\lambda_{S_i^r} - \mu \leqslant 0 \qquad\qquad S_i^r \geqslant 0 \qquad S_i^r \frac{\partial L}{\partial S_i^r} = 0 \qquad (12\text{B}.4f)$$

$$\dot{\mu} = \delta\mu - \lambda_U G' \qquad\qquad (12\text{B}.4g)$$

(The derivations in relation to the multipliers are not reproduced here.) It should be noted that the above program is formulated at current values. For purposes of simplification, the tilde for L and λ_j is left out.

Implications 12B.4a to f of the dynamic approach are equivalent to implications 4B.1 through 4B.9 of the static approach (compare Appendix 4B). The conditions (12B.4g) in both problems are identical. As an additional condition of the dynamic optimization approach, the equation of motion 12B.2 applies.

It has been assumed for the arguments presented in chapter 11 that environmental quality does not decrease to zero; thus $U > 0$. It has also been assumed that both sectors produce, so that R_i, Q_i, $S_i^p > 0$. Then, presuming that an environmental policy will be pursued, and therefore the conditions $\lambda_{S_i^r} > 0$ and $R_i^r > 0$ are fulfilled, the optimal conditions of the static optimization approach follow from the restrictions of 12B 4 for every period.

13 Economic Growth and Environmental Quality

Ecologists believe that one of the important reasons for the existence of the environmental problem stems from the emphasis on growth by the industrialized states. They point out that growth has been possible only at the expense of the environment. Ecologists postulate that growth rates were so high because the wastes and pollutants from production and increased consumption had been unscrupulously released into the environment without consideration of their effects. The destruction of the environment, the impairment in the quality of elemental environmental services, the deterioration of air quality, and the contamination of seas, rivers, and lakes were not taken into account in economic calculations. The loss and deterioration of important environmental goods went relatively unnoticed. In sum, the social costs of growth were not included in economic analyses. We have, so to speak, grown to the detriment of the environment.[1] These arguments lead to the following questions: By which indicators should growth be measured? Does a halt in growth present a convenient measure for the improvement of environmental quality? What are the effects of economic growth on environmental quality? To what extent is economic growth restricted by a limited supply of natural resources?

Zero Economic Growth

The zero economic growth demanded by ecologists has to be evaluated by two criteria: First, what kind of opportunity costs are caused by zero growth? Second, can zero growth be a suitable measure to reduce pollution and the depletion of natural resources?

Opportunity Costs of Zero Growth

A growth stop has a number of undesired effects. First, economic growth makes it possible to increase the supply of goods, and while such an increase may not seem urgent for several richer nations, it is an absolute necessity for the countries of the Third World. As a result of medical progress, life expectancy in these poorer countries has been increased while birthrates remain high. These countries have only a small industrial base and are afflicted with immense poverty, for instance, a yearly per capita income of $300 in some cases. For these countries, zero growth would mean economic and political chaos.

Second, slower economic growth in industrialized countries would adversely affect the developing countries. Their export chances would fall, and employment and national income would decrease. The economic situation of countries in the Third World would necessarily worsen if the industrialized economies experienced slower growth. Also, a solution to the international-distribution problem would become rather difficult.

Third, with slower economic growth, the industrialized nations would also be significantly affected. Although the interdependence between employment and growth cannot be studied in detail, there are some points in favor of the thesis that full employment is more easily achieved in a growing economy.

Fourth, with slower economic growth, the supply of public goods such as education and training, housing, hospitals, and medical care would be very much impaired. Social services provided by the state, especially old-age pensions, would be jeopardized.

Fifth, growth implies a moderation in the conflict over income distribution and a reduction of tension in society. A relative redistribution of income can be achieved much better in a growing economy than in a stationary one. During the 1960s and 1970s Great Britain exemplified the internal-distribution problem which a country encounters during a period of decreasing economic growth. Slower growth accompanied by increasing distribution conflicts can cause the rate of inflation to rise. Further, deficits in the balance of payment become likely.

Sixth, economic growth and environmental protection are not mutually exclusive for yet another reason. Environmental protection demands new production technologies that are favorable to the environment. It demands large investments in order to abate the wastes arising from consumption and production and to promote the recycling of materials. Environmental protection may stimulate a number of very important growth factors and thereby prompt the economy to move in a new direction of development.

Environmental Effects of Zero Economic Growth

If the opportunity costs of a zero growth are judged to be less severe, the question remains of whether zero growth has the desired effects on environmental quality and on the conservation of natural resources. Let us first consider what the effects of economic growth would be assuming that the environment is used as a common property free of charge. Then we know that increasing production raises the quantity of pollutants. The pollution-intensive sector is expanded too much with respect to the less pollution-intensive sector. The distortion of the sectoral structure implies a greater accumulation of pollutants. The zero price of environmental use does not provide any incentives to use resources in abatement, to develop new abatement technologies, or to look for more emission-favorable production technologies. The accumulation of pollutants reduces environmental quality; that is, quantitative growth with a zero price attached to environmental use leads to a negative qualitative growth. Finally, with a zero price, natural resources are overused; that is, too small a stock of resources is passed on to future generations.

Although economic growth influences environmental quality when there is a zero price assessed for environmental use, we cannot draw the conclusion that zero growth would be an appropriate measure by which one could achieve a better environmental quality and smaller depletion of resources.

Zero growth does not change the actual level of economic activities; thus, environmental pollution remains fixed at its given level. Zero growth does not even prevent a further deterioration of environmental quality; pollutants are still released into the environment and accumulated there. Environmental quality, then, can decline in spite of zero economic growth. Furthermore, zero growth does not imply that we would use resources more economically.

The relevant issue is not whether growth intensifies the conflict between the supply of goods and environmental quality, but rather the way growth has taken place previously. The structure of national output and the relationship between pollution-intensive and environmentally favorable production causes this conflict of objectives. As stated in chapter 2, the free use of the environment is the basic reason for environmental degradation. The environment cannot be used any longer as a free good for all competing uses. Instead, these competing uses must be evaluated, and the use of the environment allocated to those activities offering the highest merit.

If the zero price of environmental and resource use is abolished, the following consequences will ensue: There will be an incentive to use factors in abatement so that, production will be reduced and thus emissions decrease. The emission tax will cause a sectoral reallocation which disfavors the pollution-intensive sector and thus reduces emissions (improvement in environmental quality). We have the incentive to accumulate capital in abatement and to develop new abatement technologies. An incentive exists to use emission-favorable technologies in production. Finally, correcting the prices of natural resources implies that fewer resources will be demanded because of, for example, substitution by "cheap" raw materials or recycling. When the proper price of environmental use is taken into account, a set of adaptations takes place which improves environmental quality. The goal conflict between growth and environmental quality may be altered if these adaptations are considered. In the following analysis, the interrelationship between economic growth and environmental quality is studied in greater detail.

**Interdependencies among Environmental Quality,
Growth, and Resources**

Figure 13-1 illustrates in a very simplified way the problems discussed in this chapter. We assume that for a given technology the production function is characterized by decreasing marginal productivity (quadrant IV). With an increasing output, emissions will also rise (quadrant I). Resources can also be used in abatement (quadrant III).

    If the total resource stock $O\overline{R}$ (available in one period) is used in production, a maximal national product is attained (point B). If, on the other hand, only the resource quantity OC is used in production (and $\overline{R}C$ in abatement), emissions can be totally prevented by abatement. (Compare also figure 3-3.)

    Curve AB expresses that, under the simplified assumptions, emissions rise with output. There is a goal conflict between environmental quality and output or growth.

    Technical progress in production shifts the production function to the right (quadrant IV), the abatement function to the left (quadrant III), and the emission function downward (quadrant I). In these cases, curve AB shifts to the

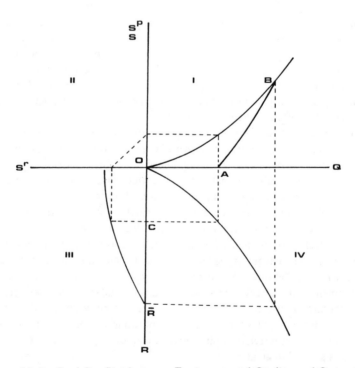

Figure 13-1. Goal Conflict between Environmental Quality and Output

right. In addition, the increase of the resource stock shifts curve AB to the right. The goal conflict between growth and environmental quality is then moderated.

Assume that the resources available for production are reduced. In this case, curve AB shifts to the left, and the goal conflict between environmental quality and output is intensified. If we then want to maintain a given output level, environmental quality will have to decline.

Growth and Environmental Degradation

In order to analyze the interdependence between economic growth and environmental quality, refer to the models in chapters 3 and 12. For purposes of simplification, we reduce the two-sector model to one sector; that is, the economy consists of one sector only. Let the resource R now be the capital stock K, so that the production function becomes $Q = F(K)$. The emission function, according to equation 3.1, is written as $S^p = Z(K)$; that is, emissions depend on input. From equation 3.1a we know that a concave production function implies a convex emission function Z; with $Z' > 0$, $Z'' > 0$. If it is assumed that pollutants are assimilated at a given rate α and if one disregards abatement, the equation of motion for pollutants[2] is

$$\dot{S} = Z(K) - \alpha S \qquad (13.1)$$

Contrary to the models in chapters 3 and 12, capital formation is explicitly taken into consideration. Net capital accumulation is given as savings minus depreciation; s denotes the propensity to save, and π is the depreciation rate of the capital stock:

$$\dot{K} = sF(K) - \pi K \qquad (13.2)$$

Equation 13.2 is explained in figure 13-2 which shows the components $sF(K)$ and πK of the $\dot{K}$ curve in the $\dot{K} + K$ space. The $\dot{K}$ curve is affected by the following: If $K < \bar{K}$, then $\dot{K} > 0$, that is, the capital stock increases. If $K > \bar{K}$, then $\dot{K} < 0$, that is, the capital stock decreases.

In the following analysis, we discuss how the system described by equations 13.1 and 13.2 behaves over time.

Zero Price of Environmental Use

In an explication model we ask toward which long-term equilibrium the economy will move if the environment can be used at a zero price. A long-run equilibrium, or steady state, is given when a capital stock and stock of pollutants are

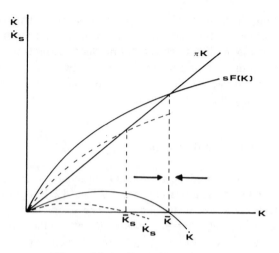

Figure 13-2. Capital Accumulation

reached which will not change; that is, we have $\dot{S} = 0$ and $\dot{K} = 0$. Consequently, we must search for conditions under which such a long-run equilibrium will come about.

When the $\dot{S} = 0$ curve holds,

$$\dot{S} = 0 \Leftrightarrow Z(K) = \alpha S$$

$$\left.\frac{dS}{dK}\right|_{\dot{S} = 0} = \frac{Z'}{\alpha} > 0$$

The $\dot{S} = 0$ curve increases progressively since $d^2S/dK^2 = Z''/\alpha > 0$. Consider a given K. A point on the $\dot{S} = 0$ curve characterizes the quantity of emissions $Z(K)$ for which $Z(K) = \alpha S$. The situation $Z(K) > \alpha S$ thus lies below the $\dot{S} = 0$ curve. There S has to rise. For $Z(K) < \alpha S$ (above the $\dot{S} = 0$ curve), we have $\dot{S} < 0$, that is, S falls (figure 13-3a). The $\dot{S} = 0$ curve shifts with a parametric change in α and the Z function. If the abatement rate of pollutants falls, the $\dot{S} = 0$ curve shifts upward. The same may be said if the emission technology deteriorates.

For the $\dot{K} = 0$ curve, we have $sF(K) = \pi K$, so that a capital stock $\overline{K}$ exists which generates exactly those savings that offset the depreciation of the capital stock. If $K < \overline{K}$, then $sF(K) > \pi K$ will hold true since with decreasing values of K, the output and thus savings decrease underproportionally. For $K < \overline{K}$, we have $\dot{K} > 0$. If $K > \overline{K}$, $sF(K) < \pi K$ holds, because with greater values of K, the output increases underproportionally. Consequently, $\dot{K} < 0$ when $K > \overline{K}$ (figure 13-3b). The locus of $\overline{K}$ varies parametrically with π and s. If the depreciation

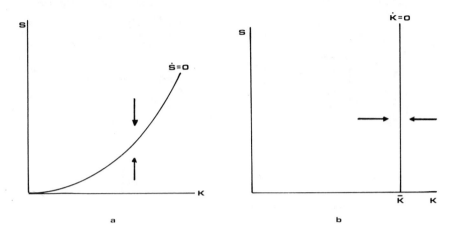

Figure 13-3. The $\dot{S} = 0$ Curve and the $\dot{K} = 0$ Curve

rate of capital becomes smaller, $\overline{K}$ shifts to the right. This is also applicable if the tendency to save rises.

Combining figures 13-2 and 13-3, we obtain a phase diagram of the economy in which no environmental policy is undertaken (figure 13-4a). Arrows indicate the directions of movement from a given location. The phase diagram is partitioned into four regions.

In the long run, a situation A with a capital stock $\overline{K}$ will be reached. The capital stock thus does not grow any more in this situation. This result is known from classical and neoclassical growth models. For a given technical knowledge and supply of labor, capital formation comes to a standstill in the long run, the growth rate of output becomes zero, and the economy reaches a stationary state. Growth is limited by the declining marginal productivity of capital. The rate of return falls, and capital accumulation becomes smaller and smaller.

In the long run, the accumulation of pollutants will also stop. The amount of pollutants absorbed by the environment (αS) will equal those pollutants simultaneously introduced into the environment by production (point A lies on the $\dot{S} = 0$ curve). Pollution comes about as a consequence of the growth process. If one were to assume an unfavorable emission technology $\widetilde{Z}$ with $\widetilde{Z}(K) > Z(K)$, a higher pollution stock for $\overline{K}$ would arise. At the same time, it becomes clear that in this context growth is interpreted "quantitatively" and not with consideration to environmental quality.

Consider region IV with an initial situation characterized by a small capital stock and a small stock of pollutants. Capital will grow. With capital accumulation, the stock of pollutants will increase. On a stable path in region IV we reach A. Assume, however, that we are in region III with a small capital stock and a large stock of pollutants. Then capital will increase and add to the stock of

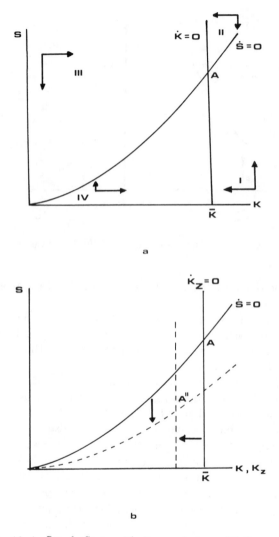

Figure 13-4. Steady State with Accumulation of Pollutants and
Environmental Constraints

pollutants; but more pollutants will be depreciated, so in the long run, situation
A can also be attained.

   If an economy is endowed with a high capital stock initially (with $K > \bar{K}$),
it will not be able to maintain this situation since this stock will wear out at a
rate stronger than that in which capital formation can take place. In region I the
emissions rise; in region II they fall.

Negative-Productivity Effect of Pollutants

Pollutants ambient in the environment may have a negative effect on output, as indicated by equation 3.8, so that[3]

$$Q = F(K, S) \quad \text{with } F_S < 0, F_{SS} < 0, F_{KS} = 0 \qquad (13.3)$$

While the $\dot{S} = 0$ curve is not influenced by this assumption, the negative productivity of pollutants affects output and the accumulation of capital. The equation of motion of the capital stock now becomes

$$\dot{K}_S = sF(K, S) - \pi K \qquad (13.4)$$

Note that equation 13.4 substitutes for equation 13.2. From figure 13-2 we see that the $\dot{K}_S = 0$ curve lies below the $\dot{K} = 0$ curve. We have

$$\left. \frac{dS}{dK} \right|_{\dot{K}=0} = \frac{sF_K - \pi}{-sF_s} \qquad (13.4a)$$

$$\frac{dS}{dK} \gtreqless 0 \Leftrightarrow K \lesseqgtr \widetilde{K} \quad \text{with } \widetilde{K} \Leftrightarrow sF_K = \pi \qquad (13.4b)$$

With an increasing capital stock, S rises at first, reaches a maximum for $\widetilde{K}$, and then falls. The negative impact of the productivity effect implies that less can be produced in comparison with the situation where $F_S = 0$ and that capital formation will also become smaller.

The $\dot{K}_S = 0$ curve is shown in figure 13-5a. Above the $\dot{K}_S = 0$ curve we have $sF(K, S) < \pi K$ since a high S has a negative effect on output and therefore on capital formation. As a consequence, the capital stock has to decrease above the $\dot{K}_S$ curve. Below the $\dot{K}_S$ curve, on the other hand, $sF(K, S) > \pi K$ holds because a smaller pollution pool allows a greater capital formation. The capital stock increases.

Figure 13-5b represents the phase diagram with four possible regions. In an economy characterized by the negative-productivity effect arising from pollutants, situation A' is reached in the long run. This situation is stable, in the sense that in all four regions a stable path exists tending toward A'. Environmental disruption is again a consequence of economic growth. An unfavorable emission function (a shift of the $\dot{S} = 0$ curve upward) would cause a greater quantity of pollutants. Given a very strong increase in pollution intensity (upward shift of the $\dot{S} = 0$ curve), it is also conceivable that the greater pollution pool could have such a strong negative effect on output and capital formation that the

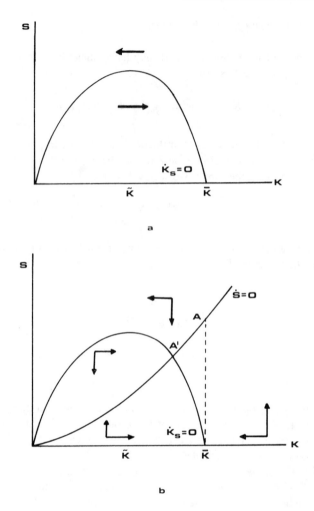

Figure 13-5. Steady State with Negative-Productivity Effect

pollution stock would be reduced in the long run (because of reduced capital accumulation).

Compare situation A in figure 13-4a with A' in figure 13-5b. The negative effect of productivity acts as a growth "brake." In the long run, the economy reaches a smaller capital stock (and thus a smaller level of output). With a smaller capital stock, a smaller pollution pool also results.

The Survival Issue

In figure 13-5*b* the negative effect of productivity can be considered as a growth brake. By way of a *Gedankenexperiment,* let the negative productivity effect become more important, that is to let F_S increase in absolute terms. This will move point A' in figure 13-5*b* downward towards the origin, because the F_S = 0-curve shifts downward and to the left. Clearly, this would be an unfavourable effect severely limiting the possibility to accumulate capital and to produce. In figure 13-6*a*, the same effect is illustrated by a movement from A' to D.[4]

Another unfavourable effect would be an increase in pollution per unit of capital, that is a larger Z', or a decline of the rate of assimilation, α. These phenomena would shift the $\dot{S}$ = 0-curve upward and to the left, implying more pollution with a given capital stock at a point D'. The combined effects will lead to a steady state D''.

If both effects keep operating, the economy would move towards the origin, suppressing economic activity. In that interpretation, the discussion can be viewed as a simple illustration of the survival issue. If some minimal capital stock is necessary for survival or if some level of pollution such as S' in figure 13-6*a* cannot be surpassed, steady state solutions such as D' or D'' may not be feasible.

Environmental Quality as a Normative Restriction for Growth

In the previous analysis, no environmental policy was undertaken. Assume now that in order to guarantee a certain environmental quality, normative restrictions fo environmental use are introduced. Assume that the government introduces an emission tax. Then an incentive is established to form capital in abatement. This implies, however, that less capital is available for production. If K in figure 13-4*b* denotes the capital stock in production, for a given capital stock in production there are fewer emissions because a part of the gross emissions is abated. The $\dot{S}$ = 0-curve shifts downward in figures 13-4*b* where the negative productivity effect is not considered.

The $\dot{K}$ = 0 curve also changes its position. The gross national product must provide consumption, capital formation in abatement $\dot{K}_A$, and capital formation in production $\dot{K}_Z$. We have

$$Q = C + \dot{K}_A + \dot{K}_Z$$

or

$$\dot{K}_Z = sF(K) - \dot{K}_A - \pi K \qquad (13.5)$$

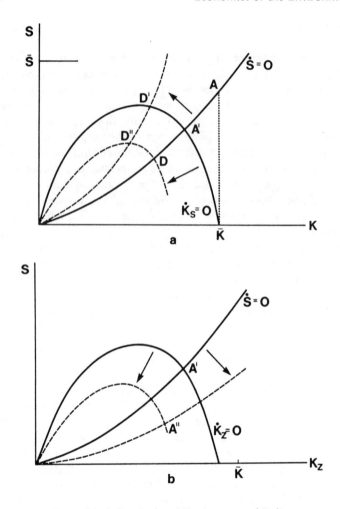

Figure 13-6. Survival and Environmental Policy

If capital is formed in abatement ($\dot{K}_A > 0$), the $\dot{K}_Z = 0$ curve shifts to the left. With the introduction of an emission tax (environmental policy), a smaller capital stock and a smaller quantity of pollutants result (situation A'' in figure 13-4b). A goal conflict exists between an improvement in environmental quality and economic growth. With environmental policy a smaller quantity of pollution comes about (and thus a better environmental quality), but this improvement is accompanied by a smaller capital stock and a smaller national product.

In figure 13-6b, the influence on environmental policy in the case of the negative productivity effect is shown. Again, the $\dot{S} = 0$-curve shifts downward.

The $\dot{K}_Z = 0$-curve shift downward, too, so that the economy moves from A' to A'' reducing pollution at the cost of capital in production.

Optimal Growth

While in the previous considerations environmental policy was introduced exogenously, one can also imagine the maximization of a welfare function for a finite or an infinite planning period. Such a model would be presented by the approach employed in chapter 12 and should be extended by an equation of motion of the capital stock in production and abatement. Although this approach is quite complex (with three state variables and three shadow prices for the state variables), the basic result is a normative decision between environmental disruption and the level of the national product, in other words, between qualitative and quantitative growth.

Growth with Finite Resources

In the previous section, environmental quality was regarded as a public-consumption good. The environment can also be viewed as a supplier of natural resources.[5] The survival issue can now be placed into a wider context with the following constituting elements. Pollutants accumulate from production (or as a function of the capital stock) and depreciate with a constant rate α according to equation 13.1. Capital is formed by savings, and the capital stock depreciates at a rate π (equation 13.2) The resource withdrawal in each period influences the change in the resource stock

$$\dot{R} = f(R) - X \tag{13.6}$$

where $f(R) = 0$ holds for nonrenewable resources. A production function describes the dependency of the output on the inputs (labor, capital, and resource use X) for a given technology T:

$$Q = F(A, K, X, T) \tag{13.7}$$

In addition, there is some restraint on the production system due to environmental considerations. Moreover, the population may increase. The question then arises under which conditions growth or survival will be possible. Whereas growth implies an increase for instance in income per capital, survival is defined with respect to some minimum level of income or consumption.[6]

In considering the production function, the relevant question is whether the resource is "essential". If one cannot produce without the resource, that is, if

$F(K, A, O) = 0$, then in the long run a situation cannot be maintained in which survival or growth are possible. The system will use up all resources in finite time and will collapse. A necessary condition therefore is that the resource is not strictly necessary for production, that is, if $F(K, A, O) > 0$.

If in a scenario of constant population and if technical progress is allowed to circumvent the resource scarcity issue, the problem remains how the environmental constraint will affect growth. It is no question that environmental constraints will reduce economic growth. Again, if enough technological progress is allowed, either in production or in abatement, growth is possible. If in addition we introduce population growth and at the same time want to guarantee survival (or growth) with giving due consideration to resource and environmental constraints, we must allow enough technological progress or sufficient adjustment in population change.

Notes

1. Compare Mishan (1969).

2. Compare equation 12.2.

3. For this model compare Forster (1972).

4. As a limiting extreme case, the curves could be suppressed to such an extent that the steady state would lie in the origin.

5. On the role of natural resources in growth compare Dasgupta and Heal or Siebert.

6. Krelle (1984, 1985) has developed the concept of a survival corridor for a society depending on the savings and the research ratio. Savings is instrumental in building the capital stock, research competing with savings and capital accumulation) is instrumental in substituting the natural resource. This concept should be extended to include environmental constraints.

14 Risk and Environmental Allocation

The frame of reference of our analysis of environmental use so far was a world of certainty. The fabrication of pollutants as a function of consumption and production, the accumulation of pollutants in the environment and their impact on environmental quality all were recognized with certainty. In reality, quite a few of the basic functions describing the role of the environment are not well known "ex ante". Emissions interact through rather complex and intricate systems and pollutants such as DDT accumulate through natural chains in a way that often is only discovered "ex post" with some delay. Variables strategic for the analysis of environmental allocation can therefore be considered as random variables. Pollutants as a by-product of our economic activities include the risk of potentially generating negative environmental impacts in the future. Risk of environmental effects may relate to small scale issues such as the eutrophication of a pond or to global problems as the heavily debated greenhouse effect from an increase in carbon dioxide or the destruction of the ozone layer. The problem arises what types of risk exist in using the environment, how these risks will influence environmental use if some optimal environmental quality is strived for, what implications will follow for environmental policy instruments and how the costs of risk reduction should be allocated to the decentral subsystems of a society.

Environmental Risks

Risks means that the implications of a decision cannot be fully determined "ex ante". Variables or interdependencies affecting a decision are random, i.e. the occurance of a specific value of a variable depends on a state of nature which cannot be controlled by the agent. Variables strategic to the problem of environmental allocation such as assimilative capacity, the stock of accumulated pollutants or environmental quality in a given moment of time diverge from a mean on both sides with the mean being defined as the expected value of the mathematical variance of possible results. Normally it is assumed that an agent can attribute probalities to a variety of outcomes, i.e. the agent knows a density function for the random variable.

Attitudes towards risk may vary between individuals. People may be risk averse, risk neutral or risk lovers. Consequently, a given probability distribution or (assuming a normal distribution) a given variance in a specific variable may not imply the same risk for different agents. Moreover, if all agents were to have the same risk attitude, the probability distribution of a specific variable may be relevant to one agent, but not to the other. Consequently, risk can only be defined with respect to the objective function and the restraint set of a specific agent. The risk that is specific to the objective function and the restraint set of an individual agent is called private risk. This type of risk is not correlated across persons and is also labelled independent risk (Dasgupta 1982, p. 81). If, however, a public good is a random variable we speak of social risk. Then the risk is correlated across persons, that is the risk is dependent. By definition, pure social risk must relate to all agents in the same way. Private risk can be shifted to another agent if he or she is willing to take over that risk possibly because a given probability distribution does not influence the target as negatively or even in a positive way. Social risk, however, cannot be shifted.

In the case of the environment, different types of risk relating to the different roles of environment can be distinguished. There is uncertainty with respect to the accumulation, the interaction and the spatial transport of pollutants. This type or risk relates to the diffusion function or to variables in the diffusion function. There is also uncertainty with respect to damages of a given quantitiy of pollutants. The magnitude of damages may not be known or the time when the damage arises may be undetermined. A specific problem may arise if threshold effects prevail and if the properties of these threshold effects cannot be determined "ex ante". Similarly, there may be the risk that a specific type of environmental use is irreversible. Other risks relate to the assimilative capacity of the environment or the generation of pollutants from consumption and production. Costs of abatement as well as production technologies may not be known "ex ante".

We are here mainly interested in the risk of environmental degradation for society as a whole where the environment is treated as a public good. Some risks in the area of environmental use may, however, be defined for specific agents. For instance, in the interpretation of the new political economy, the policy maker with the objective of being reelected faces the risk that the preferences of individuals with respect to environmental quality shift and that he may not have correctly anticipated the preference changes of individuals. The individual polluter, i.e. a firm, is exposed to the risk that he will be held liable for the pollution caused or that environmental policy instruments will vary over time.

In our analysis of environmental allocation we have stressed that the role of the environment as a consumption good relates to the public goods aspect whereas the environment as a receptacle of waste is a private good. Consequently, all risks referring to the public goods aspect of the environment are social risks where risk shifting is impossible and where the appropriate approach is risk reduction. The costs of risk reduction, however, can be attributed to those who use the environment as a receptacle of wastes.

In the discussion of the environment as a public good the free rider is a central issue. This problem also arises in the case of social risk when the probability distribution or (assuming a normal distribution) the variance in a variable representing a public good has to be evaluated. In this context, risk attitudes come into play. The risk attitude of a society can be considered as the aggregation of the risk attitudes of its individual members. Thus, determining the risk attitude of a society poses similar problems as establishing the time preference rate.

In addition to the aggregation of given individual risk attitudes, the perception of uncertain phenomena plays a decisive role for the aggregation problem and for policy making. Perception of uncertain phenomenon by a specific agent depends on his information and consequently on the distribution of information in society, so that the question arises whether perceptions and beliefs should be aggregated in the same way as individual preferences or whether time should be allowed for information to spread and for perceptions to change. Then, optimal allocation of risk should be based on ex-post and not on ex-ante perceptions (Dasgupta 1982, p. 70).

Risk and Environmental Quality

From a policy point of view, uncertainty relates to the impact of pollutants on environmental quality. A simply way to introduce risk is to interprete assimilative capacity in each period $\tilde{S}^a$ as a random variable being identically and independently distributed over time. Alternatively, risk may be introduced into the damage function

$$U = G(S, \tilde{\theta}) \tag{14.1}$$

so that environmental quality U becomes a random variable depending on the stock of pollutants and on states of nature $\tilde{\theta}$. Equation 14.1 can be simplified by assuming either that risk is additive

$$U = G(S) + \tilde{\theta} \tag{14.1a}$$

or that risk is multiplicative

$$U = \tilde{\theta} G(S) \quad \text{with} \quad \theta \leqslant 1 \tag{14.1b}$$

and $G_S, G_{SS} < 0$. Introducing randomness into a variable of the constraints in a maximization problem implies that the target variable itself becomes a random variable so that the policy maker maximizes the expected utility of the target variable subject to the constraints. Note that in equation 14.1b risk is assumed to be distributed identically and independently over time.

Assume that social welfare W depends on a private good Q and on environmental quality U. For simplifying purposes only one private good is considered. The welfare function is assumed to be well-behaved.

$$W = W(Q, U) \tag{14.2}$$

In order to model risk attitudes in the interpretation of the expected utility theory, let Γ denote a utility function indicating risk attitudes of society. Then the expected utility of social welfare in any given period is $E\Gamma[W(Q, U)]$. The policy maker maximizes the present value of expected utility from the welfare of society

$$\int_{0}^{\infty} e^{-\delta t} \{E\Gamma[W(Q, U)]\}dt \tag{14.3}$$

subject to equation 14.1b and the constraints in chapter 12. The maximization problem is spelled out in Appendix 14A.

The country is risk averse if $\Gamma' > 0$, $\Gamma'' < 0$. According to the expected utility theory the risk averse country chooses a linear combination of the possible outcomes. Thus, the country chooses the expected utility of welfare at point B instead of point A in figure 14.1a if the spread is α around the mean $\overline{U}$ and if the states $\overline{U} - \alpha$ and $\overline{U} + \alpha$ both have the probability 0.5. Consider now a mean-preserving spread in the random variable $\tilde{U}$, i.e. a stretching of the probability distribution around a constant mean. Then the country will choose point B' instead of B. Thus, an increase in the spread will reduce $E\Gamma[W(U)]$ for a given U.

Due to equation 14.1b expected disutility can be expressed as a function of the stock of pollutants S. Expected disutility of a stock of pollutants increases progressively with S due to G_S, $G_{SS} < 0$. A risk-averse agent will again choose a

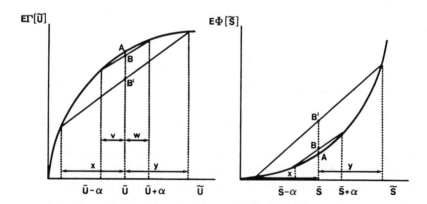

Figure 14-1. Expected Utility and Disutility

linear combination of possible outcomes such as point B in figure 14-1b. A mean-preserving spread in assimilative capacity or in $\tilde{\theta}$ will increase the expected disutility of pollutants (point B' instead of point B in figure 14-1b).

Whereas a mean-preserving spread definitely decreases expected utility of welfare from environmental quality (and increases expected disutility of welfare from pollution), the impact on expected marginal utility and disutility is indeterminate. From equations 14A.3b and 14.1b expected marginal disutility of pollutants is defined by

$$-E\Gamma'[W(Q, G(S))]W'_U \tilde{\theta}G'_S(S) = -E\phi'\{S\} \geqslant 0 \qquad (14.4)$$

The shorter term on the right hand side will be used in the text. Note that the curve $\Gamma(\cdot)$ and consequently Γ' is not affected by a mean-preserving spread but that $E\Gamma(\cdot)$ and $E\Gamma'(\cdot)$ will be influenced. The points of the curve $E\Gamma(\cdot)$ can be constructed geometrically for a given spread similar to point B in figure 14a. A mean-preserving spread will shift the $E\Gamma(\cdot)$ curve downward. However, even if we assume risk aversion, i.e. $\Gamma'' < 0$, the impact of a mean-preserving spread on marginal disutility will also depend on how risk aversion (Γ') changes with income or in our model with output Q. Neglecting the income effect and assuming that the planner is especially risk averse, a mean-preserving spread implies a higher expected marginal utility of welfare from environmental quality and thus a higher expected marginal disutility of welfare from pollution.[1] This is assumed to hold if risk is introduced as an increase in the spread of $\tilde{\theta}$; it is also assumed to hold if the spread in the random variable $\tilde{S}^a$ is increased with θ being set equal to one.

The Steady State

Conditions specifying the optimal use of the scarce input in production and abatement confirm the results of the case under certainty. The shadow price of the resource is equal to its marginal value product in production and abatement (Equations 14A.3c and d in the appendix). The contribution of a unit of output and a unit of environmental quality to welfare of society are now corrected for the marginal utility indicating a risk attitude (Equations 14A.3a and b).

Considering only the case of risk as the variance in $\tilde{\theta}$, we determine the properties of the steady state and the paths leading from a given situation to the steady state. The steady state is characterized by a situation which can be sustained indefinitely, i.e. in which the stock variables and the auxiliary variables do not change. For the shadow price, $-\mu > 0$, we have from equations 14A.3g, b and 13.4

$$-\dot{\mu} = -\delta\mu + E\phi'(S) \qquad (14.5)$$

The −μ̇ = 0 Curve

Setting −μ̇ = 0 we have

$$-\mu\big|_{\dot\mu = 0} = \frac{1}{\delta}E\phi'(S) \qquad (14.5a)$$

The −μ̇ = 0 curve increases progressively[2] with S. As in figure 12.1a, if −μ lies above the curve, −μ rises. If it lies below the curve, −μ falls.

The Ṡ = 0 curve

The resource use in production and in abatement activity depends on the level of the shadow price −μ. With an increasing −μ, more resources are used in abatement and fewer are used in production.

$$\dot S = H\{F[R(-\mu)]\} - F^r[R^r(-\mu)] - S^a \qquad (14.6)$$

A high −μ reduces the production of pollutants and increases the quantity of abated pollutants. A low −μ implies a greater production of pollutants and a smaller abatement. There is a shadow price −μ*, for which Ṡ = 0, or

$$\dot S \gtrless 0 \Leftrightarrow H\{F[R(-\mu)]\} - \tilde S^a \gtrless F^r[R^r(-\mu)] \Leftrightarrow -\mu \lessgtr -\mu^* \qquad (14.7)$$

Thus, the curve Ṡ = 0 is a horizontal line with a vertical section −μ* as in figure 12.1b. Above the straight line −μ*, Ṡ < 0 holds true, that is, S falls. Beneath the straight line −μ*, Ṡ > 0 is valid, that is, S increases.

Consider a given risk $\tilde\theta$ in the damage function and neglect the variance in the assimilative capacity. Then the steady state P with S^* and −μ* can be described in figure 14-2 in a fashion analogous to figure 12-2. Starting from a situation of high initial pollution $S(0)$, a stable situation S^* can be reached by the saddle path 1. A high initial penalty on pollution is an incentive to abate and reduce the stock of pollutants. Over time, the penalty is reduced.

Increased Risk in the Damage Function

Assume now that the risk in the damage function in each period is increased, for instance by a mean-preserving spread with more weight in the tails of the distribution. How will the steady state and the optimal path from a given initial level of pollution be affected? We consider the case that the marginal expected disutility of a given level of pollution as defined in equation 14.4 will be increased (see above). Then, the −μ̇ = 0 curve will shift upward; this implies that the steady state P moves to the left point P' in figure 14.2b.

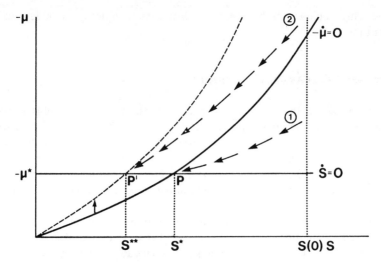

Figure 14-2. Risk in the Damage Function and Steady State

With more risk in the damage function, the time profile of the shadow price has to change if the initial level of pollution $S(0)$ is to be transformed into the new steady state S^{**}. The penalty for pollution will be higher initially as well as on the way to the steady state. In any given period before the steady state, the shadow price (in absolute terms) will be higher forcing the economy to generate less pollution. Thus, an increased uncertainty in the damage function implies a lower level of pollution.

The result depends on the assumption that increased uncertainty of environmental damages will increase the expected marginal disutility of pollution (for a given level of pollution) and that thus the $\dot{\mu} = 0$ curve is shifted upward. It can be shown that this assumption implies that the planner has an incentive to reduce the increased risk of environmental quality by just having a lower environmental quality.[3]

An increase in risk aversion of the policy maker will shift the curve of expected disutility in figure 14-2 upward, and thus will shift the $\dot{\mu} = 0$ curve upward. Consequently, if the uncertainty in the damage function remains unchanged and if risk aversion is increased, the steady state shifts to the left implying a Pontryagin path with a higher penalty on emissions.

In the analysis so far it has been assumed that risk is distributed identically and independently over time. If variance in the damage function increases over time, a lower level of pollution will be allowed in the steady state implying a higher shadow price for pollutants. Ecologists hold that threshold effects are typical for environmental damages so that information on environmental changes may only become apparent after pollutants had had their impact for a longer time. This would imply that risk is not distributed identically and independently over time.

Increased Risk in Assimilative Capacity

Assume now that the risk of the assimilative capacity in each period is increased, again by a mean-preserving spread with more weight in the tails of the distribution, whereas θ is set equal to one. How will the steady state and the optimal path from a given initial level of pollution be affected? In contrast to the discussion on $\hat{\theta}$-risk, our analysis now follows more intuitive and speculative reasoning.[4] Consequently, our results are conjectural and should be interpreted with some caution.

We assume that the marginal expected disutility of a given level of pollution as defined in equation 14.4 will be increased if there is more risk in assimilative capacity. Then, the $-\dot{\mu} = 0$ curve will shift upward; this implies that the steady state P moves to the left (point P') in figure 14.1b. Moreover, for $\dot{S} = 0$ to hold in equation 14.7, fewer emissions are required for a greater uncertainty in the assimilative capacity. This is only possible, if the shadow price $-\mu$ rises. The $\dot{S} = 0$ curve shifts upward. The steady state shifts from P to P'''.

The impact of an increase in the uncertainty of assimilation on the steady state can thus be broken down into two effects. First, an increased uncertainty in the assimilative capacity of the environment implies an increase of disutility

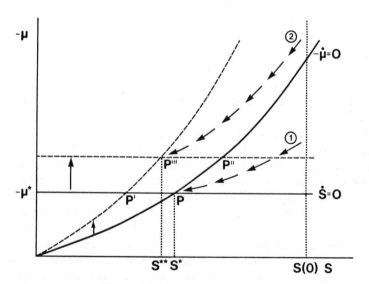

Figure 14–3. Risk and Steady State

of welfare from pollution. The $-\dot{\mu} = 0$ curve shifts upward (movement from P to P'). Second, assimilation becomes less likely, so that the $\dot{S} = 0$ curve shifts upward as if assimilative capacity would be reduced parametrically. (Movement from P to P''.) Lower assimilative capacity implies a larger stock of long-run pollution. This is due to the fact that abatement involves costs in terms of resource use foregone in production. The increase in the tolerable level of pollution, however, is restricted by welfare progressively declining with pollution.

With the increase in assimilative risk, the time profile of the shadow price has to change if the initial level of pollution $S(0)$ is to be transformed into the new steady state S^{**}. The penalty for pollution will be higher initially as well as in the steady state. In any given period, the shadow price (in absolute terms) will be higher forcing the economy to generate less pollution. Thus, an increased uncertainty in the assimilative capacity of the environment implies a lower level of pollution.

In figure 14-3 it has been assumed that the shift in the $\dot{\mu} = 0$ curve (PP') is stronger than the shift in the $\dot{S} = 0$ curve (PP''). We cannot exclude the opposite case with the movement PP'' dominating. In this case, it is conceivable that $S^{**} > S(0)$, so that $-\mu$ will actually rise over time and the system will move into a higher long-run level of pollution. This is due to the increased costs of abatement. Note, however, that $-\mu$ will be on a higher time path due to increased environmental scarcity.

Preventive Environmental Policy

Figure 14-2 illustrates the concept of preventive environmental policy (O'Riordan 1985; Simonis 1984). With the environmental impact of pollution being uncertain, a higher environmental quality is optimal in the steady state. In order to reach less pollution in the long run, a higher penalty has to be put on pollution. Thus, environmental risks make the environment more scarce. Higher environmental quality can be interpreted as an insurance against the risk of environmental degradation or as a risk premium.

Note that preventive environmental policy varies with the risk aversion of the policy maker. If he is very risk-averse, he will ask for a low level of pollution as an insurance against the risk of environmental degradation. The costs of environmental protection will be relatively high, and they will vary with risk aversion.

Preventive environmental policy also depends on the discount rate. Future disutilities are discounted thus having a lower weight in the present value of expected welfare. Therefore, the present value of welfare can be increased if the disutilities are postponed into the future, that is if a unit of pollution is accumulated at a later date. As in the case of certainty, a higher discount rate implies a lower environmental quality.

Irreversibilities

An important aspect of environmental risks are irreversibilities. When uncertain negative effects on the environment can be remidied in the future, risks may not be such a pressing problem. We only shift the costs of restoring or improving the environment to future generations. This still holds when the costs of restoration are very high. In the case of a pure irreversibility, however, the costs to remedy a negative environmental impact are infinite. Apparently, there exists a continuum of restoration costs between zero and infinity.

Environmental risks represent a serious problem if restoration costs are infinite, that is if pure irreversibilities exist. Examples are the extinction of a species or the destruction of a landscape that cannot be restored. Krutilla and Fisher (1975) have exemplified the problem with the Hells Canyon case where a Canyon is given up for a mine. Henry (1974) has discussed the problem of irreversibility with the example of turning Notre Dame in Paris into a parking lot.

Pure irreversibilities give rise to the question whether future benefits should be discounted. One solution to the problem is to use a lower discount rate, thereby giving more weight to the opportunity costs of the future. As an extreme case, if an irreversibility is judged to be crucial, a zero discount rate has to be applied. An alternative solution of handling irreversibilities is to explicitly introduce an option value being defined as the value, in addition to expected consumer's surplus from actually using a good, that arises from retaining an option to a good or service for which demand is uncertain (Krutilla and Fisher 1975, p. 70). For a risk-averse agent, the option price, i.e. the willingness-to-pay for keeping up an option, exceeds the expected consumer's surplus. Thus, the option value can be interpreted as an insurance premium or a risk premium against the irreversible loss of an alternative. Since the environment is a public good, the willingness to pay for an option cannot be determined by the market but must be established by other processes such as voting.

The concept of option value allows to introduce a specific value for avoiding an irreversibility. Note, however, that the debate on the discount rate or on the weight to be given to future generations cannot be completely separated from the determination of the option value. The option value will be affected by the discount rate.

If with the passage of time new information becomes available on the benefits and costs of a specific environmental use (Arrow and Fisher 1974), the relevance of irreversibilities will only come to light over time. Consequently, there is a positive option value even if the policy maker is not risk-averse.

Allocating Environmental Risks?

What institutional setting should be chosen in a society for the allocation of environmental risks and for the allocation of the costs for risk reduction? As an extreme answer to these two problems we perform a *Gedankenexperiment* and assume that exclusive property rights for the environment can be clearly defined so that the free rider does no longer exist. By this assumption, the environment has become a private good and environmental risks are no longer social risks. Assume bargaining costs and other transaction costs are zero. Assume also that the agents have objective probabilities for the occurence of specific states of nature. Then a Coase theorem (1960) should hold for a world with environmental risk where risk allocation will be optimal in the interpretation of Coase. Externalities relating to risk are perfectly internalized and the Coase theorem can be interpreted as the analogon to the Modigliani-Miller theorem (1958) for a world of environmental allocation. Stochastic phenomena would be transformed into deterministic market values.

We know that in the case of environmental risks such a situation cannot hold. Property rights cannot be clearly defined because the environment is a public good and not all facets of the public good can be taken away by specifying exclusive property rights. Transaction costs prevail. As a matter of fact, in an institutional setting with private property rights, transaction costs can be expected to be rather high. One aspect of transaction costs in the case of uncertainty would be liability arrangements with reliance on the judicial system. The increased role of courts would imply an ex-post allocation of risk and would give rise to a large uncertainty in private decisions. Thus, it is rather unrealistic to assume that environmental risks can be efficiently allocated through a Coase type scenario.

The risk of environmental degradation cannot be shifted because by definition the environment is a public good and the risk of its degradation is a social risk. The appropriate policy therefore is risk reduction.

Risk Reduction

The formal model presented in the previous sections takes a rather general and broad approach to risk reduction, namely to establish a higher environmental quality which can be interpreted as an insurance or a risk premium against uncertain environmental degradations. This approach of risk management may prove to be rather coarse and rough in the sense that a more detailed analysis of the risks envolved may allow to reduce the risk in a more sophisticated way. Consider for instance the case where environmental quality is measured by an index of several pollutants in different environmental media. Then preventive environmental policy requires that all pollutants are reduced in the proportion of their weight in the index. Apparently, risk management could be improved considerably if information would be available on the specific impact of different pollutants in different media. Research on the environmental impact of pollutants may increase information and thus reduce uncertainty.

A more detailed analysis of environmental risk would attempt to model these risks more specifically. An important aspect are the worst case scenarios which have a rather low probability of occuring, but would have tremendous negative impacts. An approach here is to cut off these cases. Of course, such an approach would depend on the costs involved. As an alternative approach, off-setting options for the worst case may represent an insurance premium (Dasgupta 1982, p. 74). Other aspects of a more precise modelling of environmental risks are the consideration of irreversibilities (see above) and restoration costs where applicable as well as the postponement of damages into the future (excluding irreversibilities) in the sense of diversification over time. Also a regionalization of public bads may be considered. For instance a hot spot policy, though in conflict with equity consideration, implies some type of spatial risk spreading.

Allocating the Costs of Risk Reduction

An important aspect of environmental risk management is how the costs of risk reduction are allocated to the agents causing the risks. In contrast to natural hazards such as earthquakes an important ingredient of environmental risks is man made, namely pollutants. Thus, one strategy of risk reduction is to attribute the costs of reducing the social risks to the decentralized units of the economy. By efficiently allocating the costs of risk reduction to those decentralized units that cause the social risk in the first place, an incentive is introduced to reduce the social risk. Here the results on the use of environmental policy instruments as discussed in chapter 8 hold. If the environment can be used free of charge as a receptacle of waste, no incentive is introduced to reduce emissions. If emission taxes, other pricing instruments for emissions and other policy instruments are applied, in a rather general way some of the social risk of environmental degradation is reduced. Thus, in a world with risk, we have to make use of the polluter-pays-principle; it requires that the costs of risk reduction should be attributed to the polluter.

The issue is to find not only an institutional mechanism that allows to attribute the costs of reducing environmental risks but also a mechanism that can be flexibly adjusted to new environmental situations coming to the foreground if damages are reversible. Which instruments should the regulator choose that allow a quick response to environmental degradation (Dasgupta 1982, p. 81)? When the attribution of social risks cannot follow flexibly to the arising of new damages or risk, i.e. when environmental policy cannot react quickly with its policy instruments to unforeseen damages, either the damages will be borne by the public as a public bad or the costs of damage reduction will be left with the government. Then the costs of risk reduction are not attributed to the polluter, and social risk will not be reduced in an efficient way.[5] Of course, if irreversibilities prevail, the flexibility of the policy response is not an issue.

The problem whether the political process can react swiftly to new environmental situations relates to two different aspects. First, the total quantity of tolerable pollutants ambient in the environment may have to be reduced quickly; second, instruments specifying emissions may have to be changed. The problem arises whether some policy instruments are better in taking into account the problem of uncertainty. Some people favor standards for individual facilities in order to cope with this type of uncertainty of environmental degradation claiming that the individual polluter can be controlled much better. However, it is highly questionable that in an institutional setting with emission norms for individual agents, that is non-transferable permits, the total level of pollutants ambient in the environment can be changed more easily than in a setting of emission taxes or transferable discharge permits. Emission standards and non-transferable permits may prove to be rather rigid in reality. Price mechanisms allow a better allocation of the scarce volume of tolerable emissions if emission taxes or effluent fees can be changed in some quasi-automatic way without parliamentary action for each change (see Chapter 8). Also, transferable permits will signal quickly variations in environmental scarcity. Moreover, price instruments will introduce a more stimulating incentive to reduce emissions in the long run.

The Response of the Polluter Under Uncertainty

The problem of risk reduction is more complicated than just to introduce incentives to lower emissions. The problem is that the environmental impact of pollution is uncertain. And the question is how this uncertainty should be reflected in the institutional mechanism of attributing the costs of risk reduction. The problem is aggravated by the fact that the agent drawing up the institutional setting does not only lack information on the impact of the level of pollution on the environment, but he or she also does not know how the individual firm or the individual household will react to the policy instruments chosen. The policy maker is unaware of the firm's abatement and costs function, its technology etc. When devising an institutional mechanism the regulator does not know the reactions of the different agents and, given their reaction, he does not know how their response will influence his policy target. In the German economics literature this general problem of economic policy has been studied under the heading Ordnungspolitik (Eucken 1952), more recently it has become known as the principal-agent problem.

How the individual polluter will steer this abatement processes if he faces uncertainty on the environmental policy instruments to be used (Dasgupta 1982,

Dasgupta, Hammond and Maskin 1980; Kwerel 1977) becomes relevant because the individual polluter experiences costs of adjustment when environmental policy is changed. These costs relate to capital costs, because abatement capital cannot be adjusted to new policy instruments quickly. Costs also relate to the production technology and such phenomena as location as well as sectorial and regional structure. In the case of uncertainty, the individual polluter will form expectations on the policy instruments used, and these expectations will influence his abatement behavior. Moreover, the polluter as a political group will attempt to reduce uncertainty by influencing policy instruments. Environmental policy instruments should be devised to reduce adjustment costs and to prevent "overshooting".

Notes

1. This procedure represents an ad hoc short-cut. Following Sandmo (1971, p. 67), we write the random variable $\tilde{\theta}$ as $\gamma\tilde{\theta} + \zeta$ where γ and ζ are multiplicative and additive shift parameters, respectively.

Assume

$$dE[\gamma\tilde{\theta} + \zeta] = 0 \quad \text{or} \quad E[\tilde{\theta}]d\gamma + d\zeta = 0, \quad \text{i.e.}$$

$$\frac{d\zeta}{d\gamma} = -E[\tilde{\theta}]$$

Then the optimality conditions in each period and for the steady state should be shocked by a change in γ. This exercise then would clearly indicate how the optimal solution, i.e. the optimal values for S^*, U^* and the other variables, is affected by a mean-preserving spread. Instead, we let $\tilde{\theta}$ be influenced by a parameter γ, allowing a change in the mean. Moreover, we consider a given level of pollution and thus we neglect the change in the level of pollution induced from an increased risk. Then, according to equation 14.4, the expected marginal disutility of pollutants is given by

$$-E\Gamma'(S, \gamma) = -E\{\Gamma'[W(Q, \tilde{\theta}(\gamma) \cdot G(S))] \cdot W_U[Q, \tilde{\theta}(\gamma) \cdot G(S)] \cdot \tilde{\theta}(\gamma) \cdot G'(S)\} \quad (1)$$

We neglect the impact of stretching the probability distribution on Q, that is we neglect the impact of a change in income on risk aversion. Then, derivation with respect to γ yields

$$\begin{aligned}
\partial[-E\Gamma'(S, \gamma)]/\partial\gamma = {} & -E\{\Gamma'' \cdot W_U^2 \cdot G(S) \cdot \tilde{\theta}(\gamma) \cdot G'(S) \cdot \tilde{\theta}'(\gamma)\} \\
& -E\{\Gamma' \cdot W_{UU} \cdot G(S) \cdot \tilde{\theta}(\gamma) \cdot G'(S) \cdot \tilde{\theta}'(\gamma)\} \\
& -E\{\Gamma' \cdot W_U \cdot G'(S) \cdot \tilde{\theta}'(\gamma)\}. \quad (2)
\end{aligned}$$

Rearranging terms we have

$$\frac{\partial[\ ]}{\partial\gamma} = -E\{\Gamma'' \cdot W_U^2 \cdot G(S) \cdot \tilde{\theta}(\gamma) \cdot G'(S) \cdot \tilde{\theta}'(\gamma)\}$$
$$-E\{\Gamma' \cdot G'(S) \cdot W_U \cdot [1 + U \cdot W_{UU}/W_U] \cdot \tilde{\theta}'(\gamma)\} \qquad (3)$$

Let a parametric increase in γ make a lower θ more likely and reduce environmental quality, that is $\tilde{\theta}'(\gamma) < 0$, as shown by the shift in the density function in figure 14-4a. Then

$$-U \cdot \frac{W_{UU}}{W_U} > 1 \qquad (4)$$

is a sufficient condition for the expected marginal disutility of pollutants to rise with a parametric increase in γ (neglecting the impact of a change in income on risk aversion). Note that this condition is not necessary.

Condition (4) requires a "strong" curvature of the welfare function with respect to environmental quality. Curvature in the welfare function can be a means to express risk aversion. Thus, the marginal expected disutility of pollutants will rise if the policy maker is sufficiently risk averse.

Note that introducing risk aversion into the usual utility function should not be confounded with the use of the expected utility function Γ.

The third term in equation 2 is negative; this term captures the impact of a parametric change in γ on expected marginal disutility for a given level of pollution assuming a given marginal damage and a given marginal utility. Set $\tilde{S} = \tilde{\theta}S$, then the third term of equation 2 can be written as

$$-E\left. \frac{d\Gamma}{dW} \cdot \frac{dW}{dU} \cdot \frac{dU}{d\tilde{S}} \cdot \frac{d\tilde{S}}{d\tilde{\theta}} \cdot \frac{d\tilde{\theta}}{d\gamma} \right|_{\bar{S}} < 0$$

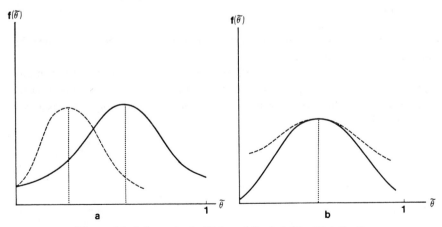

Figure 14-4. Increase in Risk and Probability Distribution

According to this effect, captured in the third term of equation 2, expected marginal disutility of pollution will be reduced, that is, marginal utility will increase due to more randomness in environmental damages. If only this effect (of the third term of equation 2) would prevail, the planner would increase pollution in order to reduce the randomness in environmental quality. If environmental quality is sufficiently low (and if the damage function 14.1b prevails which excludes for instance threshold effects) a larger spread does not imply a big loss in welfare. Thus, the planner can reduce risk by having a lower environmental quality (according to the third term). However, if the planner is sufficiently risk averse, for instance, if condition 4 prevails, he will not follow that policy. I owe the derivation and some stimulating questions on this point to Ernst Mohr.

If we assume a mean-preserving spread as in figure 14-4b, total derivation of equation 1 yields

$$d[-E\Gamma'(S, \gamma)] = -E\{\Gamma'' \cdot W_U^2 \cdot G(S) \cdot G'(S) \cdot [\tilde{\theta}d\gamma + d\zeta] \cdot [\gamma\tilde{\theta} + \zeta]$$
$$-E\{\Gamma' \cdot W_{UU} \cdot G(S) \cdot G'(S) \cdot [\tilde{\theta}d\gamma + d\zeta] \cdot [\gamma\tilde{\theta} + \zeta]$$
$$-E\{\Gamma' \cdot W_U \cdot G'(S)(\tilde{\theta}d\gamma + d\zeta)\} \tag{5}$$

Again, an increase in risk makes a lower value of θ more likely, so that $\tilde{\theta}d\gamma + d\zeta < 0$. Equation 5 can be interpreted in the same way as equation 2.

2. For a given θ, the change in $-\mu$ is given by

$$\frac{d(-\mu)}{dS} = -\frac{1}{\delta}\{E\Gamma''(\cdot)W_U'^2\theta^2 G_S'^2 + E\Gamma'(\cdot)W_U''\theta^2 G_S'^2$$
$$+ E\Gamma'(\cdot)W_U'\theta G_S''\} > 0$$

due to Γ'', W_U'', $G'' < 0$. The second derivation will be negative if $G''' < 0$, $W''' > 0$ and $\Gamma''' > 0$.

3. Compare footnote 1.

4. For a more formal analysis, a similar derivation as in footnote 1 would be necessary with respect to $\bar{S}^a$.

5. Note that there is a trade-off between flexibility and the insurance premium. If environmental policy cannot react quickly to unforeseen environmental damages, a higher insurance premium is mandated, i.e. a higher environmental quality has to be established.

Appendix 14A:
An Intertemporal
Allocation Model with Risk

The allocation problem for environmental use under uncertainty consists in maximizing the welfare function

$$\omega = \int_0^\infty e^{-\delta t} \{E\Gamma[W(Q, U)]\}\, dt \qquad (14A.1)$$

under the following restrictions:

$$\dot{S} = S^p - S^r - \overline{S^a} \qquad (14A.2)$$

Furthermore, the restrictions of the static allocation approach of equations 3.1 through 3.6 apply for every period. For simplifying purposes it is assumed that only one output is produced. If the problem is formulated in periodical values, the maximization problem is

$$
\begin{aligned}
L = {}& E\Gamma[W(Q, U) + \mu(S^p - S^r - \overline{S^a}) - \lambda_{SP}[H(Q) - S^p] \\
& -\lambda_Q[Q - F(R)] \\
& -\lambda_{Sr}[S^r - F^r(R^r)] \\
& -\lambda_U[U - \theta G(S)] \\
& -\lambda_R(R + R^r - \overline{R}) \max
\end{aligned} \qquad (14A.3)
$$

Necessary conditions for an optimum are

$$\frac{\partial L}{\partial Q} = E\Gamma'(.)W_Q' - \lambda_{SP}H' - \lambda_Q \leqslant 0 \qquad Q \geqslant 0 \qquad Q\frac{\partial L}{\partial Q} = 0 \qquad (14A.3a)$$

$$\frac{\partial L}{\partial U} = E\Gamma'(.)W_U' - \lambda_U \leqslant 0 \qquad U \geqslant 0 \qquad U\frac{\partial L}{\partial U} = 0 \qquad (14A.3b)$$

$$\frac{\partial L}{\partial R} = \lambda_Q F' - \lambda_R \leqslant 0 \qquad R \geqslant 0 \qquad R\frac{\partial L}{\partial R} = 0 \qquad (14A.3c)$$

$$\frac{\partial L}{\partial R^r} = \lambda_{Sr}F^{r\prime} - \lambda_R \leqslant 0 \qquad R^r \geqslant 0 \qquad R^r\frac{\partial L}{\partial R^r} = 0 \qquad (14A.3d)$$

$$\frac{\partial L}{\partial S^p} = \lambda_{S^p} + \mu \leqslant 0 \qquad\qquad S^p \geqslant 0 \quad S^p \frac{\partial L}{\partial S^p} = 0 \qquad (14A.3e)$$

$$\frac{\partial L}{\partial S^r} = -\lambda_{S^r} - \mu \leqslant 0 \qquad\qquad S^r \geqslant 0 \quad S^r \frac{\partial L}{\partial S^r} = 0 \qquad (14A.3f)$$

$$\dot{\mu} = \delta\mu - \lambda_U \theta G' \qquad (14A.3g)$$

Bibliography

Alchian, A., and Demsetz, H. 1973. "The Property Rights Paradigm." *Journal of Economic History* 33:16–27.

Anderson, F.R.; Kneese, A.V.; Stevenson, R.; and Taylor, S. 1977. *Environmental Improvement through Economic Incentives*. Baltimore, Md.: John Hopkins.

Anderson, R.C., and Ostro, B. 1983. "Benefit Analysis and Air Quality Standards." *Natural Resources Journal* 23:565–575.

Applegate, H.G. 1982. "A Discussion of U.S.-Mexico Experience in Managing Transboundary Air Resources: Problems, Prospects, and Recommendations for the Future." *Natural Resources Journal* 22:1169–1174.

——. 1982. "Transboundary Air Quality: Problems and Prospects from El Paso to Brownsville". *Natural Resources Journal* 22:1133–1139.

d'Arge, R.C. 1971. "Economic Growth and Environmental Quality." *Swedish Journal of Economics* 73:25–41.

d'Arge, R.C., and Kneese, A.V. 1980. "State Liability for International Environmental Degradation: An Economic Perspective." *Natural Resources Journal* 20:427–450.

d'Arge, R.C., and Schulze, W. 1974. "The Coase Proposition, Information Constraints and Long-Run Equilibrium." *American Economic Review* 64:763–772.

d'Arge, R.C.; Schulze, W.D.; and Brookshire, D.S. 1974. "Carbon Dioxide and Intergenerational Choice." *American Economic Review* 72:251–256.

Arnold, V. 1984. "Umweltschutz als internationales öffentliches Gut. Komparative Kostenvorteile und Verhandlungsgewinne." *Zeitschrift für Wirtschafts- und Sozialwissenschaften* 104:111–129.

Arrow, K.J. 1951. *Social Choice and Individual Values*. New York: John Wiley & Sons.

——. 1968. "Applications of Control Theory to Economic Growth." In *Mathematics of the Decision Sciences,* edited by G.B. Dantzig and A.F. Veinott. Providence: Mathematical Society.

——. 1971. *Essays in the Theory of Risk Bearing*. Chicago: Markham Publishing Comp.

Arrow, K.J., and Fisher, A.C. 1974. "Environmental Preservation, Uncertainty and Irreversibility." *Quarterly Journal of Economics* 88:312–319.

Asako, K. 1980. "Economic Growth and Environmental Pollution under the Max-Min Principle." *Journal of Environmental Economics and Management* 7:157–183.

Assaf, G.; Kroetch, B.C.; and Mathur, S. 1986. "Nonmarket Valuations of Accidental Oil Spills: A Survey of Economic and Legal Principles." *Marine Resource Economics* 2:211–238.

Atkinson, A.B., and Stiglitz, J.E. 1980. *Lectures on Public Economics.* New York: McGraw-Hill.

Atkinson, S.E. 1983. "Marketable Pollution Permits and Acid Rain Externalities." *The Canadian Journal of Economics* 16:704–722.

Atkinson, S.E., and Tietenberg, T. H. 1982. "The Empirical Properties of two Classes of Designs for Transferable Discharge Permit Markets." *Journal of Environmental Economics and Management* 9:101–121.

Ayres, R.U. 1972. "A Materials-Process-Product Model." In *Environmental Quality Analysis,* edited by A.V. Kneese and B.T. Bower. Baltimore, Md.: John Hopkins, 35–68.

Bailey, M.J. 1982. "Risks, Costs, and Benefits of Fluorocarbon Regulation." *American Economic Review* 72:247–250.

Baldwin, J. 1985. *Environmental Planning & Management.* Boulder, Co.: Westview.

Barnes, D.W. 1983. "Back Door Cost-Benefit Analysis under a Safety-First Clean Air Act." *Natural Resources Journal* 23:827–857.

Barnett, H.J., and Morse, C. 1963. *Scarcity and Growth: The Economics of Natural Resource Availability.* Baltimore, Md.: John Hopkins.

Baumol, W.J. 1968. "On the Social Rate of Discount." *American Economic Review* 58:788–802.

——. 1971. *Environmental Protection, International Spillovers and Trade.* Stockholm: Almqvist & Wiksell.

——. 1972. "On Taxation and the Control of Externalities." *American Economic Review* 62:307–322.

Baumol, W.J., and Oates, W.E. 1971. "The Use of Standards and Prices for Protection of the Environment." *Swedish Journal of Economics* 73:42–54.

——. 1975. *The Theory of Environmental Policy.* Englewood Cliffs, N.J.: Prentice-Hall.

——. 1979. *Economics, Environmental Policy, and the Quality of Life.* Englewood Cliffs, N.J.: Prentice-Hall.

Bayless, M. 1982. "Measuring the Benefits of Air Quality Improvements: A Hedonic Salary Approach." *Journal of Environmental Economics and Management* 9:81–99.

Beavis, B., and Walker, M. 1983a. "Random Wastes, Imperfect Monitoring and Environmental Quality Standards." *Journal of Public Economics* 21:377–387.

——. 1983*b*. "Achieving Environmental Standards with Stochastic Discharges." *Journal of Environmental Economics and Management* 10:103–111.

Becker, R.A. 1982. "Intergenerational Equity: The Capital-Environment Trade-Off." *Journal of Environmental Economics and Management* 9:165–185.

Bender, D. 1976. *Makroökonomik des Umweltschutzes.* Göttingen: Vandenhoeck & Ruprecht.

Bennett, R.J., and Chorley, R.J. 1978. *Environmental Systems.* Princeton, N.J.: Princeton University Press.

Binswanger, H.-Chr.; Bonus, H.; and Timmermann, M. (eds.) 1981. *Wirtschaft und Umwelt. Möglichkeiten einer ökologieverträglichen Wirtschaftspolitik.* Stuttgart: Kohlhammer.

Bishop, R.C.; Heberlein, T.A.; and Kealy, M.J. 1983. "Contingent Valuation of Environmental Assets: Comparisons with a Simulated Market." *Natural Resources Journal* 23:619–633.

Black, P.E. 1981. *Environmental Impact Analysis.* New York: Praeger.

Bogardi, L.; Bárdossy A.; and Duckstein, L. 1983. "Regional Management of an Aquifer for Mining and Fuzzy Environmental Objectives." *Water Resources Research* 19:1394–1402.

Bohm, P. 1970. "Pollution, Purification and the Theory of External Effects." *Swedish Journal of Economics* 72:153–166.

——. 1971. "An Approach to the Problem of Estimating Demand for Public Goods." *Swedish Journal of Economics* 73:55–66.

——. 1972*a*. "A Note on the Problem of Estimating Benefits from Pollution Control." In *Problems of Environmental Economics.* Paris: Organization of Economic Cooperation and Development.

——. 1972*b*. "Pollution: Taxation or Purification." *Kyklos* 25:501–517.

Bohm, P., and Kneese, A.V. 1971. *The Economics of Environment.* New York: MacMillan.

Bohm, P., and Russel, C.F. 1985. "Comparative Analysis of Alternative Policy Instruments." In *Handbook of Natural Resource and Energy Economics, Vol. 1,* edited by A.V. Kneese and J.L. Sweeny. Amsterdam, New York: North-Holland, 395–460.

Bonus, H. 1983. "Emissionslizenzen, Monopson und die räumliche Abschottung von Arbeitsmärkten. Bemerkungen zu Sieberts Anmerkung." *Zeitschrift für Wirtschafts- und Sozialwissenschaften* 103:57–62

Bonus, H. 1984. "Marktwirtschaftliche Instrumente im Umweltschutz." *Wirtschaftsdienst* 64:169–172.

Bonus, H. 1984. *Marktwirtschaftliche Konzepte im Umweltschutz. Auswertung amerikanischer Erfahrungen im Auftrag des Landes Baden-Württemberg.* Stuttgart: Ulmer.

Boudeville, J.R. 1966. *Problems of Regional Economic Planning.* Edinburgh: Edinburgh University Press.

Boulding, K.E. 1971a. *Economics of Pollution.* New York: New York University Press.

——. 1971b. "The Economics of the Coming Spaceship Earth." In *Environmental Quality in a Growing Economy,* edited by H. Jarret. Baltimore, Md.: John Hopkins, 3–15.

Braden, J.B., and Bromley, D.W. 1981. "The Economics of Cooperation over Collective Bads." *Journal of Environmental Economics and Management* 8:134–150.

Brady, G.L., and Cunningham, R.D. 1981. "The Economics of Pollution Control in the U.S." *Ambio* 10:171–175.

Braulke, M. 1983. "On the Effectiveness of Effluent Charges." *Zeitschrift für die gesamte Staatswissenschaft* 139:122–130.

Braulke, M., and Endres, A. 1985. "On the Economics of Efficient Charges." *Canadian Journal of Economics* 18:891–897.

Brookshire, D.S.; Eubanks, L.S.; and Randall, A. 1983. "Estimating Option Prices and Existence Values for Wildlife Resources." *Land Economics* 59:1–15.

Brown, G.J., and Max, B. 1968. "Dynamic Economic Efficiency of Water Quality Standards or Charges." *Water Resources Research* 4:1153–1159.

Brown, G.M., and Field, B.C. 1978. "Implications of Alternative Measures of Natural Resource Scarcity." *Journal of Political Economy* 86:229–243.

Brown, S.P.A. 1983. "A Note on Environmental Risk and the Rate of Discount (Environmental Externalities and the Arrow-Lind Public Investment Theorem)." *Journal of Environmental Economics and Management* 10:282–286.

Buc, L.G., and Haymore, C. 1983. "Regulating Hazardous Waste Incinerators under the Resource Conservation and Recovery Act." *Natural Resources Journal* 23:549–564.

Buchanan, J.M. 1966. "Joint Supply, Externality and Optimality." *Economica* 33:404–415.

——. 1969. "External Diseconomies, Corrective Taxes and Market Structure." *American Economic Review* 59:174–177.

Buchanan, J.M., and Stubblebine, W.C. 1962. "Externality." *Economica* 29: 371–384.

Buchanan, J.M., and Tullock, G. 1975. "Polluter's Profits and Political Response: Direct Controls versus Taxes." *American Economic Review* 65:139–147.

Buck, W. 1983. *Lenkungsstrategien für die optimale Allokation von Umweltgütern.* Frankfurt/M, Bern: Lang.

Burn, H.D., and McBean, E.A. 1985. "Optimizing Modeling of Water Quality in an Uncertain Environment." *Water Resources Research* 21:934–940.

Burness, H.S.; Cummings, R.G.; Mehr, A.F.; and Walbert, M.S. 1983. "Valuing Policies which Reduce Environmental Risk." *Natural Resources Journal* 23:675–682.

Burrows, P. 1979. *The Economic Theory of Pollution Control.* Oxford: Martin Robertson & Co. Ltd.

Burt, O.R., and Cummings, R.G. 1970. "Production and Investment in Natural Resource Industries." *American Economic Review* 60:576–590.

Burton, J. n.d. "Externalities, Property Rights and Public Policy: Private Property Rights to Prevent the Spoliation of Nature." *Mimeographed.* Kingston Polytechnic, Kingston upon Thames, England.

Byrne, R.F., and Spiro, M.H. 1973. "On Taxation as a Pollution Control Policy." *Swedish Journal of Economics* 75:105–109

Calabresi, G. 1968. "Transaction Costs, Resource Allocation and Liability Rules" *Journal of Law and Economics* 11:67–75.

Chappie, M., and Lave, L. 1982. "The Health Effects of Air Pollution: A Reanalysis." *Journal of Urban Economic* 12:346–376.

Cheung, S.N.S. 1973. "The Fable of The Bees: An Investigation." *Journal of Law and Economics* 16:11–33.

Christainsen, G.B., and Haveman R.H. 1981. "The Contribution of Environmental Regulations to the Slowdown in Productivity Growth." *Journal of Environmental Economics and Management* 8:381–390.

Clark, C.W. 1973. "Profit Maximization and the Extinction of Animal Species." *Journal of Political Economy* 81:950–961.

———. 1976. *Mathematical Bioeconomics: The Optimal Management of Renewable Resources.* New York: John Wiley.

Clarke, E.H. 1971. "Multipart Pricing of Public Goods." In *Public Choice*, Vol. 2. Den Haag: Martinus Nijdhoff, 17–33.

Coase, R.H. 1960. "The Problem of Social Cost." *Journal of Law and Economics* 3:1–44.

Cohen, M.A. 1985. *Optimal Enforcement Strategy to Prevent Oil Spills: An Application of a Principle Agent Model with Moral Hazard.* U.S. Federal Trade Commission. Bureau of Economics, Working paper No. 135.

Collinge, R.A., and Bailey M.J. 1983. "Optimal Quasi-Market Choice in the Presence of Pollution Externalities." *Journal of Environmental Economics and Management* 10:221–232.

Collinge, R.A., and Oates W.E. 1982. "Efficiency in Pollution Control in the Short and Long Runs. A System of Rental Emission Permits." *Canadian Journal of Economics* 15:346–354.

Collins, R.A., and Headley, J.C. 1983. "Optimal Investment to Reduce the Decay Rate of an Income Stream: The Case of Soil Conservation." *Journal of Environmental Economics and Management* 10:60–71.

Conrad, K. 1985. "The Use of Standards and Prices for Environmental Protection and their Impact on Costs." *Zeitschrift für die gesamte Staatswissenschaft* 141:390–400.

Conrad, K., and Morrison, C.J. 1985. *The Impact of Pollution Abatement Investment on Productivity Change: An Empirical Comparison of the U.S.,*

Germany and Canada. National Bureau for Economic Research, Working paper No. 1763.

Converse, A.O. 1971. "On the Extension of Input-Output-Analysis to Account for Environmental Externalities." *American Economic Review* 61:197–198.

———. 1974. "Environmental Controls and Economic Growth." *Journal of Economic Theory* 7:411–417.

Cummings, R.G., and Burt, O.R. 1968. "The Economics of Production from Natural Resources: A Note." *American Economic Review* 58:985–990.

Dales, J.H. 1968*a*. "Land, Water and Ownership." *Canadian Journal of Economics* 1:791–804.

———. 1968*b*. *Pollution, Property and Prices.* Toronto: University of Toronto Press.

Dasgupta, P.S. 1969. "On the Concept of Optimum Population." *Review of Economic Studies* 36:295–318.

———. 1980. "Decentralisation and Rights." *Economica* 47:107–124.

———. 1982. *The Control of Resources.* Oxford.

———. 1983. *The Control of Resources.* Cambridge, Mass.: Harvard University Press.

Dasgupta, P.S.; Hammond, P.; and Martin, E. 1980. "On Imperfect Information and Optimal Pollution Control." *Review of Economic Studies* 47:857–860.

Dasgupta, P.S., and Heal, G.M. 1979. *Economic Theory and Exhaustible Resources.* Welwyn: James Nisbet & Co, Cambridge University Press.

Dasmann, R.F. 1984. *Environmental Conservation.* 5th ed. New York: Wiley.

de Lucia, R.J. 1974. *Evaulation of Marketable Effluent Permit Systems.* Washington: U.S. Environmental Protection Agency.

de Meza, D. 1985. "Efficient Charges and Environmental Damage: A Classification." *Oxford Economic papers* 37:892–897.

Demsetz, H. 1967. "Toward a Theory of Property Rights." *American Economic Review, Papers and Proceedings* 57:347–359.

Der Rat von Sachverständigen für Umweltfragen. 1978. *Umweltgutachten 1978.* Stuttgart: Kohlhammer.

———. 1980. *Umweltprobleme der Nordsee.* Stuttgart: Kohlhammer.

———. 1981. *Energie und Umwelt.* Stuttgart: Kohlhammer.

———. 1983. *Waldschäden und Luftverunreinigungen.* Stuttgart: Kohlhammer.

Dewees, D.N. 1983. "Instrument Choice in Environmental Policy." *Economic Inquiry* 21:53–71.

Dnes, A.W. 1981. "The Case of Monopoly and Pollution." *Journal of Indian Economics* 30:213–216.

Dolbear, F.T. 1967. "On the Theory of Optimum Externality." *American Economic Review* 57:90–103

Dorfman, R., and Dorfman, N.S. 1977. *Economics of the Environment* New York: Norton & Company.

Downing, P.B. 1984. *Environmental Economics and Policy.* Boston, Toronto: Little & Brown.

Dreyhaupt, F.J. 1979. "Clean Air Plans in Air Quality Control Regions as an Instrument of Environmental Policy." In *Regional Environmental Policy: The Economic Issues,* edited by H. Siebert, I. Walter and K. Zimmermann. London, New York: New York University Press and MacMillan, 34–47.

Dudenhöffer, F. 1983. *Mehrheitswahlentscheidungen über Umweltnutzung. Eine Untersuchung von Gleichgewichtszuständen in einem Markt- und Abstimmungsmodell.* Frankfurt/M: Lang.

——. 1984. "The Regulation of Intensities and Productivities: Concepts in Environmental Policy." *Zeitschrift für die gesamte Staatswissenschaft* 140:276–287.

Eastham, G.M. 1982. "Air Pollution Abatement, Income Distribution and Interegional Labor Mobility." *Atlantic Economic Journal* 10:63.

Eisenbud, M. 1978. *Environment, Technology, and Health.* New York: MacMillan.

Endres, A. 1983. "Do Effluent Charges – Always – Reduce Environmental Damage?" *Oxford Economic Papers* 35:254–261.

——. 1982. "Taxing the Monopolistic Polluter. A Reconsideration." *Nebraska Journal of Economics and Business* 21:15–26.

——. 1985. *Umwelt- und Resourcenökonomie.* Darmstadt: Wissenschaftliche Buchgesellschaft.

England, R.W. 1982. "Workers, Capitalists, and Environmental Policy: An Economic Analysis." *American Economist* 26:39–45.

Enthoven, A.C., and Freeman, A.M. (eds.) 1973. *Pollution, Resources and the Environment.* New York: W.W. Norton.

Eucken, W. 1952. *Grundsätze der Wirtschaftspolitik.* Tübingen: Mohr.

Evans, J.S. 1984. "Theoretically Optimal Environmental Metrics and Their Surrogates." *Journal of Environmental Economics and Management* 11: 18–27.

Faber, M.; Niemes, H.; and Stephan, G. 1983. "Entropy, Environmental Protection and Raw-Material Consumption – A Natural Scientific and Economic Study." *Lecture Notes in Economics and Mathematical Systems* 214.1.

Fama, E.F. 1980. "Agency Problems and the Theory of the Firm." *Journal of Political Economy* 88:288–307.

Farber, K.D.; Dreiling F.J.; and Rutledge, G.L. 1984. "Pollution Abatement and Control Expenditures." *Survey of Current Business* 64:22–30.

Fisher, A.C. 1981. *Resource & Environmental Economics: Natural Resources & the Environment in Economics.* Cambridge, Mass.: Cambridge University Press.

Fisher, A.C., and Krutilla, I.V. 1985. "Economics of Nature Preservation." In *Handbook of Natural Resource and Energy Economics, Vol. 1,* edited by A.V. Kneese and J.L. Sweeny. Amsterdam, New York: North-Holland, 165–189.

Fisher, A.C.; Krutilla, I.V.; and Cichetti, Ch.J. 1972. "The Economics of Environmental Preservation: A Theoretical and Empirical Analysis." *American Economic Review* 62:605–619.

Fisher, A.C., and Peterson, F.M. 1976. "The Environment in Economics: A Survey." *Journal of Economic Literature* 14:1–33.

Forrester, J.W. 1971. *World Dynamics.* Cambridge, Mass.: Wright-Allen Press.

Forster, B.A. 1972. "A Note on Economic Growth and Environmental Quality." *Swedish Journal of Economics* 74:281–285.

——. 1984. "The Backward Incidence of Pollution Control: A Dual Approach." *Journal of Environmental Economics and Management* 11:14–17.

Førsund, F.R. 1972. "Allocation in Space and Environmental Pollution." *Swedish Journal of Economics* 74:19–34.

——. 1975. "The Polluter Pays Principle and Transitional Period Measures in a Dynamic Setting." *Swedish Journal of Economics* 77:56–68.

——. 1985. "Input-Output Models, National Economic Models, and the Environment." In *Handbook of Natural Resource and Energy Economics, Vol. 1,* edited by A.V. Kneese and J.L. Sweeny. Amsterdam, New York: North-Holland, 325–341.

Franke, J. 1980. "Environmental Policy and Market Structure in the Federal Republic of Germany." *Zeitschrift für Wirtschafts- und Sozialwissenschaften* 100:163–180.

Freeman, A.M. 1967. "Bribes and Charges, Some Comments." *Water Resources Research* 3.

——. 1972. "The Distribution of Environmental Quality." In *Environmental Quality Analysis,* edited by A.V. Kneese and B.T. Bower. Baltimore, Md.: John Hopkins, 243–280.

——. 1979. *The Benefits of Environmental Improvement; Theory and Practice.* Baltimore, Md.: John Hopkins.

——. 1985a. "Supply Uncertainty, Option Price, and Option Value." *Land Economics* 61:176–181.

——. 1985b. "Methods for Assessing the Benefits of Environmental Programs." In *Handbook of Natural Resource and Energy Economics, Vol. 1,* edited by A.V. Kneese and J.L. Sweeny. Amsterdam, New York: North-Holland, 223–270.

Freeman, A.M.; Haveman, R. H.; and Kneese, A.V. 1973. *The Economics of Environmental Policy.* New York: John Wiley & Sons.

Freeman, A.M. et al. 1984. *The Economics of Environmental Policy.* Melbourne: Krieger.

Frey, B.S. 1972. *Umweltökonomie.* Göttingen: Vandenhoeck & Ruprecht.

——. 1978. *Modern Political Economy.* Oxford: Martin Robertson & Co. Ltd.

——. 1979. "Interregional Welfare Comparisons and Environmental Policy." In *Regional Environmental Policy: The Economic Issues,* edited by H.

Siebert, I. Walter and K. Zimmermann. London, New York: New York University Press and MacMillan, 97–108.

——. 1985. *Umweltökonomie*. 2. erw. Aufl. Göttingen: Vandenhoeck & Ruprecht.

Frey, B.S.; Schneider, F.; Pommerehne, W.W. 1983. "Effluent Taxes and Economists, A Love Affair?" *Zeitschrift für Umweltpolitik* 6:187–194.

Friedmann, R., and Frohn, J. 1984. "Ein Konzept zur quantitativen Erfassung wirtschaftlicher Effekte umweltpolitischer Maßnahmen." *Zeitschrift für Umweltpolitik* 7:189–206.

Füllenbach, J. 1981. *European Environmental Policy: East and West*. London: Butterworth.

Furubotn, E.B., and Pejovich, S. 1972. "Property Rights and Economic Theory: A Survey of Recent Literature." *Journal of Economic Literature* 10: 1137–1162.

Gäfgen, G. 1985. "Ökonomie und Ökologie – Gegensätze und Vereinbarkeiten." Discussion paper, Konstanz.

Gallagher, D.R., and Smith, V.K. 1985. "Measuring Values for Environmental Resources under Uncertainty." *Journal of Environmental Economics and Management* 12:132–143.

Gebauer, H. 1985. *Regionale Umweltnutzungen in der Zeit. Eine intertemporale Zwei-Regionen-Analyse*. Frankfurt/M, Bern: Lang.

General Agreement on Tariffs and Trade (GATT). 1971. *Industrial Pollution Control and International Trade*. GATT Studies in International Trade. No. 1. Geneva.

Georgescu-Roegen, N. 1971. *The Entropy Law and Economics Process*. Cambridge, Mass.: Harvard University Press.

Giersch, H. (Ed.) 1974. *Das Umweltproblem in ökonomischer Sicht*. Tübingen: J.C.B. Mohr (Paul Siebeck).

Goldman, M.I. 1972. *The Spoils of Progress: Environmental Pollution in the Soviet Union*. Cambridge, Mass.: M.I.T. Press.

Gollop, F.M., and Roberts, M.J. 1983. "Environmental Regulations and Productivity Growth. The Case of Fossil-fueled Electric Power Generation." *Journal of Political Economy* 91:654–674.

Gordon, H.S. 1954. "Economic Theory of Common Property Resources." *Journal of Political Economy* 62:124–142.

Green, J., and Laffont, J.J. 1977. "Characterization of Satisfactory Mechanism for the Revelation of Preferences for Public Goods." *Econometrica* 45: 427–438.

Greenley, D.A.; Walsh, R.G.; and Young, R.A. 1981. "Option Value: Empirical Evidence from a Case Study of Recreation and Water Quality." *Quarterly Journal of Economics* 96:657–673.

Griffin, I.M. 1974. "An Econometric Evaluation of Sulfur Taxes." *Journal of Political Economy* 82:669–688.

Gronych, R. 1980. *Allokationseffekte und Außenhandelswirkungen der Umweltpolitik. Eine komparativ-statische Zwei-Sektor-Analyse.* Tübingen: J.C.B. Mohr (Paul Siebeck).

Grossman, S.J., and Hart, O.D. 1983. "An Analysis of the Principal-Agent Problem." *Econometrica* 51:7–45.

Groves, T., and Ledyard, J. 1977. "Optimal Allocation of Public Goods: A Solution to the 'Free Rider' Problem." *Econometrica* 45:783–810.

Gruenspecht, H.K. 1982. "Differentiated Regulation: The Case of Auto Emissions Standards." *American Economic Review* 72:328–331.

Hafkamp, W.A. 1984. *Economic-Environmental Modeling in a National-Regional System.* Amsterdam: Elsevier.

Hahn, R.W. 1984. "Market Power and Transferable Property Rights." *Quarterly Journal of Economics* 99:753–765.

Hardin, G. 1968. "The Tragedy of the Commons." *Science* 162:1243–1248.

Harford, J., and Ogura S. 1983. "Pollution Taxes and Standards. A Continuum of Quasi-optimal Solutions." *Journal of Environmental Economics and Management* 10:1–17.

Hartkopf, G., and Bohne, E. 1983. *Umweltpolitik. Bd. 1: Grundlagen und Perspektiven.* Wiesbaden, Opladen: Westdeutscher Verlag.

Haveman, R.H. 1973. "Common Property, Congestion, and Environmental Pollution." *Quarterly Journal of Economics* 87:278–287.

Head, J.G. 1974. *Public Goods and Public Welfare.* Durham, N.C.: Duke University Press.

Henry, C. 1974. "Option Values in the Economics of Irreplacable Assets." *The Review of Economic Studies* 41:89–104.

——. 1975. "Investment Decisions and Uncertainty: The Irreversibility Effect." *American Economic Review* 64:1006–1012.

Herfindahl, O.C., and Kneese, A.V. 1965. *Quality of the Environment.* Washington: Resources for the Future.

——. 1974. *Economic Theory of Natural Resources.* Columbus, Ohio: Merrill.

Hjalte, K.; Lidgren, K.; and Stahl, I. 1977. *Environmental Policy and Welfare Economics.* Cambridge, Mass.: Cambridge University Press.

Hotelling, H. 1931. "The Economics of Exhaustible Resources." *Journal of Political Economy* 39:137–175.

Howe, C.W., and Lee, D.R. 1983a. "Organizing the Receptor Side of Pollution Rights Markets." *Australian Economic Paper* 22:280–289.

——. 1983b. "Priority Pollution Rights. Adapting Pollution Control to a Variable Environment." *Land Economics* 59:141–149.

Hrezo, M.S., and Hrezo, W.E. 1984. "Judical Regulation of the Environment under Posner's Economic Model of the Law." *Journal of Economic Issues* 18:1071–1091.

Institut Economique et Juridique de L'Energie de Grenoble. 1975. "Alternatives au nucléaire: Réflexions sur les choix énergetiques de la France." Rapport préliminaire. Grenoble.

Isard, W. 1972. *Ecologic-Economic Analysis for Regional Development.* New York: The Free Press.

Jaenicke, M. (ed.) 1978. *Umweltpolitik: Beiträge zur Politologie des Umweltschutzes.* Opladen: Leske.

James, D.E.; Jansen, H.M.A.; and Opschoor, J.B. 1978. *Economic Approaches to Environmental Problems,* edited by R.J. Wakeman. Amsterdam: Elsevier.

Jarre, J., and Zimmermann, K. 1980. "Wettbewerbsverzerrende Wirkungen der Umweltpolitik? Der Fall des Benzinbleigesetzes." *Zeitschrift für Wirtschafts- und Sozialwissenschaften* 100:63–82.

Johnson, F.R. 1980. "Income Distributional Effects of Air Pollution Abatement. A General Equilibrium Approach." *Atlantic Economic Journal* 8: 10–21.

Johnson, R.W., and Brown, G.M., Jr. 1976. *Cleaning Up Europe's Waters.* New York: Praeger.

Joyner, C.C. 1984. "Oceanic Pollution and the Southern Ocean: Rethinking the International Legal Implications for Antarctica." *Natural Resources Journal* 24:1–40.

Kabelitz, K.R. 1983. "Nutzungslizenzen als Instrument der Luftreinhaltepolitik." *Zeitschrift für Umweltpolitik* 6:153–185.

Kamien, M.J.; Schwartz, N.L.; and Dolbear, F.T. 1966. "Asymetry between Bribes and Charges." *Water Resources Journal* 2.

Kapp, K.W. 1958. *Volkswirtschaftliche Kosten der Privatwirtschaft.* Tübingen: J.C.B. Mohr (Paul Siebeck).

——. 1970. "Environmental Disruption and Social Costs. A Challenge to Economics." *Kyklos* 23:833–848.

——. 1972. "Umweltkrise und Nationalökonomie." *Schweizerische Zeitschrift für Volkswirtschaft und Statistik.* 108:231–249.

Keeler, E.; Spence, M.; and Zeckhauser, R. 1971. "The Optimal Control of Pollution." *Journal of Economic Theory* 4:19–34.

Kennedy, W.V. 1980. "Environment Policy Review and Project Appraisal. The West German Experience." *Paper of the Internationales Institut für Umwelt und Gesellschaft des Wissenschaftszentrums,* Berlin.

Ketkar, K.W. 1983*a*. "Pollution Control and Inputs to Production." *Journal of Environmental Economics and Management* 10:50–59.

——. 1983*b*. "The Allocation and Distribution Effects of Pollution Abatement Expenditures on the U.S. Economy." *Resources and Energy* 5:261–283.

Klevorick, A.K., and Kramer, G.H. 1973. "Social Choice and Pollution Management: The Genossenschaften." *Journal of Public Economics* 2:101–146.

Kneese, A.V. 1964. *The Economics of Regional Water Quality Management.* Baltimore, Md.: John Hopkins.

——. 1971*a*. "Background for the Economic Analysis of Environmental Pollution." *Swedish Journal of Economics* 73:1–24.

——. 1971b. "Environmental Pollution: Economics and Policy." *American Economic Review, Papers and Proceedings* 61:153–166.

——. 1976. "National Resources Policy 1975–1985." *Journal of Environmental Economics and Management* 3:253–288.

——. 1977. *Economics and the Environment.* New York: Penguin Books.

——. 1984. *Measuring the Benefits of Clean Air and Water.* Baltimore, Md.: John Hopkins.

Kneese, A.V.; Ayres, R.U.; and d'Arge, R.C. 1970. *Economics and the Environment: A Materials Balance Approach.* Baltimore, Md.: John Hopkins.

Kneese, A.V., and Bower, B.T. 1968. *Managing Water Quality: Economics, Technology and Institutions.* Baltimore, Md.: John Hopkins.

——. 1972. *Environmental Quality Analysis: Theory and Methods in Social Sciences.* Baltimore, Md.. John Hopkins.

——. 1972. *Environmental Quality and Residuals Management.* Baltimore, Md.: John Hopkins.

Kneese, A.V.; Rolfe, S.E.; and Harned, J.W. 1971. *Managing the Environment: International Economic Cooperation for Pollution Control.* New York: Praeger.

Kneese, A.V., and Schulze, Ch.L. 1975. *Pollution, Prices and Public Policy.* Washington: Resources for the Future and the Brookings Institution.

Kneese, A.V., and Schulze, W.D. 1985. "Ethics and Environmental Economics." In *Handbook of Natural Resource and Energy Economics, Vol. 1,* edited by A.V. Kneese and J.L. Sweeny. Amsterdam, New York: North-Holland, 191–220.

Kneese, A.V., and Sweeny, J.L. (eds.) 1985. *Handbook of Natural Resource and Energy Economics, Vol. 1, 2.* Amsterdam, New York: Elsevier and North-Holland.

Koenig, E.F. 1984a. "Uncertainty and Pollution: The Role of Indirect Taxation." *Journal of Public Economics* 24:111–122.

——. 1984b. "Controlling Stock Externalities in a Common Property Fishery Subject to Uncertainty." *Journal of Environmental Economics and Management* 11:124–138.

Kopp, R.J., and Smith, K.V. 1980. "Environmental Regulation and Optimal Investment Behavior. A Micro-Economic Analysis." *Regional Science and Urban Economics* 10:211–224.

Kotzorek, A. 1984. "Zur Kontroverse über die Wettbewerbsbedingungen umweltpolitischer Instrumente. Eine Anmerkung." *Zeitschrift für Wirtschafts- und Sozialwissenschaften* 104:75–84.

Krelle, W. 1984. "Economic Growth with Exhaustible Resources and Environmental Protection." *Zeitschrift für die gesamte Staatswissenschaft* 140: 399–429.

——. 1985. *Theorie des wirtschaftlichen Wachstums,* Berlin: Springer.

Krutilla, J.V. 1967. "Conservation Reconsidered." *American Economic Review* 57:777–786.

———. 1972. *Natural Environments: Studies in Theoretical and Applied Analysis.* Baltimore, Md.: John Hopkins.

Krutilla, J.V., and Fisher, A.C. 1975. *The Economics of Natural Environments: Studies in the Valuation of Commodity and Amenity Resources.* Baltimore, Md.: John Hopkins.

Kühner, J. 1979. "Charge Systems in the FRG's Ruhr Area." *Mimeographed.* Washington.

Kuhl, H. 1986. *Umweltresourcen als Gegenstand internationaler Verhandlungen.* Dissertation, Mannheim.

Kwerd, E. 1977. "To Tell the Truth: Imperfect Information and Optimal Pollution Control." *Review of Economic Studies* 44:595–601.

Lancaster, K., and Lipsey, R.G. 1956–1957. "The General Theory of Second Best." *Review of Economic Studies* 24:11–32.

Lareau, T.J. 1981. "Alternate Stationary Source Air Pollution Control Policies: A Welfare Analysis." *Public Finance Quarterly* 9:281–307.

Larkin, A. 1986. "Environmental Impact and Institutional Adjustment: Application of Foster's Principles to Solid Waste Disposal." *Journal of Economic Issues* 20:43–62.

Lave, L.B., and Seskin, E.P. 1970. "Air Pollution and Human Health." *Science* 169:723–733.

Lee, J.K., and Lim, G.Ch. 1982. "Environmental Policies in Developing Countries. A Case of International Movements of Polluting Industries." *Journal of Development Economics* 13:159–173.

Lee, K. 1982. "A Generalized Input-Output Model of an Economy with Environmental Protection." *Review of Economics and Statistics* 64:466–473.

Lenihan, J., and Fletcher, W.W. (eds.) 1978. *Measuring and Monitoring the Environment.* Glasgow: Blackie & Sons Ltd.

———. 1979. *Economics of the Environment.* Glasgow: Blackie & Sons Ltd.

Leontief, W. 1970. "Environmental Repercussions and the Economic Structure: An Input-Output-Approach." *Review of Economics and Statistics* 52:262–271.

———. 1973. "National Income, Economic Structure and Environmental Externalities." In *The Measurement of Economic and Social Performance,* edited by M. Moss. New York: Columbia University Press, pp. 565–579.

Leontief, W., and Ford, D. 1972. "Air Pollution and the Economic Structure." In *Input-Output Techniques,* edited by A. Brody and A. P. Carter. London: North-Holland, pp. 9–30.

Lind R. (ed.) 1982. *Discounting for Time and Risk in Energy Policy.* Baltimore, Md.: John Hopkins.

Lindahl, E. 1919. *Die Gerechtigkeit der Besteuerung: Eine Analyse der Steuerprinzipien auf Grundlage der Grenznutzentheorie.* Berlin: Praeger.

Loehman, E., and De, V.H. 1982. "Application of Stochastic Choice Modeling to Policy Analysis of Public Goods: A Case Study of Air Quality Improvements." *Review of Economics and Statistics* 64:474–480.

Lowe, J., and Lewis, D. 1982. *Total Environmental Control: The Economics of Cross-Media Pollution.* Oxford: Pergamon.

Lyon, R.M. 1982. "Auctions and Alternative Procedures for Allocating Pollution Rights." *Land Economics* 58:16–32.

Macaulay, H.H., and Yandle, B. 1977. *Environmental Use and the Market.* Lexington, Mass.: Lexington Books, D.C. Heath.

MacDonald, G.J. 1972. "International Institutions for Environmental Management." *International Organizations* 26:372–400.

Mäler, K.-G. 1974a. "Effluent Charges versus Effluent Standards." In *The Management of Water Quality and the Environment,* edited by J. Rothenberg and P.G. Heggie. New York: MacMillan, 189–213.

———. 1974b. *Environmental Economics: A Theoretical Inquiry.* Baltimore, Md.: John Hopkins.

———. 1985. "Welfare Economics and the Environment." In *Handbook of Natural Resource and Energy Economics, Vol. 1,* edited by A.V. Kneese and J.L. Sweeny. Amsterdam, New York: North-Holland, 3–60.

Mäler, K.-G., and Wyzga, R. 1976. *Economic Measurement of Environmental Damage: A Technical Handbook.* Paris: OECD.

Magee, S.P., and Ford, W.F. 1972. "Environmental Pollution, The Terms of Trade and the Balance of Payments of the United States." *Kyklos* 25:101–118.

Malinvaud, E. 1971. "A Planning Approach to the Public Good Problem." *Swedish Journal of Economics* 73:96–112.

Maloney, M.T., and Yandle, B. 1984. "Estimation of the Cost of Air Pollution Control Regulation." *Journal of Environmental Economics and Management* 11:244–263.

Mangel, M. 1985. *Decision and Control in Uncertain Resource Systems.* London: Academic Press.

Marglin, S.A. 1963. "The Social Rate of Discount and The Optimal Rate of Investment." *Quarterly Journal of Economics* 77:95–111.

Markusen, J.R. 1975. "Cooperative Control of International Pollution and Common Property Resources." *Quarterly Journal of Economics* 89:618–632.

Martin, L.W. 1984. "The Optimal Magnitude and Enforcement of Evadable Pigouvian Charges." *Public Finance* 39:347–358.

McGartland, A.M., and Oates, W.E. 1985. "Marketable Permits for the Prevention of Environmental Deterioration." *Journal of Environmental Economics and Management* 12:207–228.

Mc Kelvoy, R. 1985. "Decentralized Regulation of a Common Property. Renewable Resource Industry with Irreversible Investment." *Journal of Environmental Economic and Management* 12:287–307.

Meade, J.E. 1952. "External Economies and Diseconomies in a Competitive Situation." *Economic Journal* 62:54–67.

——. 1973. *The Theory of Economic Externalities: The Control of Environmental Pollution and Similar Social Costs.* Leiden: Sijthoff.

Meadows, D.H.; Meadows, D.L.; Randers, J.; and Behrens, W.W. 1972. *The Limits to Growth.* New York: Universe Books.

Meadows, D.L. and Meadows, D.H. 1973. *Towards Global Equilibrium.* Cambridge, Mass.: Wright-Allen Press.

Meissner, W. 1985. "Prinzipien der Umweltpolitik." Paper presented at the IV. Zukunftskongreß der Landesregierung Baden-Württemberg 'Umwelt, Wirtschaft, Gesellschaft – Wege zu einem neuen Grundverständnis.' 17. – 18. 12. 1985.

Meissner, W., and Hödl, E. 1977. *Positive ökonomische Effekte des Umweltschutzes.* Berlin: Umweltbundesamt, Schmidt.

Mendelsohn, R. 1984. "Endogenous Technical Change and Environmental Regulation." *Journal of Environmental Economics and Management* 11: 202–207.

Mendelsohn, R., and Brown, G.M., Jr. 1983. "Revealed Preference Approaches to Valuing Outdoor Recreation." *Natural Resource Journal* 23:607–618.

Mestelman, S. 1982. "Production Externalities and Corrective Subsidies: A General Equilibrium Analysis." *Journal of Environmental Economics and Management* 9:186–193.

Miller, J.R., and Lad, F. 1984. "Flexibility, Learning, and Irreversibility in Environmental Decisions." *Journal of Environmental Economics and Management* 11:161–172.

Milleron, J.-C. 1972. "Theory of Value with Public Goods: A Survey Article." *Journal of Economic Theory* 5:419–477.

Mills, E.S. 1978. *The Economics of Environmental Quality.* New York: Norton.

Mingst, K.A. 1982. "Evaluating Public and Private Approaches to International Solutions to Acid Rain Pollution." *Natural Resources Journal* 22:5–20.

Mishan, E.J. 1969. *Growth: The Price We Pay.* London: Staples Press.

——. 1971. "The Post-War Literature on Externalities: An Interpretative Essay." *Journal of Economic Literature* 91:1–28.

Modigliani, F., and Miller M.H. 1958. "The Cost of Capital, Corporation Finance and the Theory of Investment." *American Economic Review* 48:261–297.

Möller, H.; Schneider, W., and Osterkamp, R. (eds.) 1982. *Umweltökonomik. Beiträge zur Theorie und Politik.* Königstein: Hain.

Montgomery, R. 1972. "Markets in Licenses and Efficient Pollution Control." *Journal of Economic Theory* 5:395–418.

Moore, S.A. 1981. "Environmental Repercussions and the Economic Structure." *Review of Economics and Statistics* 63:139–142.

Morgan, P. J. 1983. "Alternative Policy Instruments under Uncertainty: A Programming Model of Toxic Pollution Control" *Journal of Environmental Economics and Management* 10:248–269.

Mueller, D.C. 1979. *Public Choice.* Cambridge, Mass.: Cambridge University Press.

Müller, F.G. 1983. "Der Optionswert und seine Bedeutung für die Umweltschutzpolitik." *Zeitschrift für Umweltpolitik* 6:249–273.

Mumey, G.A. 1971. "The 'Coase Theorem': A Reexamination." *Quarterly Journal of Economics* 85:718–723.

Mumy, Gene E 1980. "Long-Run Efficiency and Property Rights Sharing for Pollution Control." *Public Choice* 35:59–74.

Musgrave, R.M., and Musgrave, P.B. 1976. *Public Finance in Theory and Practice.* New York: McGraw-Hill.

Newberry, D.M., and Stiglitz, J.E. 1981. *The Theory of Commodity Price Stabilization, A Study in the Theory of Risk.* Oxford: Clarendon Press.

Nichols, A.L. 1984. *Targeting Economic Incentives for Environmental Protection.* Cambridge, Mass.: MIT Press.

Niehans, J. 1975. "Economic Growth and Decline with Exhaustible Resources." *De Economist* 123:1–22.

Niemes, H. 1982. *Umwelt als Schadstoffempfänger. Die Wassergütewirtschaft als Beispiel.* Tübingen: J.C.B. Mohr (Paul Siebeck).

Nijkamp, P. 1977. *Theory and Application of Environmental Economics,* edited by A. Andersson and W. Isard. Amsterdam: North-Holland.

Noll, Roger G. 1982. "Implementing Marketable Emissions Permits." *American Economic Review, Papers and Proceedings* 72:120–124.

Nordhaus, W.D. 1973. "World Dynamics: Measurement without Data." *Economic Journal* 83:1156–1183.

——. 1974. "Resources as a Constraint on Growth." *American Economic Review* 64:22–26.

——. 1982. "How Fast Should We Graze the Global Commons?" *American Economic Review* 72:242–246.

Oakland, W.H. 1972. "Congestion, Public Goods and Welfare." *Journal of Public Economics* 1:339–357.

Oates, W.E., and Strassman, D.L. 1984. "Effluent Fees and Market Structure." *Journal of Public Economics* 24:29–46.

Oates, W.E., and McGartland, A.M. 1985. "Marketable Pollution Permits and Acid Rain Externalities: A Comment and Some Further Evidence." *Canadian Journal of Economics* 18:668–675.

OECD (Organization of Economic Cooperation and Development). 1972*a*. *Coûts de lutte contre les émissions dans la sidérurgie.* Paris.

——. 1972*b*. *Problems of Environmental Economics.* Paris.

——. 1972*c*. *Water Management: Basic Issues.* Paris.

——. 1973. *The Mutual Compensation Principle: An Economic Instrument for Solving Certain Transfrontier Problems*. Paris.

——. 1974a. *Environmental Damage Costs*. Paris.

——. 1974b. *The Polluter Pays Principle*. Paris.

——. 1974c. *Problems in Transnational Pollution*. Paris.

——. 1977a. *Emission Control Costs in the Fertilizer Industry*. Paris.

——. 1977b. *Emission Control Costs in the Primary Aluminium Industry*. Paris.

——. 1979. *Transfrontier Pollution, 1975–1978; Measures Related to OECD Recommendation C(74)224 on Principles Concerning Transfrontier Pollution*. Paris.

——. 1981a. *Compensation for Pollution Damage*. Paris.

——. 1981b. *Transfrontier Pollution and the Role of States*. Paris.

——. 1982a. *Photochemical Smog: Contribution of Volatile Organic Compounds*. Paris.

——. 1983a. *Hazardous Waste Problem Sites: Report of an Export Seminar*. Paris.

——. 1983b. *Wirtschaft und Umwelt. Die Verflechtung von Ökonomie und Ökologie*. Expertenbericht über besondere Umwelt- und Ressourcenprobleme für die Organisation für wirtschaftliche Zusammenarbeit und Entwicklung. Paris.

——. 1985. *Environment & Economics*. Paris.

Oehsen, J.H. v. 1984. "Ein erweitertes Standardmodell." *Jahrbücher für Nationalökonomie und Statistik* 199:49–64.

Olson, M. 1979. "On Regional Pollution and Fiscal Equivalence." In *Regional Environmental Policy: The Economic Issues*, edited by H. Siebert. I. Walter, and K. Zimmermann. New York: New York University Press, pp. 181–186.

——. 1982. "Environmental Indivisibilities and Information Costs: Fanaticism, Agnosticism, and Intellectual Progress." *American Economic Review* 72: 262–266.

Olson, M., and Zeckhauser, R. 1970. "The Efficient Production of External Economies." *American Economic Review* 60:512–517.

Opaluch, J.J. 1984. "Dynamic Aspects of Effluent Taxation under Uncertainty." *Journal of Environmental Economics and Management* 11:1–13.

Opaluch, J.J., and Grigalunas, T.A. 1984. "Controling Stochastic Pollution Events through Liability Rules: Some Evidence from OCS Leasing." *Spring* 15:142–151.

Ortolano, L. 1984. *Environmental Planning and Decision Making*. New York: Wiley.

Otway, H.J. 1980. "Perception and Acceptance of Environmental Risk." *Zeitschrift für Umweltpolitik* 3:593–616.

Page, T. 1977. *Conservation and Economic Efficiency: An Approach to Materials Policy*. Baltimore, Md.: John Hopkins.

Palmquist, R.B. 1982. "Measuring Environmental Effects on Property Values without Hedonic Regressions." *Journal of Urban Economics* 11:333–347.

Pasurka, C.A., Jr. 1984. "The Short-Run Impact of Environmental Protection Costs on U.S. Product Prices." *Journal of Environmental Economics and Management* 11:380–390.

Pearce, D.W. 1976. *Environmental Economics* New York: Longman, Inc.

Pearce, D.W., and Walter, I. 1977. *Resource Conservation: Social and Economic Dimensions of Recycling.* New York: New York University Press.

Peltzman, S., and Tideman, T.N. 1972. "Local versus National Pollution Control: Note." *American Economic Review* 62:959–963.

Pereira, P.T. 1983. "Developing Countries and the Economics of Irreversible Changes in Natural Environments." *Economia* 7:71–85.

Perl, L.J., and Dunbar, F.C. 1982. "Cost Effectiveness and Cost-Benefit Analysis of Air Quality Regulations." *American Economic Review* 72:208–213.

Perloff, H.S. 1968. *The Quality of Urban Environment.* Baltimore, Md.: John Hopkins.

Peskin, H.M. 1972. *National Accounting and the Environment.* Oslo: Aschehoug.

——. 1975/1976. "A National Accounting Framework for Environmental Assets." *Journal of Environmental Economics and Management* 2:255–262.

Peskin, H.M.; Portney, P.R.; and Kneese, A.V. (eds.) 1981. Symposium on "Environmental Regulation and the U.S. economy." *Natural Resources Journal* 21:441–587.

Peskin, H.M., and Seskin, E.P. 1975. *Cost-Benefit Analysis and Water Pollution Policy.* Washington: The Urban Institute.

Peterson, F.M., and Fisher, A.C. 1977. "The Exploitation of Extractive Resources: A Survey." *The Economic Journal* 87:682–721.

Pethig, R. 1975. "Umweltverschmutzung, Wohlfahrt und Umweltpolitik in einem Zwei-Sektoren-Gleichgewichtsmodell." *Zeitschrift für Nationalökonomie* 35:99–124.

——. 1976. "Pollution, Welfare and Environmental Policy in the Theory of Comparative Advantage." *Journal of Environmental Economics and Management* 2:160–169.

——. 1977. "Die gesamtwirtschaftlichen Kosten der Umweltpolitik." *Zeitschrift für die gesamte Staatswissenschaft* 133:322–342.

——. 1979. *Umweltökonomische Allokation mit Emissionssteuern.* Tübingen: J.C.B. Mohr (Paul Siebeck).

——. 1980. "Freifahrerverhalten und Marktversagen in einer privatisierten Umwelt." *Mimeographed.* University of Oldenburg.

——. 1982. "Reciprocal Transfrontier Pollution." In *Global Environmental Resources,* edited by H. Siebert. Frankfurt/M, Bern: Lang, pp. 57–93.

Pigou, A.C. 1920. *The Economics of Welfare.* New York: MacMillan.

Pittman, R.W. 1983. "Multilateral Productivity Comparisons with Undesirable Outputs." *Economic Journal* 93:883–891.

Plooy, L.H.E.C. 1985. "International Comparison of Industrial Pollution Control Costs." *Statistical Journal* 3:55–68.

Plott, C.R. 1966. "Externalities and Corrective Taxes." *Economica* 33:84–87.

Plourde, C.G. 1970. "A Simple Model of Replenishable Natural Resource Exploitation." *American Economic Review* 60:518–522.

——. 1972. "A Model of Waste Accumulation and Disposal." *Canadian Journal of Economics* 5:119–125.

Potier, M. 1979. "Environmental Aspects of Industrial Policy in a Regional Setting." In *Regional Environmental Policy: The Economic Issues,* edited by H. Siebert, I. Walter, and K. Zimmermann. New York: New York University Press, 221–240.

Prince, R. 1985. "A Note on Environmental Risk and the Rate of Discount: Comment." *Journal of Environmental Economics and Management* 12: 179–180.

Quirk, J., and Saposnik, R. 1968. *Introduction to General Equilibrium Theory and Welfare Economics.* New York: McGraw-Hill.

Randall, A. et al. 1974. "Bidding Games for Valuation of Aesthetic Environmental Improvements." *Journal of Environmental Economics and Management* 1:132–149.

Randall, A.; Hoehn, J.P.; and Brookshire, D.S. 1983. "Contingent Valuation Surveys for Evaluating Environmental Assets." *Natural Resources Journal* 23:635–648.

Raucher, R. 1986. "The Benefits and Costs of Policies Related to Groundwater Contermination." *Land Economics* 62:33–45.

Rawls, J. 1971. *Theory of Justice.* Cambridge, Mass.: Harvard University Press.

Reese, C.E. 1983. *Deregulation and Environmental Quality: The Use of Tax Policy to Control Pollution in North America and Western Europe.* London: Greenwood.

Reich, U.P. v., and Stahmer, C. 1983. *Gesamtwirtschaftliche Wohlfahrtsmessung und Umweltqualität. Beiträge zur Weiterentwicklung der volkswirtschaftlichen Gesamtrechnung.* Frankfurt/M: Campus.

Repullo, R. 1982. "A Note on Imperfect Information and Optimal Pollution Control." *Review of Economic Studies* 49:483–484.

Rhee, J.J., and Miranowski, J.A. 1984. "Determination of Income, Production and Employment under Pollution Control: An Input-Output Approach." *Review of Economics and Statistics* 66:146–150.

Ridker, R. G. 1967. *Economic Costs of Air Pollution.* New York: Praeger.

Ridker, R.G., and Watson, W.D. 1981. "Long-Run Effects of Environmental Regulation." *Natural Resources Journal* 21:565–587.

O'Riordan, T. 1985. "Anticipatory Environmental Policy. Impediments and Opportunities." Internationales Institut für Umwelt und Gesellschaft, IIUG, dp 85–1. Berlin.

Ro, Y.K., and Forster, D.L. 1984. "Regional Input-Output Analysis of an Environmental Regulation." *Journal of Economic and Development* 9: 167–188.

Roberts, M., and Spence, H.M. 1976. "Effluent Charges and Licenses and Uncertainty." *Journal of Public Economics* 5:193–208.

Robinson, D. 1985. "Who Pays for Industrial Pollution Abatement?" *Review of Economics and Statistics* 67:702–705.

Rolph, E.S. 1983. "Government Allocation of Property Rights: Who Gets What?" *Journal of Policy Analyses Management* 3:45–61.

Rose-Ackerman, S. 1973. "Effluent Charge: A Critique." *Canadian Journal of Economics* 6:512–528.

Rosenbaum, W.A. 1977. *The Politics of Environmental Concern.* New York: Praeger.

Rothenberg, J. 1969. "The Economics of Congestion and Pollution: An Integrated View." *American Economic Review* 60:114–121.

Rowe, R.D., and Chestnut, L.G. 1983. "Valuing Environmental Commodities: Revisited." *Land Economics* 59:404–410.

Runge, C.F. 1983. "Risk Assessment and Environmental Benefits Analysis." *Natural Resources Journal* 23:683–696.

Russel, C.S. 1971. "Models for Investigation of Industrial Response to Residuals Management Action." *Swedish Journal of Economics* 73:134–156.

——. 1973. *Residuals Management in Industry: A Case Study of Petroleum Refining.* Baltimore, Md.: John Hopkins.

Russell, C.S., and Vaughan, W.J. 1982. "The National Recreational Fishing Benefits of Water Pollution Control." *Journal of Environmental Economics and Management* 9:328–354.

Sagoff, M. 1981. "Economic Theory and Environmental Law." *Michigan Law Review* 79:1393–1419.

Samuelson, P.A. 1954. "The Pure Theory of Public Expenditure." *Review of Economics and Statistics* 36:387–389.

Sandmo, A. 1971. "On the Theory of the Competitive Firm under Price Uncertainty." *American Economic Review* 61:65–72.

Santrey, L. 1985. *Conservation and Pollution.* Mahwah, N.J.: Troll Assocs.

Savage, D.T.; Burke, M.; Coupe, J.D.; Deuchesneau, T.D.; Wihry, D.F.; and Wilson, J.A. 1974. *The Economics of Environmental Improvement.* Boston: Houghton Mifflin.

Schulz, B. 1983. *Effizienzkontrolle von Umweltpolitik. Eine integrierte ökonomisch-ökologische Analyse am Beispiel des Benzinbleigesetzes.* Frankfurt/M: Haag + Herchen.

Schulze, W.D. 1974. "The Optimal Use of Non-Renewable Resource: The Theory of Extraction." *Journal of Environmental Economics and Management* 1:53–73.

Schurr, S.H. 1971. *Energy, Economic Growth, and the Environment.* Washington: Resources for the Future, Inc.

Schwartz, Th. 1985. *The Logic of Collective Choice.* New York: Columbia University Press.

Scott, A. 1983. "Property Rights and Property Wrongs." *Canadian Journal of Economics* 16:555–573.

Segerson, K. 1985. "Unilateral Transfrontier Pollution: The Role of Economic Interdependence." *Land Economics* 61:83–87.

Sen, A.K. 1970. *Collective Choice & Social Welfare.* Amsterdam: Elsevier.

Seneca, J.J. and Taussig, M.K. 1984. *Environmental Economics.* 3rd ed. Englewood Cliffs, N.J.: Prentice Hall.

Seskin, E.P.; Anderson, R.J., Jr.; and Reid, R.O. 1983. "An Empirical Analysis of Economic Strategies for Controlling Air Pollution." *Journal of Environmental Economics and Management* 10:112–124.

Shapiro, M., and Warhit, E. 1983. "Marketable Permits: The Case of Chlorofluorocarbons." *Natural Resources Journal* 23:577–591.

Shell-Umwelt-Symposium. Bonn 7/1983. 1983. *Saubere Luft als Marktprodukt.* Stuttgart: Bonn Aktuell.

Shibata, H. 1972. "Pareto-Optimality, Trade and Pigouvian Tax." *Economica* 39:190–202.

Shibata, H., and Winrich, J.S. 1983. "Control of Pollution when the Offended Defend Themselves." *Economica* 50:425–437.

Siebert, H. 1973*a. Das produzierte Chaos. Ökonomie und Umwelt.* Stuttgart: Kohlhammer.

——. 1973*b.* "Environment and Regional Growth." *Zeitschrift für Nationalökonomie* 33:79–85.

——. 1974*a.* "Comparative Advantage and Environmental Policy: A Note." *Zeitschrift für Nationalökonomie* 34:397–402.

——. 1974*b.* "Environmental Protection and International Specialization." *Weltwirtschaftliches Archiv* 110:494–508.

——. 1974*c.* "Trade and Environment." In *The International Division of Labour. Problems and Perspectives,* edited by Herbert Giersch. Tübingen: J.C.B. Mohr (Paul Siebeck), 108–121.

——. 1975*a.* "Externalities, Environmental Quality and Allocation." *Zeitschrift für Wirtschafts- und Sozialwissenschaften* 1:17–32.

——. 1975*b.* "Regional Aspects of Environmental Allocation." *Zeitschrift für die gesamte Staatswissenschaft* 131:496–513.

——. 1975*c.* "Resource Withdrawal, Productivity Effect and Environmental Policy: Comment." *Weltwirtschaftliches Archiv* III:(3):569–572.

——. 1976*a.* "Environmental Control, Economic Structures and International Trade." *Studies in International Environmental Economics,* edited by I. Walter. New York: John Wiley & Sons, 29–56.

——. 1976*b.* "Erfolgsbedingungen einer Abgabenlösung (Steuer/Gebühren) in der Umweltpolitik." *Ökonomische Probleme der Umweltschutzpolitik,* edited by O. Issing. Schriften des Vereins für Socialpolitik, Band 91. Berlin: Duncker & Humblot, 35–64.

——. 1976*c. Analyse der Instrumente der Umweltpolitik.* Göttingen: Schwartz & Co.

——. 1977*a.* "Die Grundprobleme des Umweltschutzes. Eine wirtschaftstheoretische Analyse." In *Soziale Probleme der modernen Industriegesellschaft,* edited by B. Külp und H.-D. Haas. Schriften des Vereins für Socialpolitik, Band 92. Berlin: Duncker & Humblot, 141–182.

——. 1977*b.* "Environmental Pollution and Integration." *Contributed Papers to the Conference of the International Economic Association.* Budapest: Akadémiai Kiadó, 155–163.

——. 1977*c.* "Environmental Quality and the Gains from Trade." *Kyklos* 30: 657–673.

——. 1978*a.* "Environmental Policy, Allocation of Resources, Sector Structure and Comparative Price Advantage." *Zeitschrift für Wirtschafts- und Sozialwissenschaften* 98:281–293.

——. 1978*b. Ökonomische Theorie der Umwelt.* Tübingen: J.C.B. Mohr (Paul Siebeck).

——. 1978*c.* "Regional Planning – Land Use Approaches to Environmental Quality Management." In *Proceedings of the Seminar on Environmental Pollution Control in the Context of Regional Planning.* Kattowice, Poland.

——. 1979*a.* "Environmental Policy in the Two-Country Case." *Zeitschrift für Nationalökonomie* 39:259–274.

——. 1979*b.* "Dynamic Aspects of Regional Environmental Allocations: A Comment." In *Regional Environmental Policy: The Economic Issues,* edited by H. Siebert, I. Walter, and K. Zimmermann. London, New York: New York University Press and McMillan, pp. 148–151.

——. 1979*c.* "The Regional Dimensions of Environmental Policy." In *Regional Environmental Policy: The Economic Issues,* edited by H. Siebert, I. Walter, and K. Zimmermann. London, New York: New York University Press and McMillan, pp. 1–12.

——. (ed.) 1979*d. Umwelt und wirtschaftliche Entwicklung.* Darmstadt: Wissenschaftliche Buchgesellschaft.

——. (with A.B. Antal) 1979*e. The Political Economy of Environmental Protection.* Greenwich, Conn.: JAI Press Inc.

——. (ed.) 1979*f. Regional Environmental Policy: The Economic Issues,* edited by H. Siebert, I. Walter, and K. Zimmermann. London, New York: New York University Press and McMillan.

——. 1981*a. Economics of the Environment.* Lexington: D.C. Heath.

——. 1981*b.* "Praktische Schwierigkeiten bei der Steuerung der Umweltnutzung über Preise." In *Marktwirtschaft und Umwelt,* edited by L. Wegehenkel. Tübingen: J.C.B. Mohr (Paul Siebeck), pp. 28–53.

———. (ed.) 1982*a*. *Umweltallokation im Raum*. Schriftenreihe des Sonderforschungsbereichs 5 'Staatliche Allokationspolitik im marktwirtschaftlichen System', Vol. 1. Frankfurt/M and Bern: Lang.

———. 1982*b*. "Environmental Policy Instruments. Some Open Questions." In *Umweltallokation im Raum*. Schriftenreihe des Sonderforschungsbereichs 5 'Staatliche Allokationspolitik im marktwirtschaftlichen System', Vol. 1, edited by H. Siebert. Frankfurt/M and Bern: Lang.

———. (ed.) 1982*c*. *Global Environmental Resources*. Schriftenreihe des Sonderforschungsbereichs 5 'Staatliche Allokationspolitik im marktwirtschaftlichen System', Vol. 2. Frankfurt/M, Bern: Lang.

———. 1982*d*. "Emissionslizenzen, Monopson und die räumliche Abschottung von Arbeitsmärkten. Eine Anmerkung." *Zeitschrift für Wirtschafts- und Sozialwissenschaften* 102:279–287.

———. 1982*e*. "Instrumente der Umweltpolitik. Die ökonomische Perspektive." *Umweltökonomik*, edited by H. Möller, R. Osterkamp, and W. Schneider. Königstein: Hanstein, 284–294.

———. 1982*f*. "Nature as a Life Support System. Renewable Resources and Environmental Disruption." *Zeitschrift für die Nationalökonomie* 42.2: 133–142.

———. 1982*g*. "Negative Externalities, Environmental Quality and the Transformation Space." In *Economic Theory of Natural Resources,* edited by W. Eichhorn; R. Henn; K. Neumann; and R.W. Shephard. Wien: Würzburg, 489–506.

———. 1982*h*. "Neure Entwicklungen in der ökonomischen Analyse des Umweltschutzes." In *Umweltökonomik,* edited by H. Möller, R. Osterkamp, and W. Schneider. Königstein: Hanstein, 267–283.

———. 1982*i*. "Ökonomische Anreize in der TA-Luft." *Wirtschaftsdienst* 11: 560–564.

———. 1982*j*. "The Partitioning of Constraints." *Zeitschrift für die gesamte Staatswissenschaft* 138:109–117.

———. 1983*a*. "Luftreinhaltepolitik vom Standpunkt der Volkswirtschaftslehre." In *Funkkolleg Mensch und Umwelt, Vol. 2,* edited by T. Dahlhoff et al. Frankfurt: Fischer, 78–81.

———. 1983*b*. *Marktwirtschaftliche Ansätze in der Umweltpolitik.* Volkswirtschaftliche Korrespondenz der Adolf-Weber-Stiftung. München.

———. 1983*c*. *Ökonomische Theorie natürlicher Ressourcen.* Tübingen: J.C.B. Mohr (Paul Siebeck).

———. (ed.) 1984*a*. *Intertemporale Allokation.* Schriftenreihe des Sonderforschungsbereichs 5 'Staatliche Allokationspolitik im marktwirtschaftlichen System', Vol. 10. Frankfurt/M, Bern: Lang.

———. 1984*b*. "Umweltschutz und Wirtschaftswachstum. Überwindung eines Zielkonflikts?" *Gesellschaft der Freunde der Universität Mannheim. Mitteilungen* 4:15–23.

———. 1984*c*. "Intertemporale Interdependenzen wirtschaftlicher Entscheidungen." In *Intertemporale Allokation,* edited by H. Siebert, Frankfurt/M, Bern: Lang, 3–44.

——. 1985*a.* "Spatial Aspects of Environmental Economics." In *Handbook of Natural Resource and Energy Economics, Bd. 1,* edited by A.V. Kneese and J.L. Sweeny. Amsterdam: Elsevier.

——. 1985*b.* "TA-Luft 85: Eine verfeinerte Politik des einzelnen Schornsteins." *Wirtschaftsdienst* 65:452–455.

——. 1985*c.* "Zum Zielkonflikt zwischen Wachstum und Umwelt." In *Rationale Wirtschaftspolitik in komplexen Gesellschaften, Gérard Gäfgen zum 60. Geburtstag,* edited by H. Milde and H.G. Monissen. Stuttgart: Kohlhammer, 385–398.

——. 1986. *Umweltschäden als Problem der Unsicherheitsbewältigung: Prävention und Risikoallokation.* Discussion paper Konstanz.

Siebert, H.; Eichberger, J.; Gronych, R.; and Pethig, R. 1980. *Trade and Environment. A Theoretical Enquiry.* Amsterdam: Elsevier.

Siebert, H.; Walter, I.; and Zimmermann, K. (eds.) 1980. *Regional Environmental Policy: The Economic Issues.* London, New York: New York University Press and McMillan.

Silver, M. 1983. *Saubere Luft als Marktprodukt.* Stuttgart: Bonn Aktuell.

Simonis, U.E. (ed.) 1983. *Ökonomie und Ökologie. Auswege aus einem Konflikt.* Karlsruhe: C.F. Müller.

——. 1984. "Preventive Environmental Policy. Concept and Data Requirements." Internationales Institut für Umwelt und Gesellschaft, IIUG, dp 84–12. Berlin.

Slutzky, S. 1977. "A Voting Model for the Allocation of Public Goods: Existence of an Equilibrium." *Journal of Economic Theory* 14:299–325.

Smith, R.J. 1982. "Privatizing the Environment." *Policy Review* 20:11–50.

Smith, V.K. 1972*a.* "Dynamics of Waste Accumulation: Disposal versus Recycling." *Quarterly Journal of Economics* 86:600–616.

——. 1972*b.* "The Implication of Common Property Resources for Technical Change." *European Economic Review* 3:469–479.

——. 1975. "Relative Prices, Technical Change and Environmental Preservation." *Natural Resources Journal* 1975:283–295.

——. (ed.) 1979. *Scarcity and Growth Reconsidered,* Baltimore, Md.: John Hopkins.

——. 1981. "CO_2, Climate, and Statistical Inference: A Note on Asking the Right Questions." *Journal of Environmental Economics and Management* 8:391–394.

——. 1983*a.* "Estimating Water Quality Benefits. An Econometric Analysis." *Southern Economic Journal* 50:422–437.

——. 1983*b.* "Option Value: A Conceptional Overview." *Southern Economic Journal* 49:654–668.

——. 1984. (ed.) Environmental Policy under Reagan's Executive Order: The

Role of Benefit-Cost Analysis. Urban & Regional Policy & Development Studies. University of North Carolina Press.

Smith, V.K., and Krutilla, J.V. 1984. "Economic Growth, Resource Availability, and Environmental Quality." *American Economic Review* 74:226–230.

Snower, Dennis J. 1982. "Dynamic Environmental Targets and Technological Progress." *International Economic Review* 23:61–78.

Solow, R.M. 1974. "The Economics of Resources or the Resources of Economics." *American Economic Review* 64:1–14.

Sontheimer, K.C. 1979. "Technical Change and the Choice between Standards and Charges for Environmental Control." Paper presented at the Third Reisenberg Symposium, July 24–28, 1975. Göttingen: Vandenhoeck & Ruprecht.

Sorenson, J.B. 1984. "The Assurance of Reasonable Toxic Risk?" *Natural Resources Journal* 24:549–569.

Sprenger, R.U. (with contributions by G. Britschkat). 1979. *Beschäftigungseffekte der Umweltpolitik*. Berlin: Duncker & Humblot.

Sprenger, R.U., and Rehbinder, E. 1985. *The Emissions Trading Policy in the United States of America: An Evaluation of its Advantages and Disadvantages and Analysis of its Applicability in the Federal Republic of Germany*. München: Ifo-Institut für Wirtschaftsforschung.

Sproule-Jones, M., and Richards, P.L. 1984. "Toward a Theory of the Regulated Environment." *Canadian Public Policy* 10:305–315.

Spulber, D.F. 1985. "Effluent Regulation and Long-Run Optimality." *Journal of Environmental Economics and Management* 12:103–116.

Starret, D.A. 1972. "Fundamental Nonconvexities in the Theory of Externalities." *Journal of Economic Theory* 4:150–199.

Stevens, J.B. 1984. "Satisfaction with Environmental Change: An Empirical Analysis of Attitudes toward Air Quality by Recent Interstate Migrants." *Journal of Environmental Economics and Management* 11:264–281.

Stiglitz, J.E. 1977. "The Theory of Local Public Goods." In *The Economics of Public Services,* edited by M.S. Feldstein and R.P. Inman. London: MacMillan, pp. 274–333.

Stollery, K.R. 1985. "Environmental Controls in Extractive Industries." *Land Economics* 61:136–144.

Strom, S. 1973. "Economic Growth and Biological Equilibrium." *Swedish Journal of Economics* 75:164–175.

Strotz, R.H. 1957. "Myopia and Inconsistency in Dynamic Utility Maximization." *Review of Economic Studies* 23:165–180.

Symposium on "Environmental Management." N.Y. 12/1982. "The Policy Perspective." *Natural Resources Journal* 23:517–734.

Telcaff, L.A. 1982. "Principles for Transboundary Groundwater Pollution Control." *Natural Resources Journal* 22:1065–1079.

Terkla, D. 1984. "The Efficiency Value of Effluent Tax Revenues." *Journal of Environmental Economics and Management* 11:107–123.

Thomas, W.A. 1972. *Indicators of Environmental Quality.* New York: Plenum Press.

Tideman, T.N., and Tullock, G. 1976. "A New and Superior Process for Making Social Choices." *Journal of Political Economy* 84:1145–1159.

Tiebout, Ch.M. 1956. "A Pure Theory of Local Public Goods." *Journal of Political Economy* 64:416–424.

Tietenberg, T.H. 1973a. "Controlling Pollution by Price and Standard Systems: A General Equilibrium Analysis." *Swedish Journal of Economics* 75: 193–203.

——. 1973b. "Specific Taxes and the Control of Pollution: A General Equilibrium Analysis." *Quarterly Journal of Economics* 8:503–522.

——. 1974. "On Taxation and the Control of Externalities: A Comment." *American Economic Review* 64:462–466.

——. 1979. "On the Efficient Spatial Allocation of Air Pollution Control Responsibility." In *Regional Environmental Policy: The Economic Issues,* edited by H. Siebert, I. Walter, and K. Zimmermann. New York: New York University Press, pp. 79–93.

——. 1980. "Transferable Discharge Permits and the Control of Air Pollution: A Survey and Synthesis." *Zeitschrift für Umweltpolitik* 1:477–508.

——. 1984. *Environmental and Natural Resource Economics.* London: Scott, Foresman.

——. 1985. *Emissions Trading: An Exercise in Reforming Pollution Policy.* Baltimore, Md.: John Hopkins.

Tulkens, H. 1978. "Dynamic Processes for Public Goods." *Journal of Public Economics* 9:163–201.

Tullock, G. 1964. "The Social Rate of Discount and the Optimal Rate of Investment: Comment." *Quarterly Journal of Economics* 9:331–336.

Turvey, R. 1963. "On Divergencies between Social and Private Costs." *Economica* 30:309–313.

Ullmann, A., and Zimmermann, K. 1981. "Umweltpolitik und Umweltschutzindustrie in der Bundesrepublik Deutschland – eine Analyse ihrer ökonomischen Wirkungen." *Umweltbundesamt Bericht 6/81.* Berlin: Schmidt.

Umweltbundesamt (ed.) 1985. *Daten zur Umwelt 1984.* Berlin, Schmidt.

U.S. Council on Environmental Quality. *Environmental Quality.* Annual Reports. Washington.

U.S. Environmental Protection Agency. 1973. *Capital and Operating Costs of Pollution Control: Equipment Modules.* Washington.

Viktor, P.A. 1972. *Pollution: Economy and Environment.* London: George Allen & Unwin Ltd.

Vogt, W. 1981. *Zur intertemporal wohlfahrtsoptimalen Nutzung knapper natürlicher Resourcen – Eine kontrolltheoretische Analyse –,* Diss. 1979. Tübingen: J.C.B. Mohr (Paul Siebeck).

Vousden, N. 1973. "Basic Theoretical Issues of Resource Depletion." *Journal of Economic Theory* 6:126–143.

Walter, I. 1975. *International Economics of Pollution*. New York: MacMillan.

——. 1976. *Studies in International Environmental Economics*. New York: John Wiley & Sons.

Watson, W.D., and Ridker, R.G. 1984. "Losses from Effluent Taxes and Quotas under Uncertainty." *Journal of Environmental Economics and Management* 11:310–326.

Watts, N., and Knoepfel, P. 1985. *Environment Policy and Politics*. San Francisco: Harrow.

Wandschneider, P. 1986. "Neoclassical and Institutionalist Explanations of Changes in Northwest Wates Institution." *Journal of Economic Issues* 20: 87–108.

Wegehenkel, L. 1980. *Coase-Theorem und Marktsystem*. Tübingen: J.C.B. Mohr (Paul Siebeck).

——. 1981. *Marktwirtschaft und Umwelt*. Tübingen, J.C.B. Mohr (Paul Siebeck).

Weitzman, M.L. 1974. "Prices vs. Quantities." *Review of Economic Studies* 41:477–491.

——. 1976. "Free Access vs. Private Ownership as Alternative Systems for Managing Common Property." *Journal of Economic Theory* 8:225–234.

——. 1978. "Optimal Rewards for Economic Regulation." *American Economic Review* 68:683–691.

Welliz, S. 1964. "On External Diseconomies and the Government Assisted Invisible Hand." *Economica* 31:345–362.

Whitcomb, D.K. 1972. *Externalities and Welfare*. New York: Columbia University Press.

White, M.J., and Wittmann, D. 1982. "Pollution Taxes and Optimal Spatial Location." *Economica* 49:297–311.

Wicke, L. 1982. (with contributions of W. Franke) *Umweltökonomie eine praxisorientierte Einführung*. München: Vahlen.

Wittmann, D. 1985. "Pigouvian Taxes Which Work in the Small-Number Case." *Journal of Environmental Economics and Management* 12:144–154.

Wright, C. 1969. "Some Aspects of the Use of Corrective Taxes for Controlling Air Pollution Emissions." *Natural Resources Journal* 9:63–82.

Yandle, B. 1983. "Economic Agents and the Level of Pollution Control." *Public Choice* 40:105–109.

Zimmermann, H. 1983. *Ökonomische Anreizinstrumente in einer auflagenorientierten Umweltpolitik. Notwendigkeiten, Möglichkeiten und Grenzen am Beispiel der amerikanischen Luftreinhaltepolitik*. Stuttgart: Kohlhammer.

Zimmermann, K. 1983. "Ansatzpunkte einer verteilungsorientierten Umweltpolitik." *Kyklos* 36:420–449.

Zimmermann, K. 1986. "Die Inzidenz der Umweltpolitik in theoretischer und empirischer Sicht." *Jahrbücher für Nationalökonomie und Statistik* 199: 502–521.

Zupan, J.M. 1973. *The Distribution of Air Quality in the New York Region.* Baltimore, Md.: John Hopkins.

About the Author

Horst Siebert is professor of economics at the University of Konstanz. He received his education at the University of Cologne, the University of Münster, and Wesleyan University, Connecticut. He was assistant professor of economics at Texas A&M University (1967–1968) and professor of economics at the University of Mannheim (1969–1984). He was visiting professor of economics at Resources for the Future (1972), the University of California at Riverside (1973), New York University (1976), the University of New Mexico in Albuquerque (1977), the University of Aberdeen (1979), the Center for Energy Policy Research at the Massachusetts Institute of Technology (1980–1981), Australian National University (1982), Harvard (summer 1983) and the Sloan School of Management at the Massachusetts Institute of Technology (1986). His books include among others: *Zur Theorie des regionalen Wirtschaftswachstums* (1967); *Regional Economic Growth, Theory and Policy* (1969); *Interregionale Mobilität und regionale Entwicklung* (1970); *Das produzierte Chaos: Ökonomie und Umwelt* (1973); *Analyse der Instrumente der Umweltpolitik* (1976); *Ökonomische Theorie der Umwelt* (1978); *Umwelt und wirtschaftliche Entwicklung* (editor (1979); *The Political Economy of Environmental Protection* (with A. Berthoin Antal, 1979); *Regional Environmental Policy: The Economic Dimension* (edited with I. Walter and K. Zimmermann, 1979); *Erschöpfbare Ressourcen* (editor) (1980); *Politik und Markt. Wirtschaftspolitische Probleme der 80er Jahre* (edited with D. Duwendag, 1980); *Trade and Environment: A Theoretical Enquiry* (with J. Eichberger, R. Gronych and R. Pethig, 1980); *The Resource Sector in an Open Economy* (editor) (1983); *Ökonomische Theorie natürlicher Ressourcen* (1983); *Aussenwirtschaft* (1984, 3rd edition); *Intertemporale Allokation* (editor) (1984); *Risk and the Political Economy of Resource Development* (edited with D.W. Pearce and I. Walter, 1984); *Economics of the Resource-Exporting Country. Intertemporal Theory of Supply and Trade* (1985); and *Einführung in die Volkswirtschaftslehre*, Teil I: Markt- und Preistheorie (1986, 8th ed.), Teil II: Wirtschaftspolitische Ziele und makroökonomische Theorie (1982, 5th ed.). Professor Siebert also has contributed quite a few articles to economic journals.

Subject Index

Structural Change: The Challenge to Industrial Societies

8th German-Japanese Seminar on Economics and Social Sciences Held at Cologne, September 24–27, 1984

Editors: H. Hax, W. Kraus, K. Tsuchiya
With contributions by numerous experts

1985. Approx. 34 figures, approx. 56 tables. Approx. 210 pages. ISBN 3-540-15741-7

This volume contains contributions from Japanese and German economists and social scientists on several aspects of structural change in industrial countries. Six topics and their various interrelations are discussed: Divisions of labor and trade relations, energy supply, technology promotion, new technologies and the growth of the service sector, employment, and changes in value orientation.

M. Sattinger

Unemployment, Choice and Inequality

1985. 7 figures, 49 tables. XIV, 175 pages. ISBN 3-540-15544-9

Contents: Introduction. – Search in Labor Markets. – The Valuation of Unemployment. – The Distribution of Employment. – The Distribution of Wage Rates. – Inequality. – The Operation of Labor Markets. – Chronic Underemployment and Regression Towards the Mean. – Summary. – References. – Author Index. – Subject Index.

N. J. Schofield

Social Choice and Democracy

1985. 27 figures. XVII, 321 pages. ISBN 3-540-15604-6

Social Choice and Democracy presents, in a self-contained form, the modern analysis of voting systems, when the set of social states, W, has a geometric form. The main result is that such systems are classified by two integers v and w. If the dimension of W is no greater than v then there will exist an "equilibrium". This generalizes an early result of Downs on party competition. However, if the dimension exceeds w then there is almost always no equilibrium, and "manipulation" can lead to any outcome. This phenomenon is known as "chaos". The results derived in this book have important implications for any formal analysis of the behavior of political and other organizational systems.

E. Schlicht

Isolation and Aggregation in Exonomics

1985. XI, 112 pages. ISBN 3-540-15254-7

Contents: The Setting of the Argument. – On Isolation. – The Moving Equilibrium Method. – Econometric Implications. – The Nature of Macroeconomic Laws. – Epiloque: Economic Imagination. – References. – Author Index. – Subject Index.

Springer-Verlag
Berlin Heidelberg New York
London Paris Tokyo

G. Gandolfo

International Economics

1986. 133 figures. Approx. 830 pages.
ISBN 3-540-16707-2

Contents: The Pure Theory of International Trade: Introduction. The classical (Ricardo-Torrens) theory of comparative costs. The neoclassical theory of international trade. The Heckscher-Ohlin model. Tariffs, protection, economic integration. International trade and economic growth. Some refinements of the orthodox theory. The "new" theories of international trade. Neo-Ricardian theories of international trade. – Bibliography.

International Monetary Theory: The foreign exchange market. Balance of payments and national accounts. The role of the exchange rate in the adjustment process in a partial equilibrium framework. The role of income changes in the adjustment process. The absorption approach and interactions between exchange-rate and income in the adjustment process. Money and other assets in the adjustment process under fixed exchange rates. Money and other assets in the adjustment process under flexible exchange rates. International capital movements and other problems. Fixed versus flexible exchange rates. International liquidity and international financial markets. The problem of the integration between the pure theory of international trade and international monetary economics. – Bibliography. Name Index. – Subject Index.

E. van Damme

Stability and Perfection of Nash Equilibria

1987. ISBN 3-540-17101-0

Contents: Introduction. - Games in Normal Form. - Matrix and Bimatrix Games. - Control Costs. - Incomplete Information. - Extensive Form Games. - Bargaining and Fair Division. - Repeated Games. - Evolutionary Game Theory. - Strategic Stability and Applications. - References. - Survey Diagrams. - Index.

B. Felderer, S. Homburg

Macroeconomics and New Macroeconomics

1986. 97 figures. Approx. 320 pages.
ISBN 3-540-16961-X

From the Contents: *Fundamentals:* Some Methodological Considerations. A Historical Survey. National Income Accounting. – *Macroeconomics:* The Classical Theory. The Keynesian Theory.- Political Implications: A Comparison. – *New Macroeconomics:* The Real-Balance Effect. The Theory of Portfolio Selection. Monetarism. New Classical Economics. Neokeynesian Theory. – Mathematical Appendix. – Bibliography. – Autor Index. – Subject Index.

M. Aoki

State Space Modeling of Time Series

1986. 76 figures. Approx. 330 pages.
ISBN 3-540-17256-4

Contents: Introduction. - The Notion of State. - Representation of Time Series. - State Space and ARMA Representation. - Properties of State Space Models. - Innovation Processes. - Kalman Filters. - State Vectors and Optimality Measures. - Computation of System Matrices. - Approximated Models and Error Analysis. - Numerical Examples. - Appendices. - References. - Subject Index.

Springer-Verlag
Berlin Heidelberg New York
London Paris Tokyo

Springer